Time Traveler's Guide to Florida

Jack Powell

Pineapple Press, Inc.
Sarasota, Florida

Inquiries should be addressed to:

Pineapple Press, Inc.
P.O. Box 3889
Sarasota, Florida 34230
www.pineapplepress.com

Library of Congress Cataloging in Publication Data

Powell, Jack
Time traveler's guide to Florida / Jack Powell. -- 1st ed.
    p. cm.
Includes bibliographical references and index.
ISBN 978-1-56164-454-4 (pb : alk. paper)
1. Florida--Guidebooks. 2. Historic sites--Florida--Guidebooks. 3. Historical reenactments--Florida--Guidebooks. 4. Time travel--Guidebooks. I. Title.
F309.3.P67 2009
917.5904'44--dc22
                              2009038205

First Edition

Design by Shé Hicks
Printed in the United States of America

The author and publisher present these events for the readers' education and entertainment and do not take any responsibility for any dangers or damages that may occur. Also, the timing of a living history event is sometimes affected by the timing of holidays such as Easter or Thanksgiving. Readers are encouraged to use the contact number or web address in each chapter to confirm the schedule of an event.

All kidding aside (this only happens once, so pay attention!):

This book is for my dear great-aunt

THERESA HIGGINS

A cherished part of my past
Always welcome in the present, and
A gracious example for the future

Contents

Introduction

For those who believe that the best way to understand someone is to walk a mile in his or her shoes, Florida is the place to be. After all, the State's rich history features those whose footwear ranged from Native American moccasins to astronauts' boots, and today there are many opportunities to actually walk in those shoes. You can join in all sorts of historical reenactments—in full costume if you like. You have the chance to become a different person—be it Native American, Spanish conquistador, French colonist, rum-soaked pirate, or battlefield soldier—and relive a part of Florida's long and fascinating past.

There's more. In addition to going back to the past, you can glimpse the possibilities of the future. The Florida peninsula has been like a springboard from which human beings can rocket into space or dive beneath the surfaces of its nearly surrounding waters. And now there are places in Florida where anyone can take a peek at what the future will be (or at least, may be) like.

This unique guidebook offers you the sensation of time travel, both back into the past and forward into the future. The day has arrived for this new kind of travelogue, which reveals not only places to visit but also time periods to experience. This is a book for today's explorers of place and space, past and future. This is the *Time Traveler's Guide to Florida*.

Whether you slip into your moccasins, put on your fins, or strap on those boots that were made for walking (in space), our past and the future await you. Your first stop is not only where, but…when?

"Travel is fatal to prejudice, bigotry, and narrow-mindedness, and many of our people need it sorely on these accounts. Broad, wholesome, charitable views of men and things cannot be acquired by vegetating in one little corner of the earth all one's lifetime." —Mark Twain, *The Innocents Abroad*

Time Traveling 101:
Living History Appreciation

Here in question-and-answer format are some things to keep in mind when planning to visit a historical reenactment or other living history event:

1) **Are there any special considerations for different ages?** The sound of cannons or other gunfire may be frightening to small children. Control of children's movements is also important, especially when a weapon such as a bayonet or musket is being demonstrated. While a reenactor will never knowingly point a weapon at any spectator, even when the weapon is obviously unloaded, no one should be allowed to run into the line of fire of any gun or near a bladed weapon such as a pirate's sword.

2) **What should spectators wear?** Choose comfortable clothes appropriate for the expected weather. For any chance of rain, have umbrellas and other rain gear available. Hats and sunscreen are a must, especially for children. Sunglasses are recommended unless the day is overcast.

3) **What about seating at outdoor events such as battles?** While each entry in the text provides specific information about whether or not you'll need chairs and/or a picnic blanket, it can never hurt to keep some extras in your car just in case. Promised seating could always run out. But one thing organizers will never run out of is insects, so make sure you do bring bug repellant.

4) **Where can one get historical costumes or props?** There are almost always vendors (sutlers) present at reenactments. Ask advice from the reenactors about authenticity and period-correct items.

5) **Is there any special way of talking or acting at a living history event?** The most important thing is to keep a sense of wonder, as

if you have actually traveled back in time and have a chance to learn about how people lived back then from their viewpoint. You are encouraged to ask questions, especially if you're curious about something that surprises you. Living historians enjoy their pastime and love to talk about what they're doing. The next most important thing is to determine whether or not you are watching a third-person or first-person scenario. Let's say you are at Camp Uzita, which is a recreation of Hernando de Soto's camp at his landing site in Florida in 1539. There will probably be a person there in the garb of a sixteenth-century Spanish soldier demonstrating how to put on his armor and showing what kind of food was eaten by de Soto and his group. If the scenario is in third person, even though he'll be acting the part of a sixteenth-century Spanish soldier, he will be speaking in modern-day English, not sixteenth-century Spanish. He will talk about de Soto and the others in the third person—what "they" did, what "they" ate, and so on. In a first-person scenario, the soldier will still speak English (so you'll understand him), but will avoid using modern terms. He will not know what a digital camera is, even if you show him one. He won't know who the current president is, because there were no American presidents in 1539. He will use the words "I" and "we" when talking about himself and the rest of de Soto's group. Except for the use of English, he will truly be acting the part of a sixteenth-century Spanish soldier, as if you had gone back to the sixteenth century and somehow found someone who could speak modern English. And, of course, use common courtesy. Don't try to trip up a person doing a first-person reenactment. You're dealing with an actor who is allowing you to be part of the show, and there's no justifiable reason to be a party pooper, heckler, or other spoilsport. Play along, learn, and have fun instead.

6) **Why do some weekend events, especially the ones involving warfare, have church services?** This is for people (including the reenactors!) who want to go to a church on Sunday morning, no matter where they are. It also affords the sight of wartime opponents laying down their arms for a while in order to worship together. Especially for the children, there's a lesson in there somewhere.

7) **Why are some events assigned to the future portion of the timeline in the Table of Contents if they already exist?** A few events and attractions—such as the the Jules Undersea Lodge, listed as belonging to the year 2025—are assigned to dates in the future although they are present and operational now. That is because these events and attractions are thought to be harbingers of things that will be much more common later. So while there is only one Undersea Lodge in the world at this time, it is thought that underwater accommodations will be more common by 2025.

Before European Contact
(12,000 B.C.–1513 A.D.)

An Ancient Native Village (pre-Columbian)
Fountain of Youth Park, St. Augustine, St. Johns County

Historical Background

For Native Americans of the North American continent, Florida was where the spear of European contact first struck after the voyages of Columbus. Whether they were Apa-lachee, Timucuan, Calusan, or many others, the tribes of Florida had well-developed cultures of their own that were soon overwhelmed by European warfare, disease, and enslavement.

What You'll Find

- An authentically dressed reenactor presents a day in the life of pre-Columbian Native Americans, as if visitors are being adopted into the village's various clans and taught the ways of the tribe
- Various arts, games, crafts, and other skills are learned by the new tribal members
- With each program, a selected boy and a girl are ceremonially wed and their duties to their clans, the tribe, and each other are explained
- The new bride is also shown how to annul the marriage if she wishes
- You'll learn of the village's most precious possession

Nothing is sold at the Village itself, but there is a gift shop elsewhere within Fountain of Youth Park.

Planning Your Visit

Whom to bring: This event is open mainly by scheduled appointment with groups such as school field trips, and when there is a reenactment happening elsewhere at Fountain of Youth Park in St. Augustine. Reenactments are family events, and guide animals and well-behaved pets on a leash no longer than six feet are welcome.

Dates and times: By appointment. Except when there is a reenactment happening at Fountain of Youth Park, this experience is available only by reservation for groups of twenty or more.

Getting there: The GPS coordinates for Fountain of Youth Park are N29° 54.4141', W081° 18.9723'. The address is 11 Magnolia Avenue in St. Augustine, 32084, about half a mile north of the Castillo de San Marcos.

Parking: Free and ample for cars through buses, with ADA spaces.

Fees and tickets: Free with park admission, which ranges from less than ten dollars for adults to free for children under six years.

Facilities

Restrooms: ADA-compliant restrooms are near the parking lot.

Other ADA compliance information: Numerous paved walkways and hard-packed grounds make the park negotiable by wheelchair. There is plenty of shade.

Places to eat: A concession is on-site at Fountain of Youth Park.

Picnic facilities: There are two picnic areas without grills or pavilions.

Places to sit: There is no need to bring chairs or blankets.

Places to stay on-site: None, but many fine establishments are nearby.

Educators

The best way to experience the Ancient Native Village is via scheduled field trip. There is a villageful of curriculum aids online at AncientNative.org.

Contact Information

www.ancientnative.org

———— ◆•◆•◆ ————

Stone Age and Primitive Arts Festival (12,000 B.C. forward)
Ochlockonee River State Park, Wakulla County

Historical Background

Florida's earliest human inhabitants had arts, crafts, and technologies that have nearly been buried underneath today's avalanche of applied sciences and modern conveniences. For instance, people of centuries ago who wished to know what the weather was like had no Internet, flat-screen televisions, or weather forecasters with high-definition radar. Instead they used a primitive means known as "looking out the window" that is still effective today. Other clever solutions were fashioned for problems such as keeping warm, chasing potential meals, making containers for storage, and constructing shelters from available materials.

What You'll Find

Not everyone will be in period animal skins or fig leaves. During the Stone Age, skills counted more than fashion:

- Opportunities to try your hand at arrowhead making, deer hide tanning, making stone tools, and carving both bone and antlers
- See how bows and arrows were made
- Demonstrations of basket weaving and pottery making from locally available materials
- Primitive archery and spear-throwing competitions
- See why the period dress–authenticity award always goes to the North American flintknapper

- Find out what an atlatl is and learn to use one
- Vendors will be available

Planning Your Visit

Whom to bring: This event is for the whole family, including guide animals and well-behaved pets.

Dates and times: Held the first weekend of February from 9:30 AM to 5 PM.

Getting there: Held at Ochlockonee River State Park (GPS coordinates N29° 59.9299', W084° 29.1271'), which is four miles south of Sopchoppy or about thirty miles SSW of Tallahassee on Hwy 319. The zip code is 32358.

Parking: Adequate, with ADA spaces.

Fees and tickets: Free with a $4-per-carload park admission fee for up to eight people.

Facilities

Restrooms: ADA-accessible restrooms and portable facilities on-site.

Other ADA compliance information: Grounds are wheelchair-friendly.

Places to eat: There are no concessions.

Picnic facilities: Tables, grills, and (for rental) pavilions on-site.

Places to sit: There are few places to sit but many places to spread a blanket.

Places to stay on-site: Youth and modern camping are available by reservation.

Reenactors

Needed are pre-Columbian period impressions with the ability to demonstrate a primitive art or craft. Period dress is preferred but not required. Amenities include space to set up demonstration area, firewood, and water.

Educators

No school days, field trips, or curriculum aids are yet available.

Contact Information

Ochlockonee River SP: 850-962-2771;
www.floridastateparks.org/ochlockoneeriver/default.cfm

Naples, Collier County

Historical Background
Prior to the coming of the Spanish, present-day southwest Florida was dominated by the Calusa, a tribe of fisher-gatherers and fierce warriors who were feared throughout the southern half of the Florida peninsula. Hostilities between the Spanish and the Calusa abated somewhat after Pedro de Menéndez de Aviles (founder of St. Augustine) married the Calusa chief's sister. Afterwards the Calusa made the tactical error of isolating themselves as much as possible from Europeans and their more advanced weapons. However, they'd already been exposed to European diseases. Thus ravaged by illness, the once-dreaded Calusa were unable to withstand attacks by other Native Americans who had obtained English firearms.

What You'll See
The living history portion of this festival features:
- A recreated Calusa camp with appropriately costumed reenactors who are glad to display and share what they have learned of Calusa life
- Demonstrations of early skills such as fire starting, making clothes from animal skins, pottery making, and flintknapping (making sharp-edged stone tools)

In addition there are guest speakers for adults and special activities for children.

Planning Your visit
Whom to bring: The whole family. Guide animals are welcome. No pets.
Dates and times: From 9 AM to 4 PM on one of the last Saturdays in March. Use contact information for details.

Be sure to ask where the three souls of each Calusa are found.

Getting there: The event is held at the Collier County Museum in the county's Government Center two miles from downtown Naples. GPS coordinates are N26° 7.6256', W081° 45.9724'. The address is 3301 Tamiami Trail East (U. S. Highway 41), Naples, 34112.

Parking: Adequate and free, with ADA-compliant spaces.

Fees and tickets: Free, but donations will make you a friend of the Calusa. And everybody wants to be on the Calusa's good side.

Facilities

Restrooms: They are ADA-compliant.

Other ADA compliance information: The museum grounds and building are fully accessible to those with mobility challenges.

Places to eat: There are machines with drinks and light snacks inside the museum.

Picnic facilities: None on-site.

Places to sit: There is shaded seating. Bringing chairs or blankets is unnecessary.

Places to stay on-site: There are none, but many establishments in Naples grant refuge to those fleeing the Calusa.

Reenactors

Impressions of authentically dressed Native Americans (especially Calusa) are welcome, especially if a skill can be demonstrated.

Educators

There are no education days or field trips, but the museum's website has enough well-done curriculum aids to fill a burial mound.

Contact Information

Collier County Museum: 239-252-8476
Museum website: www.colliermuseums.com

The First Spanish Period
(1513–1763)

The School of the Sixteenth Century (1501–1600)
Fountain of Youth Park, St. Augustine, St. Johns County

Historical Background
Between the first voyage of Columbus in 1492 and the English founding of Jamestown in 1607, the North American continent wasn't exactly just sitting by idly and waiting for the Pilgrims to show up. There were European explorers scampering all over the place and, in what was to become the state of Florida, attempts at colonization. The sixteenth century saw the French begin a settlement at Fort Caroline in the area of modern-day Jacksonville, from which they were encouraged to depart (to put it politely) by the Spanish. In the meantime the first Spanish colonists of Pensacola were driven out by famine, attacks by Native Americans, and an especially vicious hurricane.

What You'll Find
- A boot camp for anyone who wants to explore sixteenth-century southeastern North America and return safely
- Displays of sixteenth-century equipment, dress, and armor
- Demonstrations of period crafts and survival skills, including needlework and tent making
- Reenactors portraying the various peoples (European explorers, soldiers, and Native Americans of different nations) of the sixteenth century who lived in what was to become Florida
- Numerous encampments show you how it was done five hundred years ago—cooking, use of armor and other forms of personal protection, etc.
- Vendors are present for those who need to be resupplied in their quests for gold, glory, and adventure
- The uses of weapons, from pikes and crossbows to muskets and cannons, are taught through training drills and demonstrations
- A unique feature of this event is that as long as adult visitors are wearing clothing of all-natural fibers (for safety reasons), they can participate in educational and weapons training

Planning Your Visit
Whom to bring: This is a family event. Guide animals are welcome, but pets are discouraged because of all the gunfire.

"Armor, n. The kind of clothing worn by a man whose tailor is a blacksmith." —Ambrose Bierce, *The Devil's Dictionary*

Dates and times: Last weekend in January, 10 AM to 4 PM on Saturday and throughout Sunday morning.

Getting there: The GPS coordinates for Fountain of Youth Park are N29° 54.4141', W081° 18.9723'. The address is 11 Magnolia Avenue in St. Augustine, 32084, about half a mile north of the Castillo de San Marcos.

Parking: Adequate and free, with ADA-compliant spaces.

Fees and tickets: Free.

Facilities

Restrooms: ADA-compliant restrooms are near the parking lot.

Other ADA compliance information: Numerous paved walkways and hard-packed grounds make the park negotiable by wheelchair. There is plenty of shade.

Places to eat: There is a concession within the park.

Picnic facilities: There are two picnic areas in the park, but no grills or pavilions.

Places to sit: There is no need to bring chairs or blankets.

Places to stay on-site: There are none, but twenty-first-century lodging is nearby.

Reenactors

Needed are military, civilians, and Native Americans in sixteenth-century dress or armor. Amenities include space for encampments, firewood, and water.

Educators

There are no school days, field trips, or curriculum aids yet.

Contact Information

(Event organizer) E-mail: lobo13@bellsouth.net

Camp Uzita (1539)

De Soto National Memorial, Bradenton, Manatee County

Historical Background

In May of 1539, Hernando de Soto landed in the Manatee County area with nine ships, two hundred and twenty horses, a herd of pigs, seven hundred soldiers (one of whom was the disguised wife of one of the soldiers), a pack of war dogs, and an eleven-year-old servant girl named Anna. There he established his base camp in an abandoned Indian village named Uzita before journeying inland in search of riches. Unfortunately for de Soto's plans to acquire *La Florida*'s legendary wealth, the Seminole Hard Rock Casinos would not be open for business for another 400 years.

What You'll Find

- Rangers and other reenactors wearing period clothing and talking about life at the camp as part of third-person impressions
- Demonstrations of Native American and conquistador crafts as well as of weapons such as crossbows and the arquebus, a primitive firearm
- Opportunities to shoot a crossbow and to try on the armor worn by the conquistadors while imagining what is what like to wear it while marching in Florida heat
- You'll find out how "tourist trees" got that name

Planning Your Visit

Whom to bring: This is for the whole family. Dogs are permitted within the park only when on a leash no longer than six feet. Guide animals are welcome.

Dates and times: The camp is open daily from mid-December to the end of April, although De Soto National Memorial is open all year.

Getting there: GPS coordinates are N27°29.3754', W082°37.7828'. The

address is 8300 De Soto Memorial Highway in Bradenton, 34209. Boaters may access the park via the Manatee River, but the park has no boat ramp. Bicycles may be used on the road and in the parking lot, but not on the walking trails. Bike racks are provided at the picnic area.

Parking: Ample. ADA spaces are provided.

Fees and tickets: Free!

Facilities

Restrooms: ADA-compliant restrooms are across the parking lot at the visitors center. There are changing tables located in the women's restroom.

Other ADA compliance information: The hard-packed ground of Camp Uzita is not as easy to negotiate in a wheelchair or a walker as the concrete pavement approach, but it is nevertheless reasonably accessible. A small but sufficient set of bleachers is provided. There is a special flat ADA-accessible surface for the parking of wheelchairs and scooters located adjacent to the bleachers. The demonstration tables area is shaded.

Places to eat: There are no concessions.

Picnic facilities: A ten-table picnic area is located adjacent to the parking lot and is available for visitors on a first-come basis. Large groups and schools should call ahead to reserve seating. Grills and alcoholic beverages are not allowed within the park.

Places to sit: Bleachers are provided at Camp Uzita, and there are benches on the walkway to the visitors center.

Places to stay on-site: None. However, generations of Spanish conquistadores have been pleased with Bradenton's numerous air-conditioned places of lodging after years of marching through Florida's heat in full armor.

Reenactors
Needed are sixteenth-century Spanish military and civilians and Native Americans, all appropriately garbed. There are no amenities except the usual benefits for volunteers. Call the park for more information.

Educators
There are no special school days, but field trips are available. Check with the local school board. Curriculum aids are at the National Park Service website for De Soto National Memorial.

Contact Information
De Soto National Memorial
8300 De Soto Memorial Hwy.
Bradenton, FL 34209
941-792-0458

The Menendez Landing Event (1565)
St. Augustine, St. Johns County

Historical Background
On September 8, 1565, Admiral Pedro Menéndez de Aviles of Spain landed at the site of present-day St. Augustine. Acting on direct orders from the king of Spain, he affirmed Spanish claims to Florida and established the first Spanish mission in what would become the United States. The New World's first Catholic Mass was immediately held, and then the local Native Americans were invited to a feast of thanksgiving for the crew's safe completion of the journey from Spain—over fifty years before the first Pilgrim's arrival. At the same time, St. Augustine (our country's first permanent European settlement) was founded. With regard to the French Huguenots who had settled at Fort Caroline to escape religious persecution in Europe, Menéndez carried a second order from Spain's king: find the French Protestants, hang them all, and then burn them.

What You'll Find
The living history aspects of this commemoration of Menéndez's arrival include:
- A Menéndez reenactor landing at the mission site in a replica small boat

- A Mass held at the mission's outdoor altar
- Sixteenth-century encampments of Spanish explorers, friars, soldiers and Native Americans at the adjacent grounds of Fountain of Youth Park
- Plenty of food in remembrance of that first feast of thanksgiving

Planning Your Visit

Whom to bring: This is a family event. Although guide animals are always welcome, pets are not allowed during the Mass. Pets may be frightened by the gunfire and cannonfire that marks Menendez's arrival.

Dates and times: Held on the Saturday of Labor Day weekend. The Mass begins at 10 AM and the landing is just before that, between 9:30 and 10 AM.

Getting there: The mission is at 27 Ocean Avenue in St. Augustine, 32084, just northeast of Fountain of Youth Park. The GPS coordinates are N29° 54.2999', W081° 19.0119'.

Parking: Free and abundant, especially at the park.

Fees and tickets: Free.

Facilities

Restrooms: ADA-accessible restrooms are adjacent to the park's parking lot.

Other ADA compliance information: Paved pathways and relatively level, hard-packed soil allow for use of wheelchairs and canes on mission grounds and at the park.

Places to eat: There's a feast.

Picnic facilities: There are not enough picnic tables at the park for the crowds, of course. Grills are neither present nor necessary.

Places to sit: There is space for your picnic blanket or folding chair.

Places to stay on-site: None, but St. Augustine's many establishments are happy to welcome those who have just arrived on slow boats from across the Atlantic.

Reenactors

Sixteenth-century civilians, military, and Native Americans in appropriate dress are welcome. Encampment space, firewood, water, and the aforementioned feast are provided.

Be sure to find out who paid the bill for the entire Menéndez expedition, and why the new city was named "St. Augustine."

Educators

There are no special school days, field trips, or curriculum aids.

Contact Information
(Event organizer) E-mail: lobo13@bellsouth.net

———◆━◆━◆◆◆━———

Drake's Raid (June 1586)
Fountain of Youth Park and city streets, St. Augustine, St. Johns County

Historical Background

This is the annual remembrance of the June 1586 attack on Spanish St. Augustine by English land and sea forces led by Sir Francis Drake. (Even after 400+ years, they're still a little sore about it.) Eighty Spanish soldiers were forced from their fort by two thousand English and their cannons. The English then crossed Matanzas Bay, drove out the remaining Spanish defenders, and began sacking the city. Once St. Augustine had been looted, burned, and every house and garden destroyed, the English departed and the Spanish colonials were able to return and rebuild, having been left little more than the clothes on their backs. Even the fruit trees had been cut down.

What You'll Find

The living history portions of this event include:

- A sixteenth-century camp in Fountain of Youth Park in which Drake's crew tries to explain why they are pillaging the city to anyone who will listen
- Military drills and demonstrations of handy weapons for those occasions when bands of the Queen's cutthroats land in your sixteenth-century neighborhood
- Demonstrations of sixteenth-century cooking and other period skills
- Sutlers selling all manner of period-appropriate goods
- An evening brawl between the Spanish militia (with their Native American allies) and the English that begins near the city gates and continues along a half-mile route to the Governor's Palace as the narrow streets fill with black-powder weapons, English pikemen, swordfights, cannonfire, armored horsemen, and terrified Spanish colonists; frantic mothers search for their children; and tourists are warned by the reenactors to go hide in the swamps
- Smoke from pistols and muskets filling the air, along with colorful Spanish curses directed at the flea-bitten English corsairs

Planning Your Visit

Whom to bring: Only in America could this be a family event. Pets are allowed if well controlled on a six-foot leash, but they may get upset by all the noise and commotion. Guide animals are always welcome.

Dates and times: The sixteenth-century encampments and living history interpretations are from 10 AM to 5 PM on the first Saturday in June at the Fountain of Youth Park in St. Augustine. The battle reenactment between Drake's party and Spanish defenders begins at 7 PM.

Getting there: The GPS coordinates for the Fountain of Youth Park are N29° 54.4141', W081° 18.9723'. The address is 11 Magnolia Avenue in St. Augustine, 32084.

Parking: Sufficient parking is available at Fountain of Youth Park to accommodate all kinds of vehicles. Metered parking is available throughout downtown St. Augustine. There is also a city parking garage nearby.

Fees and tickets: None. Admission to the encampment area of the park is free.

Facilities

Restrooms: The Park has ADA-accessible restrooms near the parking lot.

Other ADA compliance information: The grounds of the Fountain of Youth Park are hard-packed dirt with extensive paving, making it relatively easy for wheelchair, stroller, or cane users to get around. Shade is plentiful.

Places to eat: There is a small concession in the park area.

Picnic facilities: There are open tables but no grills.

Places to sit: The park has benches, but bringing a folding seat to the route of the street fighting may be helpful, as with a parade.

Places to stay on-site: Not within the park, but many splendid St. Augustine establishments are close by.

Reenactors

Sixteenth-century Native Americans, Spanish military and civilians, and English sailors or marines are needed. Note that Spanish colonial women have important roles in this event and are particularly welcome. Amenities include encampment space at Fountain of Youth Park, transportation to and from the evening's reenactment, a dinner prior to the Raid itself, and "jollification" afterwards for

Those Spanish colonial housewives and mommies aren't just running around screaming for show—they are a sneaky form of crowd control. When they try to warn bystanders away from a particular spot, they're making room for groups of soldiers and raiders who are about to arrive firing pistols and engaging in swordfights—not something you want to be caught in the middle of, especially if you're pushing a baby buggy.

the reenactors—meaning you get to party with a bunch of sixteenth-century sailors, a truly memorable experience!

Educators
There are no school days, field trips, or curriculum aids yet.

Contact information
(Event organizer) E-mail: lobo13@bellsouth.net

<hr>

A Day in Old Florida (1500s–1600s)
Faver-Dykes State Park, St. Augustine, St. Johns County

Historical Background
As more and more Europeans arrived to colonize the coasts of Spanish Florida, explorers continued to probe the interior, learning to make their living there, usually as trappers. Spanish friars built a chain of missions. European and Native American cultures met, clashed, and learned from each other. Some Native Americans resisted the missions and others joined them. European craftsmen and artisans adapted their skills to make use of materials found in their new world.

What You'll Find
The living history portions of this event include:

- A sixteenth-century Spanish camp where explorers, soldiers, and a friar seek gold, glory, and souls
- An explanation for why Native American tribes lured Spanish explorers farther and farther inland with stories of great riches to be found
- A seventeenth-century trapper trading camp
- Teaching, some of it hands-on, of centuries-old crafts and skills such as knitting a mullet net, dyeing with indigo, and making baskets from pine needles
- An array of merchants trying to make a sixteenth-century buck

Planning Your Visit
Whom to bring: This is a family event.
Dates and times: It's from 10 AM to 3 PM the first Monday in February.
Getting there: The location is Faver-Dykes State Park on 1000 Faver-Dykes Road in St. Augustine, 32086, a little over ten miles south of downtown

and almost directly west of Marineland. The GPS coordinates are N29° 40.0451', W081° 16.1254'.

Parking: Free and adequate.

Fees and tickets: Free with a few dollars per carload for park admission.

Facilities

Restrooms: ADA-compliant restrooms and portable facilities are provided.

Other ADA compliance information: The hard-packed grounds covered with pine needles are level enough for the use of wheelchairs and canes. There is abundant shade.

Places to eat: Yes! Everything from hot dogs to Minorcan clam chowder.

Picnic facilities: The park's picnic area has tables, pavilions, and grills.

Places to sit: Bringing chairs is unnecessary, though there is plenty of room to relax or picnic on a blanket.

Places to stay on-site: The park has campsites both modern and primitive.

Reenactors

Sixteenth- and seventeenth-century authentically dressed impressions of trappers, Spanish military and civilians, and Native Americans of Spanish Florida are sought. Amenities include encampment site, firewood, water, and lunch.

For educators

Field trips are available (check with your school board) since the event is on a Monday. There are no curriculum materials yet.

Contact Information

www.floridastateparks.org/faver-dykes/default.cfm
904-794-0997 or 386-446-6783

A Pirate Gathering in St. Augustine (1650–1725)

Fountain of Youth Park, St. Augustine, St. Johns County

Historical Background

Centuries ago there was often a thin line between piracy and war. Two countries at war with each other might grant "letters of marque" to private citizens who owned ships. These letters granted such citizens (known as privateers) official permission to attack, capture, and loot enemy vessels—in other words, commit acts of piracy against a specific nation. Thus a country's naval power was augmented at no expense to its government. One of the problems for privateers was that a letter of marque expired when the war ended, whether the privateers knew about the peace or not. A crew might return to home port not knowing that the war had been over for months and find themselves being tried as pirates by the same government that had granted them the letter of marque.

What You'll Find

The living history portions of this festival include:

- Pirate encampments at the De Mesa Yard in the Historic Spanish Quarter, where pirate reenactors show how they prepare on land to go back to sea
- Groups of pirate castaways busy with seventeenth-century survival skills such as knot-tying, navigation, and other facets of traveling under wind power
- Seventeenth-century pirate cooking
- The singing of authentic sea shanties and stories of their origins
- Demonstrations of weapons used by pirates with the personal safety precautions they used
- Skirmishes showing pirate fighting skills
- Storytelling about legendary pirates such as Robert Searles

Planning Your Visit

Whom to bring: The living history portions of the festival will be enjoyed by the whole family. The festival has special features, a lot of them for children.

Dates and times: The St. Augustine Pirate Gathering is held the second weekend of November, including school tours on Friday from 9 AM to 2 PM. The festival itself runs from 9 AM to 5 PM on Friday and Saturday, and from 10 AM to 5 PM on Sunday. The best hours for visiting the pirate encampments are from 2 PM to 5 PM on Saturday and Sunday.

Getting there: The GPS coordinates for the Colonial Spanish Quarter Living History Museum are N29° 53.8027', W081° 18.79'. The address is 29 St. George Street in historic downtown St. Augustine, 32084, across from the Castillo de San Marcos. Many other portions of the festival are at the Special Events Field (St. Francis Field) next to the Historic District parking garage on Castillo Street.

Parking: Available at the above-mentioned parking garage. There are few spaces along the city streets.

Fees and tickets: $1 per adult or child on Friday (the school day), and $2 ("a Buc-an-Ear") on Saturday or Sunday.

"Now and then we had a hope that if we lived and were good, God would permit us to be pirates." —Mark Twain, *Life on the Mississippi*

Facilities
Restrooms: ADA-compliant restrooms are provided.

Other ADA compliance information: Numerous paved walkways and hard-packed grounds make the park negotiable by wheelchair. There is adequate shade.

Places to eat: Concessions are present.

Picnic facilities: None.

Places to sit: Seating is available at the Special Events Field.

Places to stay: Primitive campsites are available for pre-registered pirate reenactors. For spectators needing to safely hide their whiskey and their women, St. Augustine has many secure establishments nearby.

Reenactors
Needed and invited are impressions of pirates of the late seventeenth and early eighteenth centuries. Pirate wenches of the same period are also welcome. There is a fee for participation. Amenities include primitive campsite, water, and firewood.

Educators
Friday is a school day, from 9:00 AM to 2:00 PM. Field trips can be arranged through your school board. Free curriculum aids are available at the living history site.

Contact Information
E-mail: staugustinepirategathering@yahoo.com
www.pirategathering.com

Mission San Luis (1656–1704)
Tallahassee, Leon County

Historical Background
As Spanish explorers made their way across *La Florida,* they indoctrinated native populations into Christianity. Over a hundred missions were established in Spanish Florida from the 1560s to the 1690s. Mission San Luis, home to over 1400 Spanish and Apalachee Native American souls, was the home of one of the greatest Apalachee chiefs and was the westernmost military and religious outpost of the Spanish. It was burned in 1704 to keep it out of British hands.

What You'll Find
- The only reconstructed mission in the southeastern United States, an

immersion experience so well done that a visit there should be a rite of passage for every student being educated in Florida
- Artifacts and photos from some of Florida's original people
- Living historians along with first-person impressions of Apalachee Native American or Spanish families, soldiers, friars, farmers—people making up a thriving village
- A blend of two cultures as the Spanish and the Apalachee learn to live together
- Demonstrations of the activities, arts, crafts, and skills of seventeenth-century mission life in Florida
- Reconstructions of a Spanish house, the mission's fort, the church, a friary, and one of the largest Native American council houses ever built in the Southeast
- Oxcart-loads of immersion and other educational activities for all ages
- A chance to ask the friar about his favorite black drink

Planning Your Visit

Whom to bring: Family-friendly. Pets on leashes are allowed, and guide animals are always welcome.

Dates and times: The mission is open Tuesday–Sunday from 10 AM to 4 PM. It is closed on Thanksgiving and Christmas.

Getting there: The GPS coordinates are N30° 26.8387', W084° 19.1798'. The address is 2100 West Tennessee Street in Tallahassee, 32304. The mission grounds are about half a mile west-northwest of Florida State University

Parking: Plentiful, with ADA-compliant spaces.

Fees and tickets: For a long time, admission has been free, which goes along with the friar's vow of poverty. However, the staff is taking pity upon the poor starving friar and as of January 1, 2010, admission will be $5 for adults and seniors, $3 for children five through eighteen years of age, and free for members and children under five.

Facilities

Restrooms: The restrooms are ADA-accessible.

Other ADA compliance information: The whole mission is ADA-compliant, with the obvious exception of the nature trail. Surfaces are smooth, hard, and easily negotiable with strollers, canes, or wheelchairs, but there are some hills. Although there is little shade on the walkways, the site is a beautiful green space and all structures are ADA-accessible. With prior notice, a golf-cart tour can be arranged. The list of other accommodations made for those with any type of disability is too extensive to be given here; visitors with a physical or sensory challenge should contact the main office beforehand so that suitable arrangements can be made.

Places to eat: There are vending machines, but no other concessions.

Picnic facilities: Uncovered picnic tables are available, but no grills.
Places to sit: There is no need to bring chairs or a blanket.
Places to stay on-site: None, but many are nearby in Tallahassee.

Reenactors

Mission San Luis has its own volunteer staff of people doing impressions of seventeenth-century Spanish citizens, clergy, military, and Apalachee Native Americans. Occasionally, additional reenactors are needed for special events. For details, see the mission's website or contact the volunteer coordinator.

Educators

The mission welcomes school groups and also does outreach programs. There are curriculum aids on the Mission San Luis official website.

Contact Information

www.missionsanluis.org,
    with photos at http://www.flickr.com/photos/37224609@N05/

Mission San Luis
2100 West Tennessee St.
Tallahassee, FL 32304
850-487-3711

May Military Muster at Castillo de San Luis (1690s)
Tallahassee, Leon County

Historical Background

As the seventeenth century began, Apalachee Native Americans, already beset by European diseases, found that they faced a new problem: the military threat from the English colonies north of Spanish Florida. They requested that the Spanish send missionaries to them. When the site for Mission de San Luis was chosen in 1656, one powerful Apalachee chief brought his people to live at the new mission and offered to build a blockhouse for the soldiers who defended them. By the 1690s the threat of attacks by the British and their Native American allies had increased so much that the blockhouse was upgraded to a full-scale fort, with a palisade and a dry moat filled with cacti. *El Castillo de San Luis* was manned by Spanish soldiers and the Spanish-trained Apalachee militia. Within the walls of the fort was sanctuary for the mission's population when under attack.

What You'll Find

This event focuses on the Castillo de San Luis, the military complex within Mission San Luis. On this day, visitors can observe or indulge in the following living history activities:

- Interacting with living historians doing impressions of Spanish soldiers, Apalachee militia, and civilian mission families
- Watching seventeenth-century military drills and firing demonstrations
- Seeing a formal Changing of the Guard ceremony
- Observing demonstrations of colonial arts, crafts, and other skills
- Engaging in activities for children, including archery demonstrations
- Using opportunities for children to talk to reenactors and find out why it may not be so awesome to live in a fort
- Trying one's hands at pike drills

Planning Your Visit

Whom to bring: This is for the family. Pets on leashes are allowed, and guide animals are always welcome. Because of cannon and musket fire, you may want to leave your pets at home for this event.

Dates and times: The event goes from 10 AM to 4 PM on the second Saturday in May. (Other musters are scheduled during the year; call for details and dates.)

Fees and tickets: Free until January 1, 2010, after which admission will be $5 for adults and seniors, $3 for children five through eighteen years of age, and free for members and children under five.

Reenactors

Appropriately garbed seventeenth-century Spanish soldiers, distaff, and Apalachee militia are welcome. Check with the mission offices before coming. There are no amenities.

Educators

There is no school day or field trip available. Curriculum aids are on the mission website.

Contact Information

Mission San Luis: 850-487-3711
E-mail: info@missionsanluis.org

Feeding the Flock: Foodways at Mission San Luis (1656-1704)

Tallahassee, Leon County

Historical Background

As Spanish colonists and guests learned

to live with their Apalachee neighbors at Mission San Luis, the Spanish

24

learned about new foods found in *La Florida,* and the Apalachee were introduced to new foods imported from Europe. New and unfamiliar ways of cooking and storing foods were also shared.

What You'll Find

- Illustrations of two different cultures cooperating and blending as the mission population pursues a common goal of securing nourishment
- How the technologically advanced Spanish depended on the skills and knowledge of the Apalachee in adapting to their new home
- How food was obtained in seventeenth-century *La Florida*—long before the first Publixes, and Winn-Dixies opened
- How people of differing abilities contributed to the foodways of the mission by hunting, harvesting, or storing against lean times
- How food was stored without plastic, cans, or refrigeration
- The variety of foods and cooking methods available in those times
- A multi-sensory experience involving sight, hearing, and the aromas of many kitchens

Planning Your Visit

Whom to bring: This is a family event. Pets on leashes are allowed, and guide animals are always welcome.

Dates and times: This event is held on Saturday and Sunday of Thanksgiving weekend, when everyone is either thinking of food or trying not to.

Fees and tickets: Free at the moment, but the friars give thanks for those who donate. In answer to the friars' other prayers, as of January 1, 2010, admission will be $5 for adults and seniors, $3 for children five through eighteen years of age, and free for children under five and members.

Reenactors

Impressions of seventeenth-century Spanish military, civilians, or Apalachee are welcome. Check with the administration before coming. There are no amenities.

Educators

There are no school days or field trips available, but curriculum aids are on the mission's official website.

Contact Information

Mission San Luis : 850-413-3711
E-mail: info@missionsanluis.org

Searles' Raid (1668)
St. Augustine, St. Johns County

Historical Background
Through the early half of the seventeenth century, England watched in envy as Spanish treasure galleons sailed safely past Spanish-controlled ports in the Caribbean and Spanish Florida, including St. Augustine. The lopsided balance of power changed in 1655 when England captured Jamaica, giving English privateers a safe haven from which to plunder the Spanish. Thirteen years later, Captain Robert Searle and his crew of freebooters sacked and pillaged St. Augustine, prompting Spain to fund a stone fortress at St. Augustine to protect the city and Spanish interests. The Castillo de San Marcos still stands.

What You'll Find
- More than a hundred armed men setting up encampments in Colonial Spanish Quarter
- Encampments of both English privateers and the city's Spanish defenders
- Time to visit as they explain their equipment, practice with their weapons, and keep their energy up with seventeenth-century cuisine
- At 5 PM the weapons come out and the fighting rages through the streets of downtown's historic district
- Room for you to join the terror-stricken townsfolk as they flee for their lives

Planning Your Visit

Whom to bring: This event is for the family, though small children may be upset by the gunfire and commotion. Pets are not allowed within the Spanish Quarter, but guide animals are always welcome.

Dates and times: It's held the first weekend in March. Encampments are open to the public on Saturday until the raid begins at 5 PM. Transportation of reenactors to the south end of the town plaza is at 4 PM, after which the raid begins with the English privateers coming ashore.

Getting there: The entrance to Colonial Spanish Quarter is at 29 St. George Street in historic downtown St. Augustine, 32084, across from the Castillo. GPS coordinates are N29° 53.8027', W081° 18.79'.

Parking: There is a city parking garage in the area and metered parking along the streets; otherwise parking in the Old Town section is sparse.

Fees and tickets: Free with admission to Colonial Spanish Quarter, which is less than $10.

Facilities

Restrooms: Because of the nature of historic building preservation, restrooms are present at Colonial Spanish Quarter but are not ADA-compliant.

Other ADA compliance information: There are paved paths at the Spanish Quarter, and the grounds in general are level hard-packed dirt with an occasional tree root.

Places to eat: Because the event is spread over part of downtown St. Augustine, there are numerous food establishments handy.

Picnic facilities: None available.

Places to sit: Small folding chairs might be useful at curbside while watching the parade of brigands.

Places to stay on-site: For visitors, no, but St. Augustine has many other places to conceal one's family from marauding pirates.

Reenactors

Needed are representatives of seventeenth-century Florida: Spanish townspeople, Spanish garrison soldiers, Native Americans, and English buccaneers. Native American reenactors doing im-pressions of Timucua, Apalachee, or Guale are especially welcome. Amenities include a spot at one of the primitive campsites at the park, hay, firewood, and water. Breakfast and lunch will be served to reenactors on Saturday, as well as a veritable feast during the post-raid jollification on Saturday evening.

Educators

There are no school days or field trips. Curriculum aids are on the official event website.

Contact Information

http://searlesbuccaneers.org
www.historicstaugustine.com/csq/history.html

—————◆•××•◆—————

Fort Taylor Pyrate Fest (1650–1725)

Key West, Monroe County

Historical Background

Legend has it that this was a place infested with thieves, blackguards, cutthroats, brigands, buccaneers—in general, the dregs and distilled scum of humanity, a fetid pool bubbling over with evil and villainy.

The waters around the Florida Keys have always been a treacherous place for seagoing vessels, with their shifting winds, sudden squalls, and reefs everywhere. Then there were the marooned pirates. A favorite plan of escape was to wait until a ship hove into view and then build a smoky fire as a signal, pretending to be innocent castaways. Once the luckless ship approached, the kind-hearted wretches aboard soon found themselves needing rescuing from those they had come to save.

What You'll Find

The living history part of Key West's "Pirates in Paradise" includes:

- Fort Zachary Taylor's transformation into Fort Taylor, a British fortress guarding the Crown's interests in the Florida Keys, manned by a small company of British Royal Marines unaware of their impending doom at the hands of vicious pirates
- Spectacular artillery duels between audacious seagoing buccaneers and the Fort's stalwart Royal Marines.
- An authentic pirates' pub with much merriment, jesting, japery, and raucous singing of sea shanties
- Pirate encampments as the pirates roam the island acquiring provisions (to put it discreetly); where life aboard ship and survival skills of the shipwrecked are demonstrated
- A historically accurate trial of a famous pirate
- A thieves' market of booty for sale
- Sea battles between pirate vessels and warships under full sail

Planning Your Visit

Whom to bring: This is a family event, although pets are not allowed inside Fort Zachary Taylor. Guide dogs, guide parrots, and other working animals are always welcome. Since one of the events is a "Walk the Plank" contest, consider bringing your in-laws.

Dates and times: The Fort Taylor Pyrate Fest lasts for three days, ending with the first Saturday in December. Key West's "Pirates in Paradise" festival starts on November 30. Shifty-looking denizens of the Thieves' Market will be cutting your purse on the weekend from 10 AM to 5 PM. Boasts of wickedness yet to come are brazenly scrawled onto the websites listed under "Contact information."

Getting there: Fort Zachary Taylor Historic State Park is located at the end of Southard Street through the Truman Annex in Key West. It's on the far end of the island. GPS coordinates are N24° 33.0234', W081° 48.3804'. The gate is at 1 Southard St., 33041.

Parking: Ample parking with ADA-compliant spaces is available around the fort. Remember that events take place inside and outside of the fort, as well as at sea.

Fees and tickets: Thursday is free for all students and faculty at Monroe County schools. Festival Pass: $6/adults and $4/children under twelve (park admission not included). There is also a three-day weekend pass that is $15 for adults and $10 for children under twelve (park admission not included).

Facilities

Restrooms: ADA-compliant restrooms are just outside the fort, easily accessible by those using wheelchairs, strollers, canes, peg legs, or hooks.

Other ADA compliance information: The pathways to the fort are paved, as are parts of the perimeter of the parade grounds within. The grounds are mainly hard-packed soil, level but uneven. A person using a wheelchair or cane should be able to negotiate it. Unfortunately, the upper gun decks used for observing sea battles are not ADA-accessible, but the parking lot affords views.

Places to eat: Concessions are present.

Picnic facilities: There are two uncovered tables with grills next to the restrooms. Visitors should not count on their availability.

Places to sit: It is not necessary to bring chairs or a blanket.

Places to stay on-site: There are none on-site except for primitive beach campsites. Key West has many inns to stash one's plunder while sleeping off a night at the tavern.

Reenactors

Needed are pirates, pirate wenches, other civilians, and British Royal Marines from

"Corsair, n. A politician of the seas." —Ambrose Bierce, *The Devil's Dictionary* the years 1650 to 1725. There are no amenities except for encampment space, but after enough tankards of ale no one will care.

Educators
School days, field trips, and curriculum aids are available for pint-sized apprentice pirates who are still learning how to swash their buckles. As stated above, Thursday is free for all students and faculty at Monroe County schools.

Contact Information
www.forttaylor.org/piratefest.html
E-mail: info@forttaylor.org
305-292-6713
Organizers: Bone Island Buccaneers, the most dreaded of all the pirate crews sullying the Seven Seas: www.myspace.com/boneislandbuccaneers

---

Defending St. Augustine: The Castillo de San Marcos (1675–1763)
St. Augustine, St. Johns County

Historical Background
After the sacking of St. Augustine by Robert Searles and his crew in 1668, the Spanish government allotted funds to build a stone fort to defend the city. Completed in 1695 and improved in 1756, the Castillo de San Marcos was never taken from the Spanish by force, only by treaty.

What You'll Find
- Spanish soldiers of *La Florida*'s First Spanish Period demonstrating their weapons, including cannons, and sharing their experiences of being stationed at the Castillo so far away from Spain
- The strict discipline and safety procedures used for artillery and other firearms used by professionals even so long ago
- The Castillo itself, little changed after hundreds of years, and discussion of how it was designed to be a fortress as well as a place of refuge for the people of St. Augustine
- A fascinating science lesson as the soldiers explain what happens when a cannonball hits a wall of the Castillo

Planning Your Visit
Whom to bring: This is of interest to the whole family, although small children may be frightened by the loud noises. Pets are not allowed inside the Castillo, though guide animals are always welcome.

Dates and times: The Castillo is open every day except Christmas, from 8:45 AM to 5:15 PM, although the ticket booth closes at 4:45 PM. Except during special events, staff unavailability, or bad weather, firing times are at 10:30 AM, 11:30 AM, 1:30 PM, 2:30 PM, and 3:30 PM, on Fridays through Sundays. Think of them as weekend warriors.

Getting there: The Castillo is at 1 South Castillo Drive, looming over historic downtown St. Augustine. GPS coordinates are N29° 53.9574', W081° 18.8558'. (If you can't find it, then you are probably in St. Augustine, Illinois, instead of Florida.)

Parking: Limited. There is a metered lot on the grounds that fills quickly, but has some free ADA-compliant spaces. Metered spaces on the streets are meager. There is a city parking garage four short blocks away, but it has no shuttle yet.

Fees and tickets: Castillo admission is $6 for ages sixteen and up and free for those under sixteen. Each ticket is good for seven days.

Facilities

Restrooms: ADA-accessible restrooms are provided.

Other ADA compliance information: The approach ramp to the entrance is paved but slopes upward. The Gun Deck level can only be reached by stairs. There is little shade on the Castillo's parade grounds. The interior's perimeter is paved and level.

Places to eat: There are no food concessions.

Picnic facilities: There are none.

Places to sit: There is no need to bring chairs or a blanket.

Places to stay on-site: None, but numerous lodgings are close by, although they are not as heavily fortified against unexpected attacks by offshore cannonfire.

Reenactors

First- or third-person impressions of Spanish soldiers of the sixteenth and seventeenth centuries are welcome. Black-powder weapons may only be fired by those who have been to the National Park Service Musket or Cannon schools.

Educators

There are no school days, but field trips are available. Contact your local school board. Cannonloads of curriculum aids are on the Castillo's website.

Contact Information
Castillo de San Marcos
1 South Castillo Drive
St. Augustine, FL 32084
904-829-6506
http://home.nps.gov/casa

"Gunpowder, n. An agency employed by civilized nations for the settlement of disputes which might become troublesome if left unadjusted." —Ambrose Bierce, *The Devil's Dictionary*

St. Augustine's Siege of 1702 (1702, of course)
St. Augustine, St. Johns County

Historical Background

European wars had a way of spilling over into American colonies. When King Charles II of Spain died without an heir, his will left his throne to a member of French royalty. This shifted the balance of power in Europe to France and Spain, leading to a declaration of war in 1702 by an alliance headed by Queen Anne of England. This War of Spanish Succession was known in the thirteen American colonies as Queen Anne's War. The English colony of Carolina saw Spanish-controlled St. Augustine as a major threat and decided on a pre-emptive strike. Warned by his Native American allies of the impending attack, the governor of Spanish Florida made extensive preparations as the city's inhabitants took refuge inside the Castillo. After nearly two months of siege, the frustrated Carolina forces retreated when they found themselves caught between an impenetrable Castillo and fresh Spanish relief forces from Cuba.

What You'll Find

- An outstanding nighttime immersion event in a centuries-old walled fort
- Spanish military families, civilian colonials, and Native Americans taking refuge inside the Castillo and sharing how they are preparing for the siege
- Spanish soldiers carrying out their duties and readying for the British attack
- Hearing the refugees' fears as to what might happen to the city and what they may have to deal with afterward
- The story of the secret weapon used by the Spanish troops to break up the British attack on a mission nearby

Planning Your Visit

Whom to bring: This is for the whole family. Pets are not allowed within the fort, although guide animals are always welcome.

Dates and times: This event is on the fourth Saturday evening in October. Call the Castillo or check its website for exact hours of its opening and closing.

"In our day we don't allow a hundred and thirty years to elapse between glimpses of a marvel. If somebody should discover a creek in the county next to the one the North Pole is in, Europe and America would start fifteen costly expeditions thither; one to explore the creek, and the other fourteen to hunt for each other."—Mark Twain, *Life on the Mississippi*

32

Fees and tickets: The event is free with paid admission to the Castillo.

Reenactors

Needed are authentically dressed Spanish soldiers, citizens, and Native Americans of the early 1700s. There are no amenities.

Educators

No school days or field trips are available, but enough curriculum aids are posted on the Castillo's official website to keep children occupied during a long siege.

Contact Information

Castillo de San Marcos
904-829-6506
http://home.nps.gov/casa

La Guardia de Noche—The Spanish Night Watch (1740)
St. Augustine, St. Johns County

Historical Background

After the founding of St. Augustine in 1565, the Spanish occupied the territory of *La Florida* until 1763. They were challenged numerous times. After the raid on St. Augustine by Robert Searles' brigands in 1668, a stone fort was built for St. Augustine's protection: the Castillo de San Marcos. English forces besieged the fort unsuccessfully in 1702 and in 1740. This event reenacts a securing of the city for the night during the time period leading up to the 1740 siege.

What You'll Find

- Eighteenth-century Spanish military drill, tattoo and weapons demonstrations, including the firing of artillery and muskets
- A formal Changing of the Guard at the City Gates
- Eighteenth-century Spanish family life and domestic activities in the Colonial Spanish Quarter
- An invitation to follow the soldiers and townsfolk in an evening military parade recreating the securing of the city for the evening
- The conclusion of the event with a grand musket volley at the Government House on the Plaza de la Constitución

Planning Your Visit

Whom to bring: This is a family event. Small children may be afraid of the dark. Pets are not allowed, but guide animals are always welcome.

Dates and times: The event normally takes place the first or second weekend in

March. The torchlight parade begins at 8 PM at the gates of the Castillo. The daytime events begin at 10 AM in the Colonial Spanish Quarter and the Castillo de San Marcos.

> "Cannon, n. An instrument employed in the rectification of national boundaries." —Ambrose Bierce, *The Devil's Dictionary*

Fees and tickets: The event itself is free, but getting inside the Castillo is a little over $5 for adults, less for children. The living history portion also spills to the outside grounds; access to that area and to the parade route is free.

Reenactors

Needed are impressions of mid-eighteenth-century Spanish military and civilians, as well as Native Americans and British sailors of that time. Those interested should contact the event organizers beforehand. There are no amenities other than encampment space.

Educators

There are no school days or field trips available, but curriculum aids are online at the Castillo's National Park Service website.

Contact Information

www.FloridaLivingHistory.org
877-352-4478

Flight to Freedom at Fort Mose (1738–63)
St. Augustine, St. Johns County

Historical Background

In 1738 the Spanish governor of Florida established a settlement named Mose for slaves who had escaped from the British-ruled Carolinas. The ex-slaves merely had to convert to Catholicism and (for the males) serve in the Mose militia to claim their freedom and begin their lives anew. Repeated attacks led to the building of fortifications for the town's defense, thus the name change to Fort Mose and its position as one of the defenses of St. Augustine for the Spanish. The ex-slaves at Fort Mose would fight especially fiercely against the English forces, not wanting to be returned to the English colonies and a life of renewed slavery.

What You'll Find

The living history portions of this event are arranged in stations with reenactors doing first-person impressions:

- Escaped slaves answer questions about why they fled and the hardships of their journeys
- Spanish clergy explain what the refugees must do for their freedom
- Native Americans help the fugitives and talk about why they do it
- Slave catchers hunt their quarry
- Community leaders try to solve the problems facing a place of refuge
- Residents talk about their life at Fort Mose
- Spanish military perform drills and artillery demonstrations

Planning Your Visit

Whom to bring: This is a family event. Reservations are required for the school day on Friday. Pets may be frightened by the gunfire and artillery demonstrations, but guide animals are always welcome.

Dates and times: The event is held on the first Friday and Saturday in February (to avoid conflicts with Florida school achievement testing; see website for any changes), 10 AM to 3 PM. Friday is a school day. The public day (Saturday) runs from 9 AM to 1 PM.

Getting there: This event is at Fort Mose State Historic Park. The GPS coordinates of the park's entrance are N29° 55.6613', W081° 19.5101'. The road that dead-ends into Fort Mose is the first one on the right as one passes through St. Augustine's northern city gates while going north. Zip is 32080.

Parking: Ample and ADA-compliant. There is a provision for overflow parking. A tram is provided for those parking farther away.

Fees and tickets: The event is free with a small admission fee to the park.

Facilities

Restrooms: ADA-accessible restrooms are at the visitor center.

Other ADA compliance information: The parking lot is paved. The grounds are hard-packed and without slopes; wheelchair and cane users should be able to get around without needing help. Some shade is present.

Places to eat: During the event there is a concession on-site.

Picnic facilities: One small picnic pavilion with a grill is available at no charge. There are other open picnic tables without grills.

Places to sit: This is not necessary for the event, but there are areas to spread a blanket and have a picnic.

Places to stay on-site: None.

Reenactors

Needed are impressions from the eighteenth century: Spanish (Catholic) bishops, escaped slaves, sympathetic Native Americans, and slave trappers. Eighteenth-century Spanish military (infantry or artillery) are also needed. There are no amenities.

Educators
School day is the Friday before the public event. Field trips are available if reservations are made. Curriculum aids are available online (see "Contact information")

Contact Information
Fort Mose Historical State Park
c/o Anastasia State Park
1340-A A1A S.
St. Augustine, FL 32080
904- 823-2232
www.floridastateparks.org/fortmose/default.cfm

———————◆◆◆◆◆◆———————

Life in the Colonial Spanish Quarter (1740s)
St. Augustine, St. Johns County

Historical Background
As the Castillo de San Marcos served the needs of the people of St. Augustine for protection, so the people of St. Augustine took care of the needs of the fort. Money sent from Spain to pay the soldiers and for the upkeep of the fort eventually went into the pockets of the blacksmiths, the carpenters, and women with domestic skills such as sewing. St. Augustine was a garrison town, and supporting the Castillo its major industry. For that reason, St. Augustine did not grow very much during its first two centuries of Spanish rule.

What You'll Find
- St. Augustine's only living history museum
- The sights, sounds, and aromas of life in 1740s St. Augustine
- Living historians going about their trades of blacksmithing, leatherworking, and candlemaking, among others
- Explanations for how domestic chores such as laundry were done by hand
- Reenactors discussing how St. Augustine families of the mid-1700s obtained food and drink

Planning Your Visit
Whom to bring: This will be enjoyed by the whole family. Pets are not allowed, but guide animals are always welcome.
Dates and times: Hours are 9 AM–5:30 PM, with the last ticket sold at 4:45 PM. It is closed on Thanksgiving and New Year's Day, as well as Christmas Eve and Christmas Day.
Getting there: The GPS coordinates for the Colonial Spanish Quarter Living

History Museum are N29° 53.8027', W081° 18.79'. The address is 29 St. George Street in historic downtown St. Augustine, 32084, across from the Castillo de San Marcos.

Parking: Limited metered parking is available on the streets; there is a city parking garage nearby, but no shuttle.

Fees and tickets: Rates vary from free (for military with ID) to $6.95 for adults or a family rate. Group rates are available with advance reservations.

Facilities

Restrooms: Because these are preserved historic buildings, the restrooms are not ADA-accessible.

Other ADA compliance information: Doorways and all visitor areas except the restrooms are wheelchair-accessible.

Places to eat or drink: There is a tavern next door.

Picnic facilities: None.

Places to sit: It is unnecessary to bring chairs or a blanket.

Places to stay on-site: There are none, but many are close by.

Reenactors: Volunteers should contact the museum staff.

Educators: Field trips are available, but there are no school days as such. No curriculum aids are yet available.

Contact Information

Colonial Spanish Quarter: 904-825-6830
www.historicstaugustine.com/csq/history.html

———◆━▸▪◂━◆———

The Southern Sentinel: Fort Matanzas (1742)
St. Augustine, St. Johns County

Historical Background

After the British failure in their 1740 siege of the Castillo at St. Augustine, Governor Manuel de Montiano correctly guessed that the next British attack would be from the unprotected inland waterway to the south. Realizing the urgency of the situation, he made the bold decision to order the construction of Fort Matanzas to protect the southern approach to St. Augustine without going through proper channels and getting permission from the Spanish king. While under construction, the fort was repeatedly attacked by the British, but never fell. In 1742, the British did try to attack St. Augustine from the south, but by that time Fort Matanzas had been completed and the British forces could not get past its cannons.

What You'll Find

- A beautifully preserved and restored fort from the First Spanish Period of Florida's history
- On most days, an authentically dressed reenactor doing a third-person impression of a Spanish soldier of the mid-1700s who is ready to tell about life in the fort
- Occasional special events such as artillery firings or nighttime torchlight tours
- A free ferry that takes visitors from the Visitor Center to the fort

Planning Your Visit

Whom to bring: This is a family event. Well-behaved dogs on six-foot leashes are allowed in the park but not in the Fort or on the ferry. Guide animals are welcome.

Dates and times: Fort Matanzas National Monument is open every day of the year except Christmas, from 9 AM to 5:30 PM.

Getting there: The address is 8635 A1A South in St. Augustine, 32080. The GPS coordinates of Fort Matanzas are N29° 50.2422', W081° 16.4804'.

From I-95: Take exit 305 (Route 206). Follow Route 206 east about 6 miles to Highway A1A. Turn right and follow A1A south for 4 miles to the park entrance, on the right side of the road.

From St. Augustine: Follow Highway A1A south for approximately 15 miles to the park entrance, on the right side of the road.

Parking: Limited. Can fill up on weekends, and RV parking is especially limited.

Fees and tickets: No fees. Donations gratefully accepted, especially since you will be contributing to the Fort's continuing mission to protect St. Augustine from attacks by foreign powers.

Facilities

Restrooms: ADA-accessible restrooms are just outside the Visitor Center.

Other ADA compliance information: The park is accessible by wheelchair except for the ferry and the fort itself, which is entered by a fifteen-step stairway.

Places to eat: There is a soft drink machine near the Visitor Center.

Picnic tables: Uncovered picnic tables without grills are near the Visitor Center.

Places to sit: There is no need to bring chairs or blankets.

Places to stay on-site: None.

"Abrupt, adj. Sudden, without ceremony, like the arrival of a cannon-shot and the departure of the soldier whose interests are most affected by it." Ambrose Bierce, *The Devil's Dictionary*

Reenactors

Needed are Spanish soldiers of the mid-1700s. Firing of black-powder weapons requires completion of the appropriate National Park Service course. There are no amenities.

Educators

There are no school days, but field trips and curriculum aids are available.

Contact Information

Fort Matanzas National Monument
8635 A1A South
St Augustine, FL 32080
904-471-0116
www.nps.gov/foma

> Be sure to watch your children carefully if they climb the ladder to the deck at the top of the fort's tower. The ladder is nearly vertical.

Living History Day at Fort Matanzas (1742–63)
St. Augustine, St. Johns County

Historical Background

The primary weapons at Fort Matanzas were cannons. The military strategy was simple: any ship entering the inland waterway that was the southern approach to St. Augustine was easily within range of the fort's cannons. End of story.

What You'll Find

- First- or third-person impressions by living historians of mid-1700s Spanish soldiers going about their duties, ready to talk about their lives at the fort
- Demonstrations of military drills and safety precautions taken when firing cannons and other weapons

Planning Your Visit

Whom to bring: This is a family event, although small children may be frightened by loud cannonfire. Well-behaved dogs on a leash no longer than six feet are allowed in the park, but neither on the ferry nor in the Fort. Guide animals are welcome.

Dates and times: The event is on the first Saturday of each month except in December, when it may be the second Saturday. Hours are 10:30 AM to 3:30 PM, with cannonfire each hour.

Fees and tickets: No fees. Donations to continue protecting St. Augustine from hostile invasions will be gratefully accepted.

Reenactors: Needed are Spanish soldiers of the mid-1700s. Firing of black-powder weapons requires completion of the appropriate National Park Service course. There are no amenities.

Educators: There are no school days, but field trips and curriculum aids are available.

Torchlight Tour at Fort Matanzas (1742–63)
St. Augustine, St. Johns County

Historical Background
The Spanish contingent at Fort Matanzas was rotated a month at a time from St. Augustine (some of them had families) and normally consisted of one officer and seven to ten soldiers. When hostilities threatened, the number of soldiers went to fifty. When Spain ceded *La Florida* to Britain in 1763, the British military took over the operations of the fort.

What You'll Find
- An unforgettable sensation of traveling back in time as you ride a ferry through the Stygian darkness to an isolated fort built long ago
- Living historians doing first-person impressions of mid-1700s Spanish soldiers or late-1700s British soldiers, going about their duties at Fort Matanzas and ready to answer questions about their lives at the fort
- Demonstrations of military drills and safety precautions taken when firing cannons and other weapons

Planning Your Visit
Whom to bring: This is a family event. Guide animals are always welcome, but pets are not allowed inside the fort or on the ferry.
Dates and times: The event is on the last Saturday of November (unless conflicting with Thanksgiving weekend), January, and February. Tours are every forty-five minutes starting at 6 PM, with the last one at 8:15 PM. Since tour groups are limited to thirty people, reservations are recommended.
Fees and tickets: Seven dollars; children three and under are free.

Reenactors: Needed are Spanish soldiers of the mid-1700s or British military of the late 1700s. Volunteers should check with park staff beforehand. There are no amenities.

Educators: Curriculum aids are available online, but no school days or field trips.

The British Period
(1763–1784)

Change of Flags at St. Augustine (July 21, 1763)
St. Augustine, St. Johns County

Historical Background

The first actual world war was the Seven Years' War, known as the French and Indian War in North America, which ended in 1763 with the Treaty of Paris. One result was that Spain handed over its Florida colony to England. The keys to the Castillo de San Marcos were given to the English. The Spanish population (and some of their Native American allies) then evacuated St. Augustine for Cuba.

What You'll Find

- One of only two living history events in Florida depicting a ceremonial changing of governments
- Authentic British and Spanish encampments with soldiers sharing what the change means for them, their families, and homes
- Cannon firings by both British and Spanish troops
- An explanation of how long the Seven Years' War actually lasted

Planning Your Visit

Whom to bring: This is for the whole family. Small children won't understand the historic significance, but they'll be impressed by the pageantry. However, they may be frightened by the loud cannonfire. Pets are not allowed, but guide animals are always welcome.

Dates and times: The event is on the first Saturday in May. The ceremony is at 11 AM, repeated at 2 PM.

Getting there: The Castillo is at 1 South Castillo Drive in historic downtown St. Augustine. GPS coordinates are N29° 53.9574', W081° 18.8558'.

Parking: Limited, but there are ADA spaces. There is a city parking garage nearby, but no shuttle service. Nearly all street parking is metered.

Fees and tickets: Free with admission to the Castillo.

Facilities

Restrooms: There are ADA-compliant restrooms at the Castillo.

Other ADA compliance information: The ramp leading to the Castillo entrance slopes upwards. There is almost no shade inside the fort. The parade grounds are hard-packed, and the perimeter of the parade grounds is paved. About the only parts of the Castillo that are not wheelchair-accessible are the gun towers.

Places to eat: None.

Picnic facilities: None.

Places to sit: There are benches available, and the outside grounds, although sloping, make for a good place to spread a blanket.

Places to stay on-site: None, but St. Augustine has many excellent establishments close by.

Reenactors

Needed are British and Spanish soldiers of the mid-1700s. There are no amenities except space for primitive encampments.

Educators

There are no school days or field trips, but curriculum aids are available at the Castillo's website.

Contact Information

Castillo de San Marcos
1 South Castillo Drive
St. Augustine, FL 32084
904-829-6506
http://home.nps.gov/casa

> "Diplomacy, n. The patriotic art of lying for one's country."
> Ambrose Bierce, *The Devil's Dictionary*

King's English Spoken Here: The British Garrison (1763–84)

St. Augustine, St. Johns County

Historical Background

From 1763 to the American Revolution, the British had fifteen colonies, not thirteen, in what would become the United States. Two of these colonies were Florida, split in two. In 1763, Britain gave Cuba to Spain and in return received the Florida peninsula and panhandle all the way to Pensacola. St. Augustine was made the capital of East Florida, while Pensacola was the capital of West Florida. This event commemorates the British occupation.

What You'll Find

- British Army and Royal Navy troops of the late 1700s strutting about as if they own the place, which they did from 1763 to 1784

- Native Americans, military wives, local militiamen, Loyalists, and other colonials speaking about the changes in Florida since the British took over
- Weapons demonstrations
- Opportunities to discuss the American Revolution with all the different types of people in the Castillo, including colonists still loyal to the Crown

Planning Your Visit

Whom to bring: This is a family event. Guide animals are always welcome, but pets are not allowed in the fort.

Dates and times: Held on the third Saturday of September during the regular Castillo hours of 8:45 AM to 5:15 PM. Admission gate closes at 4:45 PM.

Getting there: The Castillo is at 1 South Castillo Drive in historic downtown St. Augustine. GPS coordinates are N29° 53.9574', W081° 18.8558'.

Parking: Limited, but there are ADA spaces. There is a city parking garage nearby, but no shuttle service. Nearly all street parking is metered.

Fees and tickets: Free with paid admission to the Castillo. Occasionally the day of the garrison will coincide with "Publick Lands Day," on which admission to the Castillo is free. Check the Castillo website beforehand, or call.

Reenactors

Needed are late-eighteenth-century British Army or Royal Navy, colonial militia and Loyalists, family members, or Native Americans. Check with park staff before coming. There are no amenities.

Educators

There are no school days or field trips. Curriculum materials are available online at the Castillo's website.

Going Out in Style: The British Night Watch (1784)
St. Augustine, St. Johns County

Historical Background

The end of the Seven Years' War saw the Floridas, East and West, being ceded to Great Britain by Spain. Though the Floridas flourished under British rule, the relationship between Britain and the northern colonies deteriorated. The American Revolution began; East and West Florida remained loyal to Great Britain. St. Augustine became a staging area for British troops assigned to the South. Loyalist refugees poured into East Florida. The Castillo de San Marcos was renamed Fort St. Marks and became a British supply base as well as a prison for three signers of the Declaration of Independence. Noticing Britain's preoccupation with the little problem in North America, Spain invaded and captured West Florida. With the loss of its original thirteen colonies (as well as West Florida), Britain lost interest in its fourteenth. In 1784 East Florida was given back to Spain.

What You'll Find

The British Night Watch is a combination of pomp, pageantry, and living history. The living history components include:

- A reenactment of the last British Night Watch (celebrating the beginning of Advent) in St. Augustine while under British rule
- British encampments at the Colonial Spanish Quarter
- Period fife and drum music
- British bayonet drills, musket firings, and a military tattoo
- British troops and American Loyalists eager to share their opinions of the American Revolution and what they plan to do when Spain takes over Florida
- A "Trooping of the Colours," Drill and Pay Call at Fort St. Marks
- A proper British Country Dance Presentation, the public being invited to try their hand (and feet) at eighteenth-century dancing
- Sutlers with period wares, ready to take your pounds or dollars

In addition, there is eighteenth-century dancing and music, caroling, and an invitation to carry a lighted candle in the Grande Illumination Parade.

Planning Your Visit

Whom to bring: This is most certainly an event for the whole family, but pets are not allowed inside the Castillo or in the Colonial Spanish Quarter. Guide animals are always welcome in both places.

Dates and times: Always the first Friday and Saturday in December. Schedule details will be posted on the British Night Watch website. In general, the reading of the treaties starts the event at 4 PM in St. Augustine's Plaza de la Constitución. At 8 PM there is a free public concert and libations at Colonial Spanish Quarter's Tavern. At 9 AM Saturday the British encampments open to the public for the day as well as the British garrison in the Castillo. The parade starts at 8 PM Saturday with music and caroling afterward.

Getting there: The GPS coordinates for the Colonial Spanish Quarter Living History Museum at 29 St. George Street in St. Augustine are N29° 53.8027', W081° 18.79'. The Castillo de San Marcos is across the street at 1 South Castillo Drive in St. Augustine. Its GPS coordinates are N29°53.9574, W081°18.8558. Zip is 32084.

Parking: The Committee for the Night Watch recommends that visitors park for a small fee at the new city parking garage. There are metered parking spaces and metered lots in and about the historic downtown area.

Fees and tickets: All portions of the event are free except for the Castillo's admission fees to events inside its walls.

Facilities

Restrooms: facilities in the Castillo are ADA-compliant; those in the Colonial Spanish Quarter are not.

Other ADA compliance information: The ramp leading to the Castillo is paved but slopes upward. Its grounds are level and paved or hard-packed dirt. The fort's grounds have little shade. The Spanish Quarter is paved.

Places to eat: There is no concession at the Castillo, but the Spanish Quarter is next to a tavern, and much delicious food is being made for you close by.

Picnic facilities: There are no available picnic tables or grills.

Places to sit: There are benches at the Castillo.

Places to stay: None on-site except for the reenactors' campsites, but there are many places of lodging close by that are more substantial than tents.

Reenactors

Needed are participants dressed out as British or Provincial soldiers, Native American allies, militia, or civilian men and women of the British period. There are no amenities.

Educators

There are no school days or field trips available. Curriculum aids are on the Castillo's website.

Contact Information

The Committee for the Night Watch, Inc.
One Oak Tree Lane
St. Augustine Florida 32084
904-829-5318
E-mail: bnw@aug.com
website: www.britishnightwatch.org

"Peace, n. In international affairs, a period of cheating between two periods of fighting." Ambrose Bierce, *The Devil's Dictionary*

The Second Spanish Period: Prelude to War (1784–1821)

The Living Village of Ah-Tah-Thi-Ki (late 1700s–early 1800s)
Big Cypress Seminole Reservation, Hendry County

Historical Background

The Seminole Nation originated as an amalgamation of a number of Native American settlements already in the Florida area at the time of Spanish contact, plus groups of Creeks who had come from Georgia to several of the Spanish missions here. During the early 1800s the growing nation received thousands of Native American refugees from the taking of their homelands north of Florida.

What You'll Find

- A trail that takes you away from the museum building deeper into the Everglades where you will come upon a Seminole village of the late 1700s
- If the villagers are at home, they will be going about daily life as they did centuries ago, demonstrating Seminole skills, arts, and crafts
- See the village not as a museum exhibit but in its natural setting, showing how the early Seminoles adapted to their environment

Planning Your Visit

Whom to bring: This is for the whole family. Although pets are not allowed, guide animals are welcome.

Dates and times: The living history village is accessible every day except Christmas Eve, Christmas Day, New Year's Day, July 4, and Thanksgiving. Hours are 9 AM to 5 PM, but visitors should call beforehand to ascertain whether the villagers will be home that day.

Getting there: The museum is about seventeen miles north of Alligator Alley (I-75) once you exit at marker 49. A boardwalk takes you from the museum building about three-quarters of a mile deeper into the Everglades to the living history village, at 34725 West Boundary Rd. in Clewiston, 33440. GPS coordinates are N26°19.8626', W081°1.9792'.

Parking: There is ample parking across the street from the museum.

Fees and tickets: Access to the village is free with museum admission, which ranges from $9 for adults to free for children four and under.

Facilities

Restrooms: Modern, ADA-accessible restrooms are present at the museum building, but not the village.

Other ADA compliance information: The museum is fully accessible by wheelchair. The boardwalk is also accessible by wheelchair. A wheelchair is available for those who do not feel they can walk the entire way to the living history village and back (a round-trip of one and a half miles).

Places to eat: A restaurant is across the street from the museum.

Picnic facilities: There are no picnic areas at the museum or at the village.

Places to sit: There is no need to bring chairs or a blanket.

Places to stay: Overnight facilities are available at the Billie Swamp Safari area three miles away.

Reenactors
None are needed.

Educators
Although the museum does not have specific school days, there are a variety of educational programs involving field trips. Curriculum aids are available as well.

Contact Information
www.ahtahthiki.com
Ah-Tah-Thi-Ki
HC-61, Box 21-A
Clewiston, FL 33440
877-902-1113

———◆◆✕◆●———

Shinin' Times: The Alafia River Rendezvous (early 1800s)
Homeland, Polk County

Historical Background
In the early nineteenth century, there was still plenty of wilderness and frontier in Florida, as well as out West. Florida products such as alligator hides and feathers of exotic birds made their way through Native Americans, trappers, and pioneers to local businesses and eventually to merchants in the growing cities of more northern states. Cow hunters traversed the peninsula on a more or less regular schedule, as strings of trading posts crisscrossed the same frontier like Christmas lights. Trading camps appeared or vanished with the seasons. The Alafia River Rendezvous continues to grow larger each year as it celebrates a gathering of frontier folks, pioneers, and Native Americans for the purposes of trade, renewing friendships, and friendly competition.

What You'll Find
- Well over a thousand of the friendliest and most interesting people

you'll ever meet in pre-1840 Florida

- An overnight city whose streets are lined with the tents and tepees of Native Americans, mountain men, and merchants
- A functioning one-room school for the children of the families camped at the rendezvous
- Primitive archery, tomahawk-throwing, and musket-shooting competitions
- An array of sutlers with goods from the 1700s and early 1800s
- Displays of pre-1840 crafts, skills, and art
- A Saturday-night square dance, as it was done way back when

Because of the variety and sheer number of events and the length of the rendezvous, the schedule is best obtained from the official website.

Planning Your Visit

Whom to bring: This is a family event. Be prepared to walk a lot. Handicapped parking is available near the entry gate. No pets are allowed at any time, but service animals are welcome.

Dates and times: Main encampment begins the third Saturday of January and goes through the following Saturday; early arrival is the Wednesday before main encampment starts. Public days are the last Friday and Saturday from 9 AM to 4 PM.

Getting there: The GPS coordinates for Homeland are N27° 49.2312', W081° 49.5236'. The entrance to the rendezvous area is at the south end of Azalea Avenue in Homeland, zip 33847, which is several miles south of Bartow.

Parking: Ample, but this is a huge event. A limited number of shuttles are available for transportation to and from the parking area.

Fees and tickets: For participants, pre-registration is advised because the fees are cheaper. For public days, fees are about $10 for an adult and $5 for children and seniors (ages 65 and older).

Facilities

Restrooms: Porta-potties are available throughout the encampment, many of them ADA-compliant. They're marked on a map given upon admission. A limited number of changing tables for children are available.

Other ADA compliance information: The rendezvous is held in a large grassy, hard-packed, somewhat uneven field traversed by a dirt road. When wet, it should not be considered wheelchair accessible. A limited number of trams are provided to transport people from the parking areas to a point very close to the entrance. There is almost no shade.

Places to eat: Concessions are on-site.

Picnic facilities: A few picnic tables are at some concessions. There are no grills.

Places to sit: A few benches are scattered about. Seating is also available in front of stages and at some food concessions.

Places to stay on-site: Primitive campgrounds and RV camping for reenactors, scouts, and sutlers only. No electrical or sewer hookups are available.

Reenactors

Reenactors invited are military and civilians of the 1830s, authentically garbed. This is the best opportunity in Florida for children to be immersed in this time period. Amenities include firewood and water.

Educators

The last Friday of the encampment (same as the first public day) is a school day. Field trips are available. (Check with the local school district.) Curriculum aids are not yet available, but there is a working one-room school on-site for the encampment children.

Contact Information

www.floridafrontiersmen.org

Be sure to have sunscreen, hats, or parasols handy. There is relatively little shade.

"When I wrote my first story on the Alafia twelve years ago, a guy who was president of something like the American Teepee Pole Association said there was more knowledge of early America at a Rendezvous than there is on any college campus in the country. I can believe that." —Bill Bair, retired columnist for the *Lakeland Ledger*

Central Florida Flintknap-In (late 1700s–early 1800s)
Withlacoochee River Park, Pasco County

Historical Background

As trappers made their way into the Florida territory, adapting their tool-making skills to the materials at hand, they also adopted the technologies of the Native Americans they encountered.

What You'll Find

- Many heritage craftspeople, some in period dress, demonstrating the art of fashioning sharp-edged tools such as arrowheads or hatchets from rocks
- Teaching stations
- Demonstrations on the use of atlatls

Planning Your Visit

Whom to bring: The whole family.

Dates and times: The third weekend in February, from 9 AM to 4 PM daily.

Getting there: This is held at Withlacoochee River Park, 12449 Withlacoochee Blvd. in Dade City, zip 33525. GPS coordinates are N28° 20.7727', W082° 7.4234'.

Parking: Abundant, with numerous ADA-compliant spaces.

Fees and tickets: 2009 prices were $2 per adult or $5 a carload (up to eight people); children under twelve years old are free.

Facilities

Restrooms: There are many fixed or portable restrooms; some are ADA-accessible.

Other ADA compliance information: The grounds are level, hard-packed soil with an occasional tree root. People using wheelchairs, canes, or strollers should have no problems unless the grounds are soaked. Shady spots are abundant.

Places to eat: A concession is on-site.

Picnic facilities: Picnic tables are available, as well as many places to spread a blanket.

Places to sit: There are benches and picnic tables.

Places to stay on-site: There are primitive campsites and modern ones with electricity available. Those wishing to chip away at their rocks in more plush surroundings will find modern lodgings just a stone's throw away in Dade City.

Reenactors
Needed are flintknappers, preferably in period dress from prior to 1840.

Educators
There are no school days, field trips, or curriculum aids yet available.

Contact Information
Park Office: 352-567-0264

Fort Dade Mountain Man Rendezvous (early 1800s)
Withlacoochee River Park, Pasco County

Historical Background
Here is the early American frontier, complete with trappers, traders, Native Americans, a few pioneer families, and some hardy mountain men visiting friends and relations here in the Florida flatlands.

What You'll Find
Living historians from the fur-trading years prior to 1840, along with
- An authentic Native American (Creek) village whose residents will be in full pre-1840s regalia
- Native American music and dancing
- Early American games and competitions for young and old, including cook-offs, frying pan tosses, tug-of-wars, sack races, tomahawk and knife throwing, archery, and a black-powder gun shoot
- Cannon firings
- Lessons in bow making
- Demonstrations of heritage skills such as candle making, clothes dyeing, soap making, and making pies or biscuits over an open fire
- Mountain men with astounding stories to tell
- Merchants of pre-1840s goods graciously accepting twenty-first-century cash
- Encampments of pioneers, trappers, and mountain men who truly have hair of the bear, all in period clothes

Planning Your Visit
Whom to bring: The whole family will talk about this one for a long time.
Dates and times: The last weekend in January through the first weekend in February, from 9 AM to 4 PM daily.
Getting there: This is held at Withlacoochee River Park, 12449 Withlacoochee Blvd. in Dade City, zip 33525. GPS coordinates are N28° 20.7727', W082° 7.4234'.

Parking: Enough for any size wagon train, with numerous ADA-compliant spaces.

Fees and tickets: Admissions is $2 per adult or $5 a carload. Free for those under twelve. Payments in furs must be negotiated with event organizers.

Facilities

Restrooms: There are many fixed or portable restrooms; some are ADA-accessible. Unfortunately, doing what real mountain men do is illegal here.

Other ADA compliance information: The grounds are level, hard-packed soil with an occasional tree root. People using wheelchairs, canes, or strollers should have no problems unless the grounds are soaked. Shady spots are abundant.

Places to eat: A concession is on-site.

Picnic facilities: Picnic tables are available, as well as many places to spread a blanket.

Places to sit: There are benches and picnic tables to rest one's bones after a long walk in from the Smokies or wherever.

Places to stay on-site: There are primitive campsites and modern ones with electricity available. Less hardy pilgrims will find a hotel seven miles away in Dade City.

Reenactors

Needed are impressions of Native Americans, trapper, pioneers, and mountain men of the fur-trading years before 1840, in period dress. Ability to demonstrate a heritage skill is especially welcome. Amenities include a primitive campsite and exhibit space.

Educators

The first day (Friday) of the rendezvous is a school day, from 9 AM to 4 PM. Field trips are available through your local school board. No curriculum aids exist yet.

Contact Information

Park Office: 352-567-0264

The Seminole Wars
(1821–1860)

Ambush: The Dade Battle Reenactment (1835)
Dade Battlefield Historic State Park, Bushnell, Sumter County

Historical Background

"Have a good heart; our difficulties and dangers are over now, and as soon as we arrive at Fort King you'll have three days to rest and keep Christmas gaily," Major Francis L. Dade said to his weary troops in a pine forest on the chilly morning of December 28, 1835. Within eight hours, they were ambushed by Seminoles determined to preserve their homeland and their freedom. Only three of one hundred and eight Federals survived. The Second Seminole War had begun.

What You'll Find

- A full-scale narrated battle between Seminole and Federal forces, showing the different tactics used by each side
- Authentic soldier, civilian, and Seminole camps, including Black Seminoles
- Sutlers anxious to ambush your most recent paycheck
- Demonstrations of historic crafts and skills
- Musket-shooting and tomahawk-throwing competitions
- A camp meeting–style Sunday morning service
- Period music throughout the day

Planning Your Visit

Whom to bring: This is a family event. Pets are allowed, but may be frightened by gunshots and cannonfire. They must be well behaved, on a leash no longer than six feet, and cleaned up after.

Dates and times: Dade Battle reenactment dates vary, but are always the weekend either just before or after New Year's Day.

Getting there: Dade Battlefield Historic State Park is in Bushnell, Florida, at 7200 CR 603 South Battlefield Drive. The GPS coordinates of the park entrance are N28° 39.2242', W082° 7.5098'. Zip is 33513.

Parking: Ample, although parking for the reenactment has always been an issue. Check with the Dade Battlefield Society's website for the parking location. Trams

> "Hostility, n. A peculiarly sharp and specially applied sense of the earth's overpopulation"
> —Ambrose Bierce, *The Devil's Dictionary*

are provided to the soldier camp, Seminole camp, sutler/vendor, and reenactment areas.

Fees and tickets: Admission is $5 per person, with children under six free.

Facilities

Restrooms: Portable units are provided that are ADA-compliant.

Other ADA compliance information: A tram is provided to help people get around, especially from the parking area to the battlefield. The grounds are hard-packed dirt but uneven. Those using wheelchairs may need help.

Places to eat or drink on-site? Yes.

Picnic facilities: Six covered tables with electricity and lights. They are first come, first served, and there is plenty of competition.

Places to sit: Because this event is so popular, the provision of bleachers doesn't guarantee a seat. The tram transportation to the reenactment area from the parking lot makes it easier to bring one's own lawn chairs or blanket.

Places to stay on-site: For reenactor encampments, yes.

Reenactors

Reenactors needed are Federal troops and civilians of the 1830s and Seminole warriors and civilians of the same period. Walk-ons are not permitted, but volunteers are welcome and should contact the Dade Battlefield Society beforehand. Amenities include food rations, powder rations, commemorative medallions, firewood, and hay. Reenactment participants may also purchase $20 meal tickets (good for a total of five meals) for immediate family members.

Educators

There are no school days, field trips, or curriculum aids yet.

Contact Information

www.floridastateparks.org/dadebattlefield/default.cfm
Dade Battlefield Historic State Park
7200 CR 603 South Battlefield Drive
Bushnell, FL 33513
352-793-4781

Under Fire: Fort Cooper Days (1836)

Fort Cooper State Park, Inverness, Citrus County

Historical Background

Fort Cooper got its start during the

Second Seminole War when Major Mark Anthony Cooper stayed behind

at the present location on the west bluff of Lake Holathlikaha to protect sick and wounded troops until the arrival of reinforcements. A fortification was built for the medical camp. Although Seminole War Chief Osceola and his warriors camped across the lake and often clashed with the soldiers at Fort Cooper, a stalemate resulted until supplies and reinforcements arrived for the Federals.

What You'll Find
Living history events such as:
* Authentic encampments of Seminoles, civilians, and U.S. military of the 1830s–1840s. They will all be glad to discuss their sides of the Second Seminole War
* Reenactments of the skirmishes between the U. S. military and the Seminoles at 11 AM and 2 PM each weekend day
* Demonstrations of period arts, crafts, and other skills
* Sutlers, especially of handmade Native American clothing and jewelry
There will also be food vendors with barbecue, seafood, kettle corn, and such, as well as music, dancing, and more modern crafts

Planning Your Visit
Whom to bring: This is a family event. Pets may be frightened by the sounds of gunfire and artillery.
Dates and times: Third weekend in March, from 9 AM to 4 PM. Battle

reenactments between Seminoles and Federal troops take place daily at 11 AM and 2 PM.

Getting there: Fort Cooper State Park is located just off US 41, at 3100 South Old Floral City Road, two miles south of Inverness. Zip is 33450. Park entrance GPS coordinates are N28° 48.9871', W082° 18.2294'.

Parking: Ample parking is available. An overflow lot has also been designated with tram service. It is about a quarter-mile walk from the main parking lot to the event site at the fort.

Fees and tickets: Children under six get in free, while admission for children six through seventeen is $1 and adults pay $5.

Facilities
Restrooms: All the park's restrooms are ADA-compliant.

Other ADA compliance information: In prolonged dry weather, some of the trails get sandy and inaccessible by wheelchair. If considering a visit, let the park know at least two weeks in advance if you will be using a wheelchair. A shuttle is available for those needing assistance to get from the parking area to the event site.

Places to eat: A variety of food vendors will be on-site.

Picnic facilities: Covered and uncovered picnic tables are on-site, as are grills.

Places to sit: Bleachers are provided for viewing the skirmishes but they can fill up; there is space for one's own chairs or a blanket.

Places to stay on-site: The park has primitive and youth camping sites.

Reenactors
Needed are Federal troops and Seminoles from the 1830s, and civilians from the same. Military includes infantry, cavalry, artillery, and medics. Amenities

include firewood, water, ice, and space for the exhibits and period campsites.

Educators
There are no school days, field trips, or curriculum materials yet.

Contact Information
Fort Cooper State Park
3100 South Old Floral City Road
Inverness, FL 34450
352-726-0315
www.floridastateparks.org/fortcooper

> Be sure to get to the park at least an hour before any skirmish you want to see, especially if you'll be using the tram to get to it.

Serving in Hades: Fort Foster's Garrison (1836-38)
Fort Foster State Historic Site, Hillsborough County

Historical Background
Fort Foster is the second fort to have been built to protect the bridge across the Hillsborough River used by the Fort King Military Road. The original structure, Fort Alabama, was abandoned a few months after being built. The soldiers boobytrapped the fort on leaving it; someone set off the trap and blew it up. The remains were burned by Seminoles. Fort Foster was then established in the same spot, but was plagued by mosquitoes and diseases such as yellow fever, rendering the fort indefensible at times before being abandoned two years after being built.

What You'll Find
- The only authentically reconstructed fort from the era of the Second Seminole War
- Fort Foster alive with soldiers in authentic uniforms going about their duties within the fort as if they had been there for months
- Soldiers happy to find a willing ear for their comments about what it is like to be stationed in 1830s Florida, as well as their take on the Seminole Wars

Planning Your Visit
Whom to bring: The family. Guide animals are welcome. Pets are not allowed.
Dates and times: Garrison weekends are on the third weekend of the month with occasional exceptions. (See the Calendar in this book's Appendix.) There is no garrison in January. The garrison opens to the public at 2 PM

on Saturdays and 11 AM on Sundays. (An updated calendar can be found at www.floridastateparks.org/fortfoster/default.cfm.)

Getting there: All visitors to Fort Foster must enter through Hillsborough River State Park first. Hillsborough River State Park is located nine miles north of Tampa and six miles south of Zephyrhills on US Highway 301. The address is 15402 US 301 North, Thonotosassa, 33592. GPS coordinates for the entrance to Hillsborough River State Park are N28° 8.686', W082° 13.4844'.

Parking: Ample parking with some ADA-compliant spaces is provided.

Fees and tickets: Six dollars a carload (up to eight passengers) to get into the park, and a little more for the tour of Fort Foster.

Facilities

Restrooms: ADA-accessible restrooms are in Hillsborough River State Park. There are no restrooms at the Fort Foster site itself.

Other ADA compliance information: The fort is about 1800 feet (a third of a mile) from the parking lot. The path is hard-packed dirt and level.

Places to eat: Spirit of the Woods Café is in Hillsborough River State Park.

Picnic facilities: Covered and uncovered tables are available at Hillsborough River State Park, as well as grills.

Places to sit: It is not necessary to bring chairs or a blanket for the garrison event.

Places to stay on-site: Hillsborough River State Park has primitive and RV campsites. Camping reservations are recommended.

Reenactors

Needed are Federal troops of the 1830s in authentic garb. There are no amenities.

Educators

Please review www.floridastateparks.org/fortfoster/default.cfm for school program information (currently found in the "FAQ" section).

Contact Information
Fort Foster State Historic Site
Hillsborough River State Park
15402 US 301 North
Thonotosassa, FL 33592
813-987-6771
www.floridastateparks.org/fortfoster/default.cfm
www.floridastateparks.org/hillsboroughriver/default.cfm

Rendezvous at Fort Foster (1836–38)
Fort Foster State Historic Site, Hillsborough County

What You'll Find
- Historical reenactors portraying Federal troops, Florida militia, Seminole Indians, Creek Indian guides, civilians, and settlers in period dress
- Sutlers selling period items to all sides, including you
- Period weaponry (tomahawk throws, cannon firing, period rifles, and archery demonstrations)
- Demonstrations of heritage crafts, arts, and skills
- Period encampments to visit and hear differing sides of the Fort Foster story; you can talk with civilians, Native Americans, and a contingent of soldiers living and working at Fort Foster
- The opportunity to find out who secretly used Fort Foster during the summertime

Planning Your Visit
Whom to bring: This event will be enjoyed by the whole family. Guide animals always welcome. Pets are not allowed.

Dates and times: One weekend in February each year (check website as to which one). School days are the prior Thursday and Friday, making this a four-day event. The general public is welcome all four days. The event starts at 10 AM and ends at 3 PM each day.

Getting there: All visitors to Fort Foster must enter through Hillsborough River State Park first. Hillsborough River State Park is located nine miles north of Tampa and six miles south of Zephyrhills on US Highway 301. The

address is 15402 US 301 North, Thonotosassa, 33592. GPS coordinates for the entrance to Hillsborough River State Park are N28° 8.686', W082° 13.4844'.

Parking: Event signs will guide you toward the parking area.

Fees and tickets: 2010 prices are $5 per person for those thirteen or over for the event. Children twelve and under are free. Student admission is $2 apiece on school days. Teachers and chaperones are free. "Scholarships" may be available for area classes and homeschool students.

Facilities

Restrooms: ADA-accessible restrooms are available during this annual event.

Other ADA compliance information: The fort is about 1800 feet (a third of a mile) from the parking lot. The path is dirt, negotiable by wheelchairs or canes unless muddy.

Places to eat: There are vendors at the fort during the event.

Picnic facilities: Covered and uncovered tables and grills are available at Hillsborough River State Park. Pavilions are available for picnicking within Hillsborough River State Park.

Places to sit: This is a walking tour. Places to sit are sparse.

Places to stay: There are primitive and RV campsites at the park, and there are motels within ten miles.

Reenactors

Needed are impressions of white civilians, Seminole civilians and warriors, Creek guides, and Federal troops from the era of the Second and Third Seminole Wars (1830s–1850s). Although mosquitoes played an important role in eventually driving U.S. troops from Fort Foster, mosquito reenactors are not needed; the Park has an adequately sized staff of volunteer mosquitoes (but fortunately without authentic 1800s mosquito-borne diseases). Amenities include free firewood, water, straw, on-site parking, and a site for period encampment.

Educators

Thursday and Friday of the event are school days. Hours are 10 AM to 3 PM. Contact your school board for field trip arrangements. Lesson plans and curriculum aids are not yet available. Registration forms are available at the fort's website. More information is available on the park's website under "FAQ."

Living History Weekend and Holiday Garrison at Fort Foster (1836–38)

Fort Foster State Historic Site, Hillsborough County

What You'll Find
- Historical reenactors portraying Federal troops, Florida militia, Seminole Indians, Creek guides, civilians, and settlers in period dress
- Frantic sutlers selling holiday gift items before either war or Christmas begins
- Period weaponry (tomahawk throws, cannon and period-rifle firing, and archery demonstrations)
- Skirmish reenactments on the weekend days as the soldiers and militia try to defend the bridge and Seminoles try to burn it
- Demonstrations of heritage crafts, arts, and skills
- Period encampments to visit and hear differing sides of the Fort Foster story; you can talk with civilians, Native Americans, and a contingent of soldiers living and working at Fort Foster
- Reenactments of many aspects of holiday life at the fort, such as torchlight tours on Friday evening in which captain gives a holiday address to the troops. Native American allies are invited to share in the celebration. The officers have a Christmas dinner, and the enlisted troops in the barracks lift their spirits by lifting spirits.
- Holiday and other music of the Victorian era

Planning Your Visit
Whom to bring: This event will be enjoyed by the whole family. Guide reindeer with red noses and other working animals always welcome. Pets are not allowed.

Dates and times: Second weekend in December. School day is the prior Friday, making it a three-day event. The general public is welcome all three days, but no battles will be fought on Friday. Skirmishes start after 1 PM on Saturday and Sunday. The event starts at 10 AM and ends at 3 PM each day.

Getting there: All visitors to Fort Foster must enter through Hillsborough River State Park first. Hillsborough River State Park is located nine miles north of Tampa and six miles south of Zephyrhills on US Highway 301. The address is 15402 US 301 North, in Thonotosassa, 33592. GPS coordinates for the entrance to Hillsborough River State Park are N28° 8.686', W082° 13.4844'.

Parking: Event signs will guide you toward the parking area

Fees and tickets: The event is $5 per adult; children twelve and under get in free. Organized school groups and homeschoolers admitted for $2 per student, but "scholarships" may be available. Teachers and chaperones with students are free on school days.

Facilities

Restrooms: ADA-accessible restrooms are in Hillsborough River State Park. No restrooms are at the Fort Foster site itself.

Other ADA compliance information: The fort is about 1800 feet (a third of a mile) from the parking lot. The path is hard-packed dirt, negotiable by wheelchair, stroller, cane, or sleigh unless soaked.

Places to eat: There are vendors at the fort during the event.

Picnic facilities: Covered and uncovered tables and grills are available at Hillsborough River State Park. Pavilions are available for picnicking within Hillsborough River State Park.

Places to sit: Bleachers are provided to watch the skirmishes.

Places to stay: There are primitive and RV campsites at the park and motels within six miles.

Reenactors

Needed are impressions of white civilians, Creek guides, Seminole civilians and warriors, and Federal troops from the era of the Second and Third Seminole Wars (1830s–1850s). Amenities include free firewood, water, straw, on-site parking, and a site for period encampment.

Educators

Friday of the event is a school day. Hours are 10 AM to 3 PM. Contact your school board for field trip arrangements. Lesson plans and curriculum aids are not yet available. Registration forms and event updates are available at the fort's website at www.floridastateparks.org/fortfoster/default.cfm.

*Another Day, Another Fort: Encampment at
Fort Christmas (1837–38)*
Fort Christmas, Orange County

Historical Background
One of over two hundred forts built during the Second Seminole War, Fort Christmas had a short military life. Construction began on Christmas Day in 1837; three months later (March 1838) the fort was abandoned because the fighting had moved so far south that the fort was no longer needed as a supply depot.

What You'll Find
- An encampment of the Florida militia of the 1840s in front of a full-scale replica of Fort Christmas
- Firing of muskets and cannons from the time of the Second Seminole War
- Programs presented by the militia twice a day inside the fort that about the Second Seminole War and the difficulties faced by soldiers in frontier Florida

Planning Your Visit
Whom to Bring (including pets): This is for the whole family, except that pets are not allowed.

Dates and times: This event occurs the first weekend in April and the weekend before Thanksgiving. Presentations within the fort are at 12:30 PM and 2:30 PM.

Getting there: Fort Christmas is at 1300 Fort Christmas Road in Christmas, 32709. It is just off SR 50, twenty miles east of Orlando. The turnoff is marked by a giant artificial Christmas tree. GPS coordinates are N28°33.6401, W081°1.2821.

Parking: Ample, with ADA-compliant spaces.

Fees and tickets: Free.

Facilities
Restrooms: ADA-accessible restrooms are provided.

Other ADA compliance information: The first floor of every building within the fort and one of the pioneer homes is wheelchair-accessible.

Places to eat: There are no concessions on-site.

Picnic facilities: Picnic tables and grills are available, as are rental pavilions.

Places to sit: There is no need to bring chairs or a blanket.

Places to stay: There are none on-site.

Reenactors
Not needed.

Educators
There are no school days, field trips, or curriculum aids yet available for this event.

Contact Information
Fort Christmas Park
1300 Fort Christmas Road
Christmas, FL 32709
407-568-4149
www.nbbd.com/godo/FortChristmas

The Battle of Okeechobee (Christmas Day, 1837)
Okeechobee, Okeechobee County

Historical Background
Acting on President Andrew Jackson's Indian Removal Act, the U.S. Army marched southward through the Florida peninsula to force the remaining Miccosukee and Seminole tribal groups to relocate to reservations west of the Mississippi River. On Christmas Day, 1837, a force of over a thousand troops led by Colonel Zachary Taylor and Missouri volunteers led by Colonel

Richard Gentry caught up with about a thousand Native Americans (mostly Seminole) on the north side of Lake Okeechobee. The majority were women, children, and elderly being evacuated to the Everglades area under the protection of fewer than 400 warriors.

As the noncombatants continued moving to relative safety, the warriors positioned themselves and their rifles to hold off the Federal troops as long as possible. The result was that Colonel Taylor had 138 casualties, including most of his officers and noncoms. The Seminoles lost 11 warriors and had 14 injured before withdrawing and rejoining their tribal group. No Native Americans were taken prisoner, but after the last Seminole had vanished, Colonel Taylor's forces were able to capture and detain 100 Seminole ponies and 600 head of Seminole cattle without sustaining a single casualty. For this self-proclaimed victory, Colonel Taylor was promoted to brigadier general and then elected president. (It is not known if his equine and bovine prisoners of war were ever relocated to reservations west of the Mississippi.)

What You'll Find

- Reenactments of the Battle of Okeechobee, largest and fiercest battle of the Seminole Wars
- Narrations of the battles by representatives of both the Seminole Tribe of Florida and of the battlefield's citizen support group
- Period sutlers doing a little war profiteering

- Authentic Seminole and soldier encampments to visit and hear different sides of the story and why they were fighting
- Historical displays and booths

In addition there are alligator demonstrations, music, horse rides, shows featuring rarely seen Florida wildlife, and demonstrations of Seminole Indian arts, crafts, and foods.

Planning Your Visit

Whom to bring: This is a family event. Guide animals are welcome, but guide alligators should be pre-registered.

Dates and times: First weekend in February (Saturday-Sunday). Gates open at 10 AM. Check the event website for battle times and other updated information. All day events are from 10 AM to 4 PM.

Getting there: Okeechobee Battlefield Historic State Park (3500 S.E. 38th Avenue, Okeechobee, 34974) is on the north shore of Lake Okeechobee. GPS coordinates are N27° 12.7102', W080° 47.3648'.

Parking: Small and reasonable fee.

Fees and tickets: Admission is free with parking fee.

Facilities

Restrooms: ADA-compliant portable restrooms are provided.

Other ADA compliance information: Parking is abundant, and a sufficient amount of ADA-compliant parking is provided. Although there are patches of ground that may be difficult for a wheelchair, the event organizers will make every attempt to accommodate those with special needs. After all, they want you to come! Please contact them beforehand.

Places to eat: Food and drink vendors are on-site.

Picnic facilities: A temporary tent and tables are provided during this event—limited seating available.

Places to sit: Limited bleachers and seating available during the event only. It is recommended that you bring your own chairs or blanket for watching the battles.

Places to stay on-site: For vendors, sutlers, and reenactors only.

Reenactors

Needed are Seminole reenactors (male and female) and mid-1800s Federal Army reenactors for U. S. militia. Volunteers are welcome and should contact event officials beforehand. Amenities include lunch, dinner, firewood, powder ration, and raffle door prizes.

Educators

Contact the event committee with specific needs or inquiries—educational programs are under development at this time.

Contact Information

Website (check here for updates and current information): www. OkeechobeeBattlefield.com

Coordinators: Okeechobee Battlefield Friends and Florida State Park Service

Be sure to point out to children that although hostilities between the U.S. military (representing white settlers) and the Seminoles are reenacted, the event itself is a cooperative effort between the two former antagonists. Also ask the Seminole reenactors why they chose this spot for the battle and how they prepared for it.

Second Seminole War Weekend at the Castillo (1835–42)
St. Augustine, St. Johns County

Historical Background

It was in 1837, twelve years after the Castillo de San Marcos had been renamed Fort Marion, that the fort played its part in one of the more despicable episodes of the Second Seminole War. Seminole War Chief Osceola had responded to a U.S. government offer of peaceful negotiations. Approaching nearby Fort Payton under a white flag of truce, Osceola and his band of warriors were taken prisoner. Osceola was locked up in Fort Marion. Despite howls of outrage from U.S. citizens and from within the government itself, he was eventually transferred to a prison in South Carolina, where he died in 1838 of malaria.

What You'll Find

- An immersion experience within the Castillo as the fort's interior reverts to Florida's early territorial period during the Second Seminole War
- Opportunities to hear the viewpoints of territorial citizens, U.S. soldiers, local militia, and Seminole Indians
- Cannon or musket firings throughout the day
- Period-correct U.S. military and Seminole encampments at the Colonial Spanish Quarter Museum
- A demonstration of nineteenth-century medicine

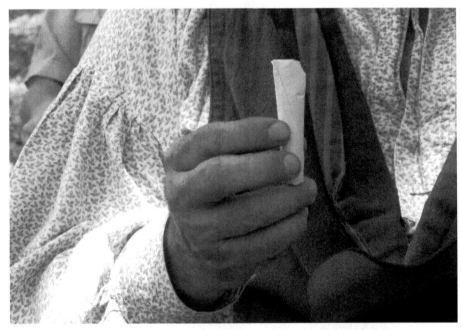

A hand-rolled paper cartridge with gunpowder for a single shot from a nine-teenth-century musket.

Planning Your Visit

Whom to bring: This is a family event. Guide animals are always welcome, but pets are not allowed.

Dates and times: The event is held the last weekend of April from 9:30 AM to 4:30 PM each day.

Getting there: GPS coordinates are N29°53.9574, W081°18.8558. The Castillo dominates downtown St. Augustine at 1 South Castillo Drive. Zip is 32084.

Parking: The lot has metered parking and fills up quickly, as does the metered parking on the streets nearby. ADA-compliant spaces are provided. There is a city garage within walking distance, but no tram servicing it.

Fees and tickets: Free with paid admission to the Castillo.

Facilities

Restrooms: ADA-compliant restrooms are located inside the Castillo.

Other ADA compliance information: The approach to the Castillo is a paved ramp that slopes upwards. The parade grounds are hard-packed level dirt that is paved along the perimeter. The gun turrets and upper deck are not ADA-accessible. The area of the Colonial Spanish Quarter is level with paved walkways.

Places to eat or drink: There are no concessions at the Castillo, but there is a tavern at the Colonial Spanish Quarter at which one can drink enough to forget about eating.

Picnic facilities: There are none at the Castillo or at the Spanish Quarter.

Places to sit: There are places to sit within and outside of the Castillo.

Places to stay on-site: None, but many fine establishments are close by.

Reenactors

Needed are impressions of Seminole Indians, Florida civilian militia, U.S. Army soldiers, and civilians of the 1830s. There are no amenities except sites provided for the encampments.

Educators

School days and field trips are not yet available. There are curriculum aids on the Castillo's website.

Contact information

Organizers: Rangers Jeffrey Edel and Jeffrey Jones
904-829-6506, ext. 233
E-mail edelj@yahoo.com or Jeffrey_M_Jones@nps.gov

Big Cypress Shootout (1835–42)
Big Cypress Seminole Reservation, Hendry County

Historical Background
Faced in the 1830s with loss of their freedom and homeland because of the U.S. government's policy of Indian removal, the Seminoles took up arms after a series of broken treaties and unsuccessful peace parleys. The result was the fiercest of all wars ever waged between the U.S. Government and Native Peoples, as fifty-two thousand Federal soldiers fought against fewer than two thousand warriors. There were casualties on both sides, and some Seminoles were removed to Oklahoma; the rest are still in their homeland, flourishing and known as The Unconquered Seminole Tribe of Florida.

What You'll Find
The living history portions of this multifaceted event focus on the Second Seminole War. Included are:
- Authentic Seminole, U. S. Army, and civilian (white settler) camps for visiting and finding different views of the conflicts between the Native Americans, the Army, and the white settlers
- A school day full of special presentations on Seminole crafts, tools, and weapons, as well as presentations on Florida animals
- Battle reenactments showing tactics that the Seminoles used to hold off forces of much greater size
- Demonstrations of weapons, tools, and crafts of the era of the Seminole Wars
- Primitive archery competitions

Also featured are tomahawk throws (allowed for younger ages than permitted by the Florida State Park system), alligator wrestling, venomous snake shows, a fireworks display, storytelling, music, and dancing.

Planning Your Visit

Whom to bring: This event is for the entire family, but because of the wildlife exhibits, pets are not allowed. Guide animals are welcome. A nearly irresistible package has been put together for Scout troops; see the details on the website.

Dates and times: This is held the last weekend in February, including Friday as a school day from 11 AM to 4 PM. The battle reenactments will take place at 2 PM on Saturday and Sunday. Hours on Saturday and Sunday are 10 AM to 5 PM.

Getting there: Billie Swamp Safari is located between Fort Lauderdale and Naples, on the Big Cypress Reservation just north of I-75 (Alligator Alley). Take Exit 49. Go about 17 miles north. GPS coordinates are N 26° 15.608, W 080° 51.318.

Parking: There is an abundance of guided parking.

Fees and tickets: Between $5 and $10 dollars per adult, less per child. *Important: cash only*

Facilities

Restrooms: The restrooms are ADA-compliant. Portable facilities are also provided and are ADA-accessible.

Other ADA compliance information: The grounds are hard-packed level dirt and should be negotiable by those using wheelchairs, strollers, or canes, unless it has been raining recently. Shady spots are plentiful.

Places to eat: There are concessions at the festival. The full-service Swamp Water Café is also close by.

Picnic facilities: There are no picnic tables or grills.

Places to sit: Chairs would be cumbersome to carry around, but a blanket can be spread for watching the battle reenactments. There are no bleachers.

Places to stay on-site: There are campsites for reenactors and for Scout troops.

Reenactors

Needed are Seminoles, other civilians, and Federal soldiers of the 1830s. For amenities, reenactors will be given breakfast and dinner on Saturday and Sunday, as well as bottled water, ice, a gasoline allowance, access to Billie Swamp Safari's indoor bathrooms and showers, primitive camping sites in the woods next to the battlefield, and use of a limited number of chickees.

Educators

The first day of the event (Friday) is a school day starting at 11 AM. There is no battle on that day. Check with your school board regarding field trips. There are no curriculum aids yet.

Contact Information

Billie Swamp Safari

800-949-6101, ext. 12125

E-mail: shootout@semtribe.com

The following website is where current schedules and updated information may be found: www.seminoletribe.com/calendar/shootout/index.html

---

Fort Chokonikla's Living History Weekend (1849)

Bowling Green, Hardee County

Historical Overview

Situated within Paynes Creek Historic State Park, the area of Fort Chokonikla started out as a trading post serving the local white settlers and the region's Native Americans, especially the Seminoles, who were used to having to travel all the way to the coast to do some shopping. The real purpose of the trading post was to help keep the Seminoles bottled up within a small portion of their own land. The trading post was eventually attacked by a renegade band of Seminoles. Although the renegades were swiftly brought to justice by their people, the U. S. government ordered the fort to be built. After its completion the Army troops were relentlessly assaulted and nearly driven out—not by Native Americans, but by native Florida mosquitoes.

What You'll Find

The year 1849 and a functioning trading camp, where frontiersmen and Seminoles come by foot or horseback to set up temporary camps and buy or sell goods. Without an actual building to serve as the trading post, it seems like a very small-scale rendezvous. You'll also find:

- Tomahawk-throwing contests
- Authentic Seminole encampments and U. S. Army encampments of the era of the Second and Third Seminole Wars, where you can see a Seminole star fire
- Living historians happy to show and tell visitors what life was like before automobiles and Wal-Mart
- Sutlers with period wares

Planning Your Visit

Whom to bring: This event is for the whole family.

Dates and times: The second weekend in January, from 10 AM to 4 PM daily.

Getting there: The park is a half-mile southeast of Bowling Green, in the center of the Florida peninsula. Highway 17 runs through town from north to south; turn east onto East Main Street or Hardee Street to access Lake Branch Road and follow the signs southeastward for a short distance. The address is 888 Lake Branch Road, Bowling Green, 33834. GPS coordinates for the park entrance are N27° 37.5663', W081° 48.5241'.

Parking: Ample free parking is available within the park, including spaces for RVs.

Fees and tickets: There is a small fee (a few dollars) for admission to the park, but the event itself is free.

Facilities

Restrooms: Portable units are on-site. The visitor center has two ADA-compliant family restrooms with changing tables.

Other ADA compliance information: The site itself is hard-packed dirt. The service road leading to it cannot be negotiated by wheelchair. Because the parking lot is between the visitor center and the event, the ADA spaces are closer to the visitor center and farthest from the event. Those with special needs should use the shuttles provided by the park staff, even within the event site.

Places to eat: A large tent with tables and benches is set up on-site, and is also a source of shade.

Picnic facilities: Elsewhere in the park.

Places to sit: Plentiful seating is available under the tent.

Places to stay on-site: For reenactors and sutlers only.

Reenactors

Needed are Seminoles of all ages, Federal troops (pre-Civil War), and civilians of the mid-1800s of all ages. Amenities include primitive campsites, dry RV campsites, firewood, and water.

Educators

There are no school days or field trips, but curriculum aids are available.

Contact information

Paynes Creek Historic State Park
888 Lake Branch Road
Bowling Green, FL 33834
863-375-4717
www.floridastateparks.org/paynescreek/default.cfm

The American Civil War (1861–1865)

The Olustee Civil War Expo (1861–65)

Olustee Battlefield Historic State Park, Baker County

Historical Background
This event focuses more on the Civil War in general than it does on the Battle of Olustee, although it happens to be held at Olustee Battlefield Historic State Park, the site of Florida's largest Civil War battle.

What You'll Find
- A "boot camp," or introduction to the living history of the Civil War era
- Reenactors doing impressions of Union or Confederate military of the Civil War era, including infantry, cavalry, and artillery
- Impressions of civilians sharing in the hardships, defeats, and the triumphs of war
- Authentic military or civilian encampments to visit and learn from
- An authentic Civil War era camp meal for all—tasty and free
- Music of the 1800s throughout the day
- Artisans and sutlers
- Exhibits of weapons and other artifacts from the Civil War
- Demonstrations of fighting tactics of the time
- Infantry drills and artillery firing
- Demonstrations of period skills such as blacksmithing and tool-making

Planning Your Visit
Whom to bring: This is for the whole family, but pets are not allowed. Guide animals are welcome.
Dates and times: Held the fourth Saturday in September, 10 AM to 3 PM.
Getting there: Olustee Battlefield State Historic Site is on Highway 90, just off Interstate 10, 15 miles east of Lake City and 50 miles west of Jacksonville. Park entrance GPS coordinates are N30° 12.7613', W082° 23.328'.
Parking: Adequate parking is available in the park, with ADA-compliant spaces.
Fees and tickets: $5 a carload (includes free lunch for everyone).

Facilities
Restrooms: Modern, ADA-compliant facilities are available.
Other ADA compliance information: Grounds and footpaths are hard-packed, level dirt that should be easily negotiable by wheelchairs, strollers, or canes unless soaking wet.

Places to eat: Lunch will be served.

Picnic facilities: There are a few picnic tables provided, but they may be claimed for use for the expo. There are no grills.

Places to sit: Visitors are advised to bring their own chairs or blankets.

Places to stay on-site: None for visitors. Many establishments are in Lake City.

Reenactors

Needed are Union or Confederate military impressions including cavalry, infantry, and artillery, as well as civilian impressions of the Civil War era. There are no amenities other than the lunch.

> "What a cruel thing war is...to fill our hearts with hatred instead of love for our neighbors." —General Robert E. Lee

Educators: There are no school days or field trips yet. An army of curriculum aids is available online at the citizen support organization's website.

Contact Information

www.battleofolustee.org (Citizen Support Organization)
www.floridastateparks.org/olustee/default.cfm

Christmas at Gamble Plantation (1861–65)
Ellenton, Manatee County

Historical Background

This historic state park surrounds the only surviving plantation house in south Florida. Formerly the centerpiece of a large sugar plantation, the Gamble House is thought to have been a temporary refuge for Confederate Secretary of State Judah P. Benjamin before he could safely travel to England after the fall of the Confederacy.

What You'll Find

- A fully restored plantation house decorated in nineteenth-century holiday fashion, with guides in authentic Civil War-era finery
- A group of weary, grungy Confederate troops politely camped outside on the lawn rather than tracking dirt all over milady's living room
- Period music
- Living historians demonstrating period crafts and skills
- Sutlers providing nineteenth-century holiday shopping
- A nineteenth-century medical display for husbands after they see how much was spent at the sutler booths

- Displays of artillery and infantry weapons
- Fine Southern holiday cooking

Planning Your Visit

Whom to bring: This is a family event, although pets are not allowed inside the mansion. Guide animals are always welcome.

Dates and times: The event is from 10 AM to 4 PM on the second Sunday in December.

Getting there: The park is off I-75 in Ellenton, north of Bradenton and Sarasota. Take exit 224 from I-75 and go west on US 301 for a mile. Look to the right for a white picket fence and then the park entrance. The GPS coordinates are N27°31.401594, W082°31.606542. The address is 3708 Patten Avenue, Ellenton, 34222.

Parking: Ample. ADA-compliant spaces are provided.

Fees and tickets: It's free.

Reenactors

Needed are Confederate troops (infantry and artillery). Volunteers should contact park officials beforehand. There are no amenities.

Educators

There are no school days, field trips, or curriculum aids yet.

Contact Information

Gamble Plantation Historic State Park
3708 Patten Avenue
Ellenton, FL 34222
941-723-4536
www.floridastateparks.org/gambleplantation

"Do your duty in all things. You cannot do more, you should never wish to do less." —General Robert E. Lee

---

Spring Encampment at the Gamble Plantation (1861–65)
Ellenton, Manatee County

Historical Background

Once scheduled for demolition, the Gamble House and sixteen acres of the old sugar plantation were bought by the United Daughters of the Confederacy and donated to the State of Florida.

What You'll Find

- Confederate troops camping on the lawn and ready to talk about a soldier's life

- Free tours of the Gamble Mansion and the Patten House, with guides in fashions of the mid-1800s
- Period music
- Demonstrations of 1800s workmanship and skills, such as black-smithing, gardening, basket weaving, and other crafts

Planning Your Visit

Whom to bring: This is for the whole family. Pets are not allowed in the house, but guide animals are always welcome.

Dates and times: Part of the Manatee Heritage Days celebration, this event is held on the second Sunday in March from 8 AM to 4:30 PM.

Fees and tickets: It's free.

Reenactors

Needed are Confederate soldiers, infantry, and artillery. Volunteers should contact park officials beforehand (no walk-ons). There are no amenities.

Educators

There are no school days, field trips, or curriculum aids yet.

Christmas Camp Walton (1861)
Valparaiso, Okaloosa County

Historical Background

The "Yule of Yesteryear" event at the Heritage Museum of Northwest Florida celebrates a Victorian Christmas in the Florida Panhandle, complete with a remembrance of those serving away from home in the military.

What You'll Find

- A Confederate encampment in Valparaiso's Perrine Park, with soldiers going about their duties while spending the holidays away from home
- The same soldiers trying to be at their best when invited inside to a Victorian tea with its customs and etiquette
- Troops who are glad to have company and to discuss their equipment, what they think of the war, and how they feel about being away from home (especially during the holidays)
- Families of some of the soldiers who have shown up to visit

Planning Your Visit

Whom to bring: The encampment is a family event. Pets are allowed in Perrine Park, but not at the tea. Guide animals are always welcome in either place.

Dates and times: The encampment is from 8 AM to 4 PM on the second Saturday in December. The Victorian tea is at 2 PM.

Getting there: Perrine Park is nearly in the center of Valparaiso, which is squished between Eglin Air Force Base and Choctawhatchee Bay. The museum is across the street at 115 Westview Avenue. GPS coordinates are N30° 30.2782', W086° 29.4001'.

> "I have been up to see the Congress and they do not seem to be able to do anything except to eat peanuts and chew tobacco, while my army is starving." —General Robert E. Lee

Parking: Adequate, with ADA-compliant spaces.

Fees and tickets: The encampment is free. The tea is $10 apiece.

Facilities

Restrooms: The museum has ADA-accessible restrooms.

Other ADA compliance information: The park grounds are easily negotiated by those using wheelchairs, strollers, or canes.

Places to eat: There are no concessions at the park or inside the museum, but there is a great Victorian tea at 2 PM.

Picnic facilities: There are uncovered picnic tables at the park, but no grills.

Places to sit: The park has benches and picnic tables.

Places to stay on-site: None, but motels are nearby.

Reenactors

Needed are Confederate infantry appropriate to 1861, in uniform, and period-dressed civilians to portray family members. There are no amenities.

Educators

There are no school days, field trips, or curriculum aids yet.

Contact Information
www.heritage-museum.org

◆◆×◆◆

A Nineteenth-Century Saturday at the Park (1851–1900)
Valparaiso, Okaloosa County

Historical Background
This annual event commemorates the latter half of the nineteenth century in the Fort Walton Beach area.

What You'll Find
- A Confederate encampment in Perrine Park, with soldiers going about their daily chores but always ready to take a break to talk with visitors about a soldier's life
- Demonstrations of pioneer crafts and skills such as pine-needle basketry, wood turning, and pottery
- A special children's hands-on section where they can learn pioneer skills (such as butter churning) and old-time games

Planning Your Visit
Whom to bring: The encampment is a family event.

Dates and times: It is held the last Saturday in April, from 9 AM to 5 PM.

Getting there: Perrine Park is nearly in the center of Valparaiso, which is squished between Eglin Air Force Base and Choctawhatchee Bay. The museum is across the street at 115 Westview Avenue. GPS coordinates are N30° 30.2782', W086° 29.4001'.

Parking: Adequate.

Fees and tickets: It's free!

Facilities
Restrooms: The museum has ADA-accessible restrooms.

Other ADA compliance information: The park grounds are easily negotiated by those using wheelchairs or canes. Shade is abundant.

Places to eat: There will be concessions in the park during this event.

Picnic facilities: There are uncovered picnic tables at the park, but no grills.

Places to sit: There are benches and tables at the park.

Places to stay on-site: None, but motels are close by.

> "Rope, n. An obsolescent appliance for reminding assassins that they too are mortal. It is put about the neck and remains in place one's whole life long." —Ambrose Bierce, *The Devil's Dictionary*

Reenactors
Needed are Confederate infantry appropriate to 1861, in uniform. Amenities include firewood and water.

Educators
There are no school days, field trips, or curriculum aids yet.

Contact Information
www.heritage-museum.org
www.waltonguards.org

The Anclote River Raid (1861–65)
Jay B. Starkey Wilderness Park, Pasco County
(Note: This event was cancelled for a while due to construction. The organizers plan to restart in 2011.)

Historical Background
During the Civil War, Florida's ports were nearly constantly blockaded by Union naval forces, especially in the latter half of the war. The Federals had much less success when they tried to go inland. Although they destroyed many farms and saltworks, Northern raiding parties were repeatedly evicted by Florida's Confederate forces. The event is a demonstration of what one such raid might have been like.

What You'll Find

- Battles at 2 PM on Saturday and Sunday with use of mortars and cannons
- Skirmishes throughout the weekend days
- Some poor wretch will be accused of a heinous crime and the townspeople will decide whether his fair trial should be before or after they hang him
- Gunfights on Sutler's Row
- Sutlers with period wares who will dive for cover during the gunfights
- A ladies' tea Saturday morning
- A Blue-Gray Dance on Saturday evening
- Church services on Sunday morning for those left over from the gunfights
- Blacksmithing demonstrations
- Activities especially for children after church services

Planning Your Visit:

Whom to bring: This is a family event.

Dates and times: Third or fourth weekend in April (see contact address for current information). Friday is a school day and will open at 9:30 AM. Battles are on Saturday and Sunday at 2 PM.

Getting there: The event is at Jay P. Starkey Wilderness Park, east of New Port Richey, at 10500 Wilderness Park Road, New Port Richey, 34655. The Park's GPS coordinates are N28° 15.1258', W082° 38.9318'.

Parking: Abundant and guided.

Fees and tickets: Free.

Facilities

Restrooms: There are at least four ADA-compliant restrooms in the park. Showers and water fountains are also ADA-accessible.

Other ADA compliance information: The grounds consist of hard-packed dirt. Unless very wet, they should be negotiable by wheelchair or with a cane.

Places to eat: A food concession will be on-site during the event.

Picnic facilities: The park has five picnic shelters that have grills and will seat up to 50 people each, and two larger ones with big grills, running water, and electricity.

Places to sit: There are no bleachers at the park for watching the battles. Bringing one's own chairs or a blanket is advised.

Places to stay on-site? There are cabins and primitive campsites available for rental at the park.

> Be sure to take heat and sun exposure precautions.

Reenactors
Needed are Civil War soldiers, including cavalry, infantry, and artillery, as well as civilians. Amenities include four bounties available for artillery, firewood, and ice.

Educators
Friday is a school day, starting at 9:30 AM. Field trips are available (check with your school board); curriculum aids are not yet available.

Contact Information
E-mail: AncloteRiverRaid@yahoo.com

------◆◆◆◆◆◆------

Raid on Fort Pierce (1861–65)
Savanna County Park, St. Lucie County

Historical Background
Although there was never an actual raid on Fort Pierce during the Civil War, this event illustrates the many Union raids up and down Florida's coasts during that time. Even as Union troops marched through Dixie leaving wide paths of total devastation, Florida was becoming a progressively more important supplier of salt and farm goods to the Confederacy. Union raiders kept busy trying to destroy the Florida farms, the supply lines, and the shipping that carried the supplies so badly needed in the Confederate war effort.

What You'll Find
- Period-correct Federal and Confederate encampments, both winter camps and campaign camps for comparison.
- Demonstrations of cooking, blacksmithing, and other period skills
- On school day, station changes for the students will be signaled by cannonfire—no mistaking when to change!
- A narrated pitched battle with plenty of gunfire and hand-to-hand combat on each weekend day. (However, for sheer ferocity, these reenactments pale in comparison to holiday shopping—they are highly recommended for battle-weary bargain hunters needing a little respite and new ideas on tactics)
- Sutlers selling that perfect Confederate holiday gift

Planning Your Visit
Whom to bring: This is a family event. Guide animals are always welcome. Pets are discouraged since they may become frightened by the sounds of battle and the pyrotechnics.

Dates and times: Starting with a school day on Friday, this Civil War reenactment is on the second weekend in December, extending through Sunday. School day starts at 9 AM and ends when the last bus leaves, between 1 and 2 PM. Weekend hours are from 9 AM to 5:30 PM. Battles are on Saturday at 2 PM and Sunday at 1 PM.

Getting there: I-95 to exit 126. This is Midway Road (SR 712). Go east about 5.5 miles to Savanna County Park (on the left). Follow the signs. The GPS coordinates of Savanna Park are N27° 22.8656', W080° 18.4327'. The Park is at 1400 East Midway Road in Fort Pierce. Zip is 34982.

Parking: Parking is abundant, and attendants will guide visitors to their spaces. ADA-compliant parking is available. A tram is also provided on Saturday and Sunday for those who are parked farther away than they would have liked.

Fees and tickets: Parking is free.

Facilities

Restrooms: Porta-potties are available, and some of them are ADA-compliant.

Other ADA compliance information: The grounds are level and either paved or consist of hard-packed dirt relatively easy to negotiate by wheelchair or with a cane.

Places to eat: A concession will be on-site.

Picnic tables: An extensive number of picnic tables and other seating, all covered, is provided. There are no grills.

Places to sit: Bleachers are provided for the battles, with space on either side for those who bring their own chairs or blankets to sit on.

Places to stay on-site: There are campsites with hookups for RVs; fees are charged for electricity and water. Bathrooms are indoor, and hot showers are available.

Reenactors

Needed are Civil War military of both sides and civilians of the 1860s era. Cavalry and artillery are welcome. Sutlers are by invitation only. Walk-ons are not permitted; volunteers should contact the event organizers beforehand. Amenities include firewood and water. Powder rations are distributed to the first two artillery pieces registered for the Federal and for the Confederate sides.

Be sure to tell the children what an "arsenal" is. There is one at the battlefield, or at least until it gets blown sky-high during the first battle and into its component atoms during the second one, courtesy of your friendly St. Lucie County Sheriff's explosives division.

Educators

The first day (Friday) of the event is a school day and starts at 9 AM. Field trips are available, but no curriculum aids yet.

Hillsborough River Raid (1863)
Tampa, Hillsborough County

Historical Background

This was the largest land action of the Civil War in Tampa. Late at night on October 16, 1863, U.S. naval forces landed near Tampa and marched fourteen miles inland to the shipyard on the Hillsborough River, where two notorious Confederate-manned blockade runners were docked. Early the next day, the naval force destroyed both vessels. They were then faced with getting back to their pickup point (Ballast Point) despite mounting Confederate resistance.

What You'll Find

- Battles with amphibious landings at 2:30 PM on Saturday and Sunday
- Sutlers trying to sell everything before it's destroyed by the Yankees
- A great photographic backdrop on the water with a wooded far shore
- A Grand Review, or military parade
- Infantry and artillery drills with rifles and cannons
- Period-appropriate music
- Union sailors and marines, and Army infantry as well as Confederate infantry encampments to visit

Planning Your Visit

Whom to bring: This is a family event. Guide animals are welcome. Pets may become upset by the gunfire, but are allowed as long as they are well behaved and on a leash no longer than six feet. Pets must not be left alone. Bring cameras and sunscreen.

Dates and times: First weekend in October, open to the public from 10 AM to 5:30 PM. There will be a skirmish at 2:30 PM both days.

Getting there: Veterans' Memorial Park is on Highway 301, a quarter-mile south of Martin Luther King Blvd. on the north side of the Tampa Bypass Canal, and about a mile north of East Broadway. GPS coordinates are N27° 58.5727', W082° 21.6374'. The park's address is 3602 U.S. Highway 301 North, in Tampa. Zip is 33619.

Parking: Overflow parking is available when needed. The small size of the park and the layout preclude the need for trams.

Fees and tickets: Free, except sutlers pay a small registration fee.

Facilities

Restrooms: All restrooms are ADA-accessible. They can be found both inside and outside the nearby Veterans Museum.

Other ADA compliance information: ADA-compliant parking spaces are provided. The picnic areas are shaded. The park grounds are level hard-packed dirt.

Places to eat: Food and drink vendors are on-site.

Picnic facilities: There are two pavilions with picnic tables and grills.

Places to sit: Bleachers are provided for watching the skirmishes, but there is space for blankets or one's own seats.

Places to stay on-site: None, except that primitive campsites are available for the reenactor camps. Hotels and motels are nearby.

Reenactors

Needed are naval forces from both sides and Confederate infantry, with period-appropriate uniforms. The small size of the site does not allow mounted troops. Artillery units are by invitation only. Amenities include a free Saturday-evening meal and a primitive encampment site.

> Be sure to talk with the troops. This is a rare chance to learn about the naval aspects of the Civil War in Florida. Few people know that the South had a navy.

Educators

School days, field trips, and curriculum aids are not yet available.

Contact Information

Veterans Memorial Park
3602 Hwy 301 N.
Tampa, FL 33619
813-744-5502
Organizers' e-mail: floridawar@msn.com or gunboat@ussforthenry.com

---

Battle of Ballast Point (October 1863)
Fort De Soto Park, Tierra Verde, Pinellas County

Historical Background

One of the few historical reenactments in Florida that is a sequel to another, this is the follow-up to the events memorialized by the "Hillsborough River Raid" (see previous entry). A U.S. naval raiding party has landed and destroyed two Confederate blockade runners that had just picked up a new cargo. Confederate troops catch up to them as they reach their designated pickup site at Ballast Point in the Tampa area. The Union sailors are retreating on boats sent by two of their nearby ships, but they are under heavy fire from the Rebels, including shots from a cannon loaded with buckshot.

What You'll Find

- An American Civil War encampment and historical weekend
- A raiding party's amphibious landing
- A mock military trial and execution
- Artillery demonstrations and infantry drills
- A ladies' afternoon tea
- Drum and fife music performances
- Civil War medical demonstrations
- Sutlers on hand to take your Confederate money
- Battle reenactments on both Saturday and Sunday afternoons
- A skirmish on Friday, the school day

Planning Your Visit

Whom to bring: This is for the whole family. Guide animals are welcome. Pets are discouraged because so many are frightened by gunfire.

Dates and times: For three days over the last full weekend of February. Civil War camps will be open to the public each day from 10 AM to 5 PM. School day is on Friday of the event weekend from 9:30 AM to 2:30 PM, with a brief skirmish at noon. Battle reenactments are at 1:30 PM on Saturday and Sunday.

Getting there: Fort De Soto Park is the southernmost point of Pinellas County, at the end of the Pinellas Bayway off I-275 in the area of St. Petersburg. GPS coordinates are N27° 38.8525', W082° 42.9149'. The address is 3500 Pinellas Bayway S., Tierra Verde, 33715.

Parking: Ample parking is available, with overflow space if necessary. The parking lot is placed between the battlefield and the camps, so there is really no inconvenient parking space. ADA-compliant parking is on the side of the permanent concession, which is the far end of the lot as one enters it.

Fees and tickets: Free.

Facilities

Restrooms: Restrooms are ADA compliant.

Other ADA compliance information: There are paved walkways along one side of the sutler and encampment area. The grounds are covered with hard-packed dirt and shell. Bleachers are immediately between the battlefield and the parking lot, so the whole area is accessible by users of wheelchairs, strollers, and canes.

Places to eat: Food and drink concessions are on-site.

Picnic facilities: Some of the picnic tables under the pavilion are likely going to be used for the event. Other tables are scattered about and have grills.

Places to sit: Benches are available in the park, as well as many places to spread a picnic blanket or place one's own chairs. Bleachers are provided to view the battlefield. Shady places from which to watch the battles are rare, except for the pavilion.

Places to stay on-site: For reenactors only, a limited number of modern camping spaces are available on a first-contact, first-served basis. There are other campsites in the park that are primitive and open to anyone.

Reenactors

Needed are Union and Confederate infantry, artillery, cavalry (limited), and civilian impressions. Units and artillery are asked to let the organizers know if they are coming. Sutlers are by invitation only because of space considerations. Amenities include free firewood, hay for sleeping, and ice. There is a $50 cash bounty for the first three pre-registered artillery units with a cannon on the Federal and on the Confederate side. There is also a $10 cash bounty for the first ten pre-registered cavalries who attend.

Educators

Friday is a school day, with field trips available. Curriculum aids are not yet available.

Contact Information

http://www.angelfire.com/pa5/97pavolinf/2008fortdesoto.html

A Regional Fife and Drum Muster Event
Fort De Soto Park, Tierra Verde, Pinellas County

Historical Background

Whether it's the bugling during battles or a little drummer boy lending a cadence to the marching of the troops, musicians have been part of the military for a long time. This event is held concurrently with the "Battle of Ballast Point" reenactment at Fort De Soto Park in Pinellas County, Florida.

What You'll Find

Informal playing sessions of musicians from different time periods, and they're all unplugged. There are also formal marches while playing.

Planning Your Visit

Dates and times: Held concurrently with the Fort De Soto Civil War Event (or "Battle at Ballast Point") on the third weekend of February, including the Friday school day.

Fees: Free!

Reenactors

Musicians in authentic costume from all time periods are invited, including Revolutionary War era. Amenities include firewood, hay for sleeping, and ice.

<hr />

Battle at Townsend's Plantation (1861–65)

Mount Dora, Lake County

Historical Background

Although no Civil War battle was ever fought in this area, the event is a series of living history demonstrations ranging from a telegraph station to a full-scale battle with infantry, cavalry, and artillery.

What You'll Find

- A Civil War–era battle each weekend day on a forty-acre battlefield with infantry, cavalry, and artillery
- Authentic Union and Confederate military camps
- Living history exhibits, such as a Civil War–era medicine demonstration and a telegraph station
- A ladies' tea
- An old-time chapel service on Sunday morning
- Sutlers with period wares trying to compete with the huge antique and flea market next to the event site
- A Civil War–era dress ball on Saturday night
- Period music throughout the day

Planning Your Visit

Whom to bring: This is a family event.

Dates and times: First weekend in February, including Friday as a school day. (Note: Check the event website as to whether there will be a school day that year, since there is no school day if it would conflict with achievement testing.) Hours are 10 AM–5 PM on Saturday and Sunday. Battles are at 3 PM on Saturday and 2 PM on Sunday. Dress ball is at 8 PM on Saturday, and chapel service is at 11:30 AM on Sunday.

Getting there: North of Orlando on Highway 441, about two miles from Mt. Dora. Look for the Renninger's Flea Market sign. GPS coordinates are

N 28° 48.414', W 081° 37.511'. Address is 20651 U. S. Hwy 441, Mount Dora, 32757.

Parking: Ample for bicycles through RVs.

Fees and tickets: Children twelve and under: $2. Ages thirteen and up: $5.

Facilities

Restrooms: Ample porta-potties, some of which are ADA accessible.

Other ADA compliance information: The grounds are hard-packed, gently rolling dirt and, if wet, may be difficult to negotiate for those using wheelchairs or canes.

Places to eat: There is a restaurant at the adjacent flea market.

Picnic facilities: None, but there's plenty of space to spread a blanket.

Places to sit: There are no bleachers; bringing chairs or a blanket would be helpful.

Places to stay on-site: Campsites (primitive or modern) for the reenactors.

Reenactors

Needed are Civil War soldiers for both sides and period-appropriate civilians. Cavalry and artillery are welcome. Amenities include campsites, straw, hay, firewood, and water. There are bounties for artillery and cavalry.

Educators

School day (if one is held) is the Friday of the event weekend. Field trips are available—contact your local school board. No curriculum aids are yet available.

Contact Information

Infantry and artillery: colvaughn@cfl.rr.com
Sutlers: drhooch@comcast.net
Cavalry: mayorbob@embarqmail.com
www.renningers.com

Raid on the Suwannee River (1861–65)
Spirit of the Suwannee Music Park, Live Oak, Suwannee County

Historical Background

This is a "what if" scenario. There were no skirmishes or battles on the Suwannee—not that the North didn't try. The railroad bridge over the Suwannee was one of the goals of the Union forces that marched out of Jacksonville in February 1864 before being sent packing back from Olustee.

What You'll Find

- A battle on Saturday and on Sunday
- A large group of period merchants selling period wares and trying to collect old debts before everyone gets killed in battle
- Authentic Civil War encampments to visit and from which to hear all sides of the story
- One of the best sites for a large-scale living history event in Florida
- A military ball with period dress on Saturday evening

Planning Your Visit

Whom to bring: This is a family event.

Dates and times: It's the third weekend in November, including Friday. Battles are at 2 PM weekend days. Camps open at 9 AM, closing at 5 PM Saturday and 4:30 PM Sunday.

Getting there: The location, Spirit of the Suwannee Music Park, is on Highway 129 north of Live Oak, halfway between I-10 and I-75. Address is 3076 95th Drive in Live Oak, 32060. GPS coordinates are N30°23.8193, W082°56.7668.

Parking: Plentiful, with ADA-compliant spaces.

Facilities

Other ADA compliance information: Paved pathways and level, hard-packed grounds make it easy for those in wheelchairs to get around.

Places to eat: There is a full-service restaurant on-site.

Places to sit: No bleachers are available. Spectators may bring their own chairs or a blanket for watching the battles.

Places to stay on-site: Available lodging ranges from primitive campsites to cabins and lodges.

Reenactors

Needed are infantry, artillery, and cavalry of both Federals and Confederates, as well as civilian camp followers. Usual amenities.

Educators

Friday is a school day. Field trips are available, but curriculum aids are not yet provided.

Contact Information

The park's website is www.musicliveshere.com
Organizer: bobgomillion@yahoo.com
Cavalry registration: mayorbob@embarqmail.com

Battle at Narcoossee Mill (1861–65)

Ralph V. Chisholm Regional Park, St. Cloud, Osceola County

Historical Background

There was never a battle here. This is a "what if" scenario demonstrating a full-scale Civil War battle as realistically as possible without anyone getting killed or arrested. This particular event is especially popular among reenactors and is legendary for its pyrotechnics. The event's proceeds go to the Jacob Summerlin Scholarship Fund as well as to many other efforts for the community.

What You'll Find

- A mock narrated battle each weekend day on 150 acres of open and wooded land
- A ladies' tea
- A military ball with period music on Saturday night
- Period Union and Confederate camps
- The most spectacular battle pyrotechnics in Florida
- Sutlers hoping the organizers were careful as to where they put the explosives
- A dazzling nighttime artillery firing over East Lake Tohopekaliga
- Storytelling by descendants of Florida Civil War veterans

Planning Your Visit

Whom to bring: This is a family event. Guide animals are always welcome, but pets and small children may get upset by the gunfire and pyrotechnics.

Dates and times: Last weekend in March. School day is that Friday, starting at 9 AM. Note that this event often falls during spring break, so many of the visiting students are homeschooled. Friday's education tours start at 9:30 AM. On weekend days the park opens at 10 AM. Battles are at 2 PM Saturday and 2:30 PM Sunday. Dress ball starts at sundown and goes to 10 PM. Church is at 10 AM Sunday.

Getting there: The address is 4700 Chisholm Park Trail in St. Cloud, on the eastern shore of East Lake Tohopekaliga. GPS position: N28° 16.748', W081° 15.102'. This is the northeast part of the St. Cloud area. Zip is 34771.

Parking: Abundant.

Fees and tickets: Small fee on Education Day includes lunch and a drink. On weekend days, there is a small admission per adult, free for children under twelve years old.

Facilities

Restrooms: ADA-compliant portable units are provided.

Other ADA compliance information: The grounds are hard-packed soil, but

Buffalo soldiers: Troops of the Third U.S. Colored Cavalry with one of their mounts.

uneven. Those using wheelchairs may need assistance.

Places to eat: There are food and drink vendors on Sutler Row.

Picnic tables: There are none, and no grills.

Places to sit: Bleachers are provided, but bringing one's own chairs or blankets is okay too. The battlefield is such that there are no bad places to sit and watch the action.

Places to stay on-site: The campsites are for the reenactors and sutlers only, but your luxurious suite awaits you in the Kissimmee–St. Cloud area.

Reenactors

Needed are Civil War–era reenactors of any type, including Union or Confederate infantry, cavalry, and artillery, as well as camp followers and other civilians. Registration deadline for all groups is two weeks before the event. Amenities include a lunch to be provided to those helping with the Education Day on Friday.

After much scholarly inquiry, modern-day anthropologists dispute the assertion that the lake's name, "Tohopekaliga," is an ancient Native American term meaning "great place to hang out with the guys and have a few cold ones."

Be sure to see Tom Torso. Get a photo if you can!

Educators

Friday is a school day. Field trips are available. Check with your school board. No curriculum aids are yet available.

Contact Information

Website: www.jacobsummerlin.org (Registration can be done here.)
For Education Day information, contact Education@JacobSummerlin.org or call the Jacob Summerlin Camp Hotline at 407-931-7003

Civil War Heritage Days (1864)
Fort Zachary Taylor Historic State Park, Key West, Monroe County

Historical Background

Built in the mid-1800s to help defend the southeastern U. S. coastline, Fort Zachary Taylor sits serenely at the far end of Key West, bristling with cannons pointed in every direction except at each other. Some of those cannons could hurl a red-hot or explosive cannonball accurately up to four miles out, blowing their hapless targets all the way back to their home ports, a piece at a time. Union troops possessed the fort throughout the Civil War, using it as part of the naval blockade of Florida's coastline.

What You'll Find

- An infinite variety of "what if" scenarios of Civil War action on land, sea, or both, ranging from skirmishes between troops on land to Confederate ships trying to run a Union blockade amid cannonfire from the ships and the fort.
- Authentic Union and Confederate encampments
- One of the best immersion experiences in Florida that includes a torchlight tour of Fort Zachary Taylor at night, as the fort and everything within reverts to 1864 and the reenactors become Civil War military and civilians
- Nighttime artillery firings, like no fireworks you have ever seen
- A ball with period musicians on Saturday evening for reenactors
- A town hall–style worship service on Sunday morning
- Sutlers with period wares (including toys, notions, and food)
- The trial of a blockade-runner ship's captain
- Living history demonstrations, including medical
- A ladies' tea

Planning Your Visit

Whom to bring: This is a family event.

Dates and times: Civil War Days is on the second or third weekend in February. Early registration and setup for reenactors, sutlers, and volunteers is the Thursday before. School day is the Friday before from 10 AM to 3 PM. Candlelight tours are from 7 PM to 9 PM on Friday evening. Weekend hours are from 10 AM to 5 PM.

Getting there: Fort Zachary Taylor Historic State Park is located at the end of Southard Street through the Truman Annex in Key West. It's the far end of the island. GPS coordinates are N24°33.38322, W081°47.97552. Zip is 33041.

Parking: Ample parking is available around Fort Taylor. Remember that events take place both inside and outside of Fort Taylor, as well as at sea.

Fees and tickets: There is a small fee (a few dollars) to enter the park and a very reasonable fee to enter the event.

Facilities

Restrooms: There are ADA-accessible restrooms just outside the fort.

Other ADA compliance information: Pathways are ADA compliant; parade grounds where most exhibits and camps are consist of hard-packed dirt suitable for wheelchair access. There is no wheelchair access to the top deck of the fort; sea battles can be watched from the parking lot or the grounds near the beach.

Places to eat: There's a concession outside the fort near the beach.

Picnic tables: Two uncovered tables with grills are adjacent to the fort.

Places to sit: There are many benches about, and no need for a blanket inside the fort. However, blankets are great for a beach picnic.

Places to stay on-site: There is primitive and dry RV camping available for reenactors, volunteers, and sutlers only during the event. Shell-shocked visitors needing a little R & R have a wide choice of bars and places of lodging in Key West.

Reenactors

Needed are all Civil War types, including civilians. Walk-ons are not permitted; volunteers should contact park officials beforehand.

> "Projectile, n. The final arbiter in international disputes." —Ambrose Bierce, *The Devil's Dictionary*

Amenities include on-site primitive and dry RV campsites. Several meals are provided, including breakfasts and suppers. A small fee is charged for each, but the food is delicious and well worth the price. There is a $100 bounty on powder for the first six cannon crews that sign up.

> Be sure to visit me at the medical tent! Autographs gladly given, but don't expect much from my handwriting. Copies of this book will not be with me; it's 1864 and it hasn't been written yet.

Educators
School day is Friday from 10 AM to 3 PM. Field trips are available Contact your local school board. A variety of curriculum aids are available online.

> "It is foolish and wrong to mourn the men who died. Rather we should thank God that such men lived." —Gen. George Patton

Contact Information
http://www.floridastateparks.org/forttaylor/default.cfm
www.forttaylor.org
Fort Zachary Taylor Historic State Park
P.O. Box 6560
Key West, FL 33041

Eden Gardens Christmas Candlelight Tour with Holiday Encampment (1861–1900s)

Eden Gardens State Park, Point Washington, Walton County

Historical Background
The last two decades of the nineteenth century and the early years of the twentieth were the high times of Florida's timber barons. With millions of acres of longleaf pine to be harvested for their wood and naval stores (resin and turpentine), fortunes were made as quickly as the forests could be depleted.

One such businessman began a timber operation in Florida's panhandle and, in 1897, built his 5600-square-foot home nearby. The two-story mansion and its meticulously landscaped grounds are the focal points of Eden Gardens State Park. Each year there is a Holiday Open House.

What You'll Find

- This unique holiday event is probably the only example in Florida of a reenactment of a reenactment. The mansion is resplendent in 1900s-period holiday decorations, including electric Christmas lights, which were invented in 1882 and could only be afforded by the wealthy at that time. Inside the Wesley House the guides and hostesses are dressed in Civil War–era clothing.
- A Civil War encampment is on the north lawn near the reflecting pool for several days and nights.
- The soldiers outside are lonely and will be glad for some company. Visitors can learn what it's like for them to be away from home and at war during the holidays, and why they do it. Children will have a better understanding of the isolation of soldiers even today.

Planning Your Visit

Whom to bring: Definitely a family event. No pets are allowed, but guide animals are welcome.

Dates and times: From 5 PM to 8 PM on the Saturday before Christmas for the holiday open house, although the encampment is there all day and evening.

Getting there: Eden Gardens is roughly halfway between Panama City and Fort Walton Beach. Take CR 395 north from Highway 98 about one mile before arriving at the park. The address is 181 Eden Garden Road, Santa Rosa Beach, 32459. GPS coordinates: N30° 22.2298', W086° 6.9904.

Parking: Adequate.

Fees and tickets: During the Holiday Christmas Candlelight Tour, the park admission fee is waived in lieu of a donation to the Friends of Eden, the Citizen Support Organization for Eden Gardens. There is a charge of a few dollars for entrance to the park at other times if one wishes to see the Wesley House on an occasion other than the Open House evening.

Facilities

Restrooms: ADA-accessible restrooms are by the ranger station, down near the picnic pavilions, and within a screened-in pavilion on the grounds.

Other ADA compliance information: The grounds are gently rolling to level hard-packed dirt and negotiable by users of wheelchairs or canes. The first floor of the Wesley House is accessible by wheelchairs via a lift.

Places to eat: Refreshments are served during the Holiday Open House.

Picnic facilities: Uncovered picnic tables are by the bayou, with grills. There are also four picnic pavilions complete with tables and grills in the wooded area northwest of the house off the bayou.

Places to sit: No need to bring chairs or a blanket.

Places to stay on-site: None.

Reenactors

Needed are Civil War infantry. No cavalry or artillery are needed. Walk-ons permitted, but volunteers should contact park officials beforehand. Amenities include firewood, water, and a camping space.

> "I think it is better to do right, even if we suffer in so doing, than to incur the reproach of our consciences and posterity." —General Robert E. Lee

Educators

There are no school days, field trips, or curriculum aids yet.

Contact Information

Eden Gardens State Park
181 Eden Garden Road
Santa Rosa Beach, FL 32459
www.floridastateparks.org/EdenGardens/default.cfm
850-231-4214 (Interested volunteers should call the staff directly at this number.)

The School of the Soldier and Point Washington Skirmish (1864)

Eden Gardens State Park, Point Washington, Walton County

Historical Background

The skirmishes in this event are based on an actual skirmish that occurred between Union and Confederate forces near Point Washington on February 9, 1864.

What You'll Find

- An authentic Civil War military camp
- Drills and artillery firing
- A ladies' tea
- Period camp cooking and blacksmithing

- Medical demonstrations, where one can learn the proper dosage of brandy for anesthesia during wartime surgery

Planning Your Visit

Whom to bring: This is a family event. No pets are allowed, but guide animals are welcome.

Dates and times: The event is in the second to last full weekend of January, from Friday (school day) through Sunday. Saturday hours are 9 AM to 5 PM; Sunday hours are 9 AM to 2 PM.

Fees and tickets: The event is free, but the usual park admission rates apply (less than five dollars per carload).

Facilities

Restrooms: ADA-accessible restrooms are by the ranger station, down near the picnic pavilions, and within a screened-in pavilion on the grounds.

Other ADA compliance information: The grounds are hard-packed level dirt. Only the first floor of the Wesley House is accessible by wheelchair, via a lift.

Places to eat: None on-site.

Reenactors

Needed are Civil War infantry and artillery. Walk-ons are permitted, but volunteers should contact park officials beforehand. Amenities include firewood, water, and an authentic camping space (no modern camping facilities).

Educators

There is one school day. A field trip can be arranged beforehand. There are no curriculum aids as yet. Teachers must contact the park prior to the school day to be included in the event and to get the day's schedule.

Contact Information

Event organizers: jimbusby3@cox.net, or contact the Eden Gardens State Park directly at 850-231-4214 for more information or to volunteer.

"Brandy, n. A cordial composed of one part thunder-and-lightning, one part remorse, two parts bloody murder, one part death-hell-and-the-grave, and four parts clarified Satan. Dose, a headful all the time." Ambrose Bierce, *The Devil's Dictionary*

Dade City's Pioneer Days (1861–1900)
Dade City, Pasco County

Historical Background
The Pioneer Museum at Dade City is a year-round attraction that has its annual Pioneer Days event on the Sunday and Monday of Labor Day weekend.

What You'll Find
The living history portion of this festival consists of:
- Period Federal and Confederate encampments arranged on the edge of the fair in a semicircle facing the open battlefield
- Reenactors doing third-person impressions of Civil War–era troops and civilians
- Sutlers with period wares
- A mock court-martial on the second day of the festival at 12:30 PM
- A battle between Union and Confederate forces each afternoon at 2 PM with artillery, not narrated

A unique feature of this event is that there is an auditory illusion of bullets and cannonballs flying through the air. Because the area used as the battlefield is a shallow bowl–shaped open field, the sounds of gunshots and cannonfire cause echoes that sound like bullets and cannonballs whizzing overhead and through the spectators. This occurs no matter where the troops are on the field. (Three families near me had to leave the area until their children saw that people were not dropping to the ground all around them.)

Planning Your Visit
Whom to bring: This is a family event. No pets are allowed, although guide animals are always welcome.
Dates and times: Labor Day and the Sunday before. Open both days 9 AM–4 PM. The battles are at 2 PM each day. The court-martial is on the second day at 12:30 PM.
Getting there: One mile north of Dade City off Highway 301 North, east on Pioneer Museum Road. The GPS coordinates of the museum are N28° 23.1317', W082° 11.4717'. Zip is 33525.
Parking: Free with admission, on a large field that wraps around the village. The area is well policed by guides on horseback. ADA-compliant spaces are available.
Fees and tickets: Tickets are a couple of dollars above the usual fees for entrance to the museum, and of course include full admission to the museum itself.

Facilities

Restrooms: Some of the fixed-facility restrooms are ADA-compliant, but the porta-potties are not. Near the battlefield in front of a bank of porta-potties was a well-stocked, ADA-accessible handwashing station easily used even by children.

Other ADA compliance information: Paved paths are conveniently located throughout the fair area.

Places to eat: Delicious food and sweetened drink are plentiful enough to keep Dade City dentists busy for months.

Picnic facilities: There are none on-site, and no grills.

Places to sit: Benches are blessedly plentiful throughout the site, nearly always located in shade.

Places to stay on-site: None, but there are accomodations on the south end of town.

Reenactors

Needed are Civil War soldiers, both Union and Confederate, and civilians of the mid-1800s. Amenities include water, firewood, and encampment sites.

Educators

There are no school days, field trips, or curriculum aids yet.

Contact Information

Pioneer Florida Museum: 352-567-0262
www.pioneerfloridamuseum.org

The Crystal River Reenactment (1863–65)
Holcim Mine property, Citrus County

Historical Background

Although no actual hostilities between Union and Confederate forces occurred there, Florida's Citrus County certainly didn't miss out on the Civil War. Both the Crystal and Homosassa rivers were used as ports by Confederate blockade runners as they brought in goods from other nations, as well as ferried homegrown agricultural products to the rest of the Confederacy.

What You'll Find

- A "what if" scenario imagining what might have happened if one of the Union raiding forces had met Confederate resistance
- Two Civil War battle reenactments
- Authentic Union and Confederate period encampments
- Artillery firings, as well as musket and mortar competitions

- Civil War–era medical demonstrations
- Two concerts by the 97th Regimental String Band
- For those who have spent the previous two days finding religion while getting shot at, maimed, and blown sky-high, there's a church service Sunday morning that is open to reenactors as well as the public
- A ladies' tea
- A period dance (for reenactors)
- A Civil War–era telegraph station

Planning Your Visit

Whom to bring: This is a family event. Be aware that animals and small children may become frightened by all the gunfire, artillery, and pyrotechnics.

Dates and times: Held during the second weekend in March; school day is Friday from 9:30 AM to 2 PM. Gates open at 9 AM on Saturday and Sunday. Camps will remain open to the public until 5 PM each day.

Getting there: The event is located along the west side of US Hwy 19/98, about seven miles northwest of Crystal River. The GPS position is N28° 56.596, W082° 37.329. Signs are posted as one nears the one-lane turnoff from the highway.

Parking: The general-admission parking area is located near the entrance to the site. The Citrus County Sheriff's Posse will be on hand (and on horseback) to assist you in parking your vehicle. There is a continuous shuttle service between the parking lot and the spectator area (usually on bales of hay).

Fees and tickets: General Admission is $5 for adults and $3 for students, ages nine to seventeen years. Children eight years old and under are admitted free of charge.

Facilities

Restrooms: Portable restroom facilities and handwashing stations are provided, some of them ADA-accessible.

Other ADA compliance information: The grounds are hard-packed dirt, but uneven; wheelchair users may need assistance.

Places to eat: Food choices feature both period items and modern concessions.

Picnic facilities: There are no picnic tables or grills on-site.

Places to sit: You may bring your own chairs or blanket. Folding chairs will be available to rent, for a nominal charge.

Places to stay on-site: There are no facilities for the public to stay on-site. Primitive and modern (although without hookups) campsites are available for event participants.

Reenactors

Needed are Civil War–era civilians, as well as Union and Confederate military, including infantry, artillery, and cavalry. Artillery must pre-register. Medallions will be given to all reenactors ages nine years old and up; they must be worn while on-site. Amenities include powder ration for all pre-registered artillery pieces. A free BBQ meal is on Friday night for reenactors who help with School Day activities. Hay, wood, and water are available for campsites. Reenactors pay a fee of $2 at the time of registration.

Educators
School day is Friday. Field trips are available (check with your school board). There are no curriculum materials yet.

> Be sure to ask the telegraph operator about wiretapping during the Civil War.

Contact Information
www.crystalriverreenactment.org

Birney's Raid (1864)
De Leon Springs State Park, De Leon Springs, Volusia County

Historical Background
Explore the camp of the Union troops involved in the largest Union raid into central Florida. The targets were the mill and plantation at Spring Garden, now known as De Leon Springs. Despite fatigue, homesickness, frightful wounds and disease, the stalwart Federal troops had resolutely overcome all obstacles in their fervor to stop the Rebels from tearing apart their beloved Union. (Southern readers: Please be aware that my Massachusetts-born wife is watching me write this. Feel free to contact me privately for an alternate introduction.)

What You'll Find
- A first-person Union encampment (no battles)
- Demonstrations of how they drilled, as well as how they slept, ate, and otherwise fended for themselves
- Artisans demonstrating woodworking, spinning, and weaving
- A Civil War–era cow camp

Planning Your Visit
Whom to bring: This is a family event.
Dates and times: It's held the second weekend in January. Park hours are 8 AM to sunset.

Getting there: Follow the state park signs for about six miles on US Hwy 17 North out of DeLand. At Ponce de Leon Blvd., turn left and go one mile to the park's entrance. The GPS coordinates for the entrance to De Leon State Park are N29° 7.8163', W081° 21.5418'. Zip is 32130.

Parking: Limited. Carpooling and early arrival are recommended.

Fees and tickets: A small admission fee is charged. The event is free, but a nice donation will endear you to the park staff forever.

Facilities

Restrooms: ADA-accessible restrooms are available at the visitor center and at the concession (restaurant).

Other ADA compliance information: Wheelchairs are available to help get around the park, including the nature trail. Those with special needs are strongly encouraged to call the park headquarters beforehand in order to help them prepare for the most ideal experience. The staff at this park work hard to make it one of the best state parks in the system with regard to accommodating those with physical challenges.

Places to eat: Yes—Old Spanish Sugar Mill Restaurant, open 9 AM to 5 PM Mon–Fri and 8 AM to 5 PM Sat–Sun, serving till 4 PM. You can make your own pancakes right at the table!

Picnic facilities: Picnic tables with grills are available on a first-come, first-served basis. Four pavilions are available for rental.

Places to sit: There is no need to bring one's own chairs or blanket unless a picnic is planned at the park.

Places to stay on-site: No, except at the encampment itself for the reenactors.

Reenactors

Needed are Civil War–era Union soldiers for first-person impressions. Cow hunters of the Civil War years are also invited. Rations are provided. Other amenities include firewood, water, ice, straw for the asking, and encampment space.

Educators

There are no school days, field trips, or curriculum materials yet.

Contact Information

De Leon Springs State Park
601 Ponce De Leon Blvd., P.O. Box 1338
De Leon Springs, FL 32130
386-985-4212

Skirmish at Open Pond (1864)
DeFuniak Springs, Walton County

Historical Background

There was never a documented skirmish at this precise site, but there were encampments in the area by cavalry units of the Confederate Army. Passing nearby were the forces of Brigadier General Alexander Asboth, whose Union forces mounted a raid into northwest Florida that was so destructive that it would take decades for full recovery. General Asboth didn't do so well either. It took four years, but the wounds he received during this raid eventually killed him.

What You'll Find

The living history components of the annual Chatauqua Assembly include:

- Authentic Union, civilian, and Confederate encampments for visiting
- Skirmishes between both Union infantry and Confederate navy/marines including an amphibious landing on the shore of Open Pond and use of artillery, based on General Asboth's Florida raids
- The chance to visit with and ask questions of chaplains in the civilian camps
- Displays of military equipment
- Civil War–era medical displays
- Nineteenth-century skills such as candlemaking and blacksmithing
- Sunday morning church services

Planning Your visit

Whom to bring: This is a family event. Guide animals are always welcome. Although pets are not recommended because they can become frightened by the artillery and gunfire, people living in the area of the lake are often seen out walking their dogs around the edge of the battlefield anyway, oblivious to the cannons being fired and Civil War–era military types running all over the place.

Dates and times: The event is held the first weekend in February. The skirmishes are on Saturday and Sunday and start after 2 PM. Encampment visiting hours are 8:30 AM–3 PM on Friday, 9 AM–5 PM on Saturday, and 9 AM–2:30 PM on Sunday. Friday's weapons firings are at 9:45 AM, 11:45 AM, and 2:45 PM.

Getting there: The GPS coordinates are N30° 43.0149', W086° 6.9633'. The address is 95 Circle Drive, DeFuniak Springs, 32435.

Parking: Available not only at the Chatauqua complex itself, but all around the lake. The battlefield area is a shallow bowl with the lake in the center.

Fees and tickets: The living history portion of the Assembly is free.

Facilities

Restrooms: Restrooms are available within the buildings and are ADA-compliant.

Other ADA compliance information: The grounds are hard-packed dirt, sloping and not completely level. There is a paved path circling the lake from which the battlefield can be seen, but the path does not run near the camps.

Places to eat: There are none on-site.

Picnic facilities: None.

Places to sit: There are no bleachers for watching the skirmishes.

Places to stay on-site: None, but the event site is surrounded by the town of DeFuniak Springs with its places of lodging.

Reenactors

Needed are Union and Confederate artillery and infantry. No cavalry is needed because of the limited space involved. Confederate naval/marine impressions are also needed. Amenities include firewood, water, a free evening meal, and free admission to all the other Chatauqua Assembly events.

Educators

There is a school day on Friday from 8:30 AM to 2 PM. Field trips are available. Curriculum aids are not yet available.

Contact Information

The Florida Chautauqua Center
Post Office Box 1273
DeFuniak Springs, FL 32435
850-892-7613
www.Florida-Chautauqua-Center.org
Living History organizer: ectrader@gulftel.com

The Civil War in Jacksonville (1861–65)

Fort Caroline National Memorial, Jacksonville, Duval County

Historical Background

Bull Run, Gettysburg, and Andersonville are all place names associated with the Civil War, more so than the name "Jacksonville." Yet the war was real enough to the people of the Jacksonville area—as real as the Union blockade of the St. Johns River or the occupation of the city itself.

What You'll Find

- A cross-section of the population of northeast Florida during the Civil War years, ranging from Union gunboat sailors to civilian nurses, all in authentic dress or uniform and each with a different story to share

- Period encampments at the visitor center and at the fort
- A period camp-style church service on Sunday morning
- Demonstrations of period skills and crafts such as quilting, spinning, and candle making
- Aromas of fine camp cooking
- Foods the Civil War soldiers lived on
- Southern women's fashions of the day, such as hoop skirts

Planning Your Visit

Whom to bring: This is a family event. Although guide animals are always welcome, pets are discouraged because they are not allowed inside the visitor center or the fort.

Dates and times: This event is held the weekend before Thanksgiving from 10 AM to 4 PM each day.

Getting there: The GPS coordinates of Fort Caroline National Memorial are N30° 23.0323', W081° 29.9713'. The address is 12713 Fort Caroline Road in Jacksonville, 32225. It is about fourteen miles east-northeast of Jacksonville's downtown.

Parking: Adequate, with ADA spaces and provision for overflow.

Fees and tickets: Free. Your tax dollars at work!

Facilities

Restrooms: The restrooms at the visitor center are ADA-compliant.

Other ADA compliance information: The trail from the visitor center to the event (at the fort) is inaccessible by wheelchair. Transportation is available for those with mobility challenges who are patient during the busiest part of the day. There is little shade in the fort area.

Places to eat: There are no concessions at the event.

Picnic facilities: There are none in the event area.

Places to sit: There are places to spread a blanket and relax in the area of the fort. Benches are provided within a covered breezeway at the visitor center.

Places to stay on-site: There are none for visitors.

Reenactors

Needed are military, civilian, and medical/nursing impressions from the Civil War era. Military includes infantry of North or South, gunboat sailors, marines, artillerymen, musicians, and chaplains. Amenities include meals and powder (courtesy of the National Park Service).

Educators

There are no school days or field trips. The National Park Service's Fort Caroline website has a gunboat-load of curriculum aids.

Battle of Lake City (1864)
Lake City, Columbia County

Historical Background
After landing at Jacksonville on February 7, 1864, Federal forces began raiding northeastern Florida in preparation for a large-scale operation, possibly a march on Tallahassee. One of those raids was to Lake City. The outcome of this action and many others led to a recommendation that all Federal forces be withdrawn from Florida's interior. It was ignored. Over five thousand Union troops set out from Jacksonville on an unauthorized march toward Olustee. Those who think that Lake City played an insignificant role in the Olustee events are overlooking one grim and important part of the story: while struggling to take care of its own despite the war, the Federal raids, and the Union blockade, Lake City ended up having to take care of both sides' casualties.

What You'll Find
The living history portions of the Olustee Battle Festival in Lake City include:
- A skirmish between Federal infantry and cavalry versus Confederate marines on the shores of Lake De Soto
- Firing of artillery pieces
- Demonstrations of life as it was in the mid-1800s, including cooking techniques, sewing, laundry, and storytelling
- Angels of Mercy, an active multi-room active Civil War field hospital with reenactors portraying battle casualties as well as medical and nursing staff

Planning Your Visit
Whom to bring: This is a family event.

Dates and times: Second Friday in February, concurrent with the Battle of Olustee reenactment and Lake City's Olustee Battle Festival. The battle reenactment is at 5 PM behind the Columbia County Courthouse, near the SW corner of the lake. (A bus for the reenactors leaves the entrance of the Olustee Battlefield at 3:30 PM.) The Angels of Mercy event is from 6 PM to 9 PM on Friday and Saturday. Other living history demonstrations at the museum are from 10 AM to 5 PM.

Getting there: Lake De Soto is part of downtown Lake City, nearly the center of town. The museum, where the living history exhibits (including Angels of

Mercy) is two blocks away. The museum's address is 105 South Hernando Street in Lake City, 32025. The museum's GPS coordinates are N30° 11.3504', W082° 38.1748'.

Parking: Scattered but adequate, within a block of the lakeshore. Traffic control is by the local police force, and has always been done well.

Fees and tickets: Free!

Facilities

Restrooms: Porta-potties are set up within a block because there is a big festival also going on downtown; many of them are ADA-compliant.

Other ADA compliance information: The spectator viewing area is either paved or has hard-packed dirt and is easily accessible by those using wheelchairs or canes.

Places to eat: All manner of food concessions are at the festival, and the local pharmacies are well stocked with Tums, Rolaids, Pepto-Bismol, and Alka-Seltzer.

Picnic tables: There are no picnic tables, pavilions, or grills at the lake.

Places to sit: This is a short event without bleachers, but there is seating along the lakeshore and places to spread blankets.

Places to stay on-site: Lake City has places to stay, but they may be booked because of the Olustee reenactment going on nearby.

Reenactors

Needed are Confederate marines and infantry, and Federal infantry and cavalry. There are no amenities.

Educators

There are no school days, field trips, or curriculum aids yet.

Contact Information

Organizer: d_eversole@bellsouth.net
www.olusteefestival.com

> Be sure to visit the Angels of Mercy living history depiction of a working Civil War hospital at nearby Lake City/Columbia County Historical Museum. There's no interaction with the players, but it is an effective reminder of a war's aftermath.

The Road to Olustee (1864)
Camp Milton, Duval County

Historical Background

The Federal occupation of Jacksonville during the Civil War gave the Union troops a stronghold from which they could make destructive raids into Florida as well as prepare for larger operations that they were considering. One such operation was a march to destroy the railroad bridge across the Suwannee River. Confederate resistance was met and overcome at what is now Camp Milton Historic Preserve. The overconfident Federals then marched west on the road to their trouncing at Olustee.

What You'll Find
- A Civil War immersion experience involving spectators as citizens of a town during Civil War hostilities
- Confederate camps going about activities such as inspecting and cleaning weapons and building earthworks
- Civilians engaged in daily Jacksonville life (shopping, household chores, spinning, etc.)
- Union troops scouting and then raiding the town and encampments
- Sutlers playing their part of the town scenario as merchants
- Raids and skirmishes on Saturday and Sunday
- A school day on Friday
- A period church service on Sunday morning
- Period games for the children to learn

Planning Your Visit
Whom to bring: This is a family event, although dogs and cats are not allowed. Contact the event organizers about other animals such as goats or chickens, which contribute to the authenticity of the town scenarios. No one knows if Duval County's leash laws apply to pet chickens.

Dates and times: The event is held the first full weekend in February, which is the weekend before the Battle of Olustee reenactment. School groups can come on Friday from 8 AM to 3 PM. Hours on Saturday and Sunday are 9 AM to 4 PM.

Getting there: GPS coordinates are N30° 17.7542', W081° 52.1651'. The address of Camp Milton is 1175 Halsema Rd in Jacksonville, 32221.

Parking: Adequate, with ADA-compliant spaces.

Fees and tickets: Free for reenactors, $5 for spectators thirteen and up.

Facilities
Restrooms: ADA-accessible conventional and portable restrooms are provided.

Other ADA compliance information: The grounds are hard-packed dirt and level. Those using wheelchairs get around easily.

Places to eat: There are no food concessions on-site.

Picnic facilities: There are none on-site.

Places to sit: No bleachers or places to sit are needed.

Places to stay: There are primitive campsites for the participants, but no lodging or campsites for spectators.

Reenactors

Needed are Confederates of 1864 who were present at Camp Milton and Federals of 1864 who were present in Jacksonville. Civilians of 1864 Jacksonville are also welcome. Authenticity guidelines are posted on the event website. Sutlers are by invitation only. Specialty impressions must be pre-approved by the event organizers. The number of Confederate participants will be limited.

Educators

Friday is an unofficial school day from 8 AM to 3 PM. Field trips are available. No curriculum aids are available yet.

Contact Information

Camp Milton website: www.campmilton.com

A Call to Olustee (1864)
Live Oak, Suwannee County

Historical Background

As Federal soldiers under General Seymour marched west from Jacksonville in February of 1864, it was anticipated that they would destroy the railroad bridge across the Suwannee River. A call went out across the northern Florida peninsula for Confederate troops to gather at Olustee, squarely in General Seymour's path.

What You'll Find

- A Confederate encampment learning of the threat to their duty station and preparing to join their fellows at Olustee for the anticipated battle
- A military parade
- Ample opportunity to talk with the soldiers about their equipment, preparations for war, and what they are thinking as they prepare to leave their home and loved ones

Planning Your Visit

Whom to bring: The whole family will enjoy attending this event.

Dates and times: The event is from 8 AM to 4 PM the second Saturday of February, which is the Saturday before the Battle of Olustee reenactment.

Getting there: The encampment is on the grounds of the Suwannee County Historical Museum at 208 N. Ohio Avenue in Live Oak. GPS coordinates are N30°17.850756, W082°59.01567.

Parking: There is adequate parking and ADA spaces are provided.
Fees and tickets: It's free!

Facilities
Restrooms: Modern, ADA-accessible restrooms are available at the museum.
Other ADA compliance information: The grounds are level, hard-packed dirt and easily negotiable by those using canes or wheelchairs. There is abundant shade.
Places to eat: There are food vendors on-site during this event.
Picnic tables: Uncovered picnic tables are provided, but there are no grills.
Places to sit: Benches and picnic tables are available.
Places to stay on-site: None, but motels are nearby.

Reenactors
Needed are Confederate infantry and artillery appropriate to Suwannee County of 1864. There are no amenities.

Educators
As yet there are no school days, field trips, or curriculum aids available.

Contact Information
Suwannee County Historical Museum
208 N. Ohio Avenue
Live Oak, FL 32060
386-362-1776
www.suwanneemuseum.org

The Florida Expedition (1864)
Olustee Battlefield Historic State Park, Baker County

(Note: The public is not invited. This is for reenactors only.)

Historical Background
As Union forces marched across northern Florida toward Olustee, they began to encounter Confederate resistance. The Federal commander, Brigadier General Truman Seymour, thought he was encountering the same sporadic resistance that he had previously and easily defeated. He sent his units piecemeal toward what turned out to be an entrenched Confederate force of over five thousand men.

What You'll Find
- A forced three-mile march beginning at dawn through the pine forests near the main Federal camp

- Occasional unscripted clashes with Confederates, possibly including an ambush
- A bivouac by late afternoon for the night
- A high probability of a night attack by Confederate forces
- As complete and intense an immersion experience for reenactors as you'll find anywhere in Florida

Planning Your Visit

Whom to bring: This is a campaign-style private event, by invitation only. There will be no spectators. Because fur-bearing pets are not allowed at Olustee during the event weekend, only Civil War–era pet rocks may be brought along. Rocks must be pre-registered, have negative Coggins documentation, and will be inspected for authenticity.

Dates and times: Friday of the Battle of Olustee weekend, or the second Friday of February. Saturday morning the participants will rendezvous with the main Federal Army at the Olustee Battlefield.

Getting there: The location of the initial bivouac will be sent to all pre-registered participants.

Parking: N/A

Fees and tickets: This event is free. The organizers only ask that the participants stay and engage in the weekend battles of the main Battle of Olustee event.

Facilities

A professionally designed pine forest has been provided by your Creator. Restroom facilities are the same as used by the local bears.

Reenactors

Cavalry, artillery, and citizen's participation is by invitation only. Although Confederate infantry registration will be limited to fifty, there will be no limit on Federal infantry participants. Infantry participants must be able to meet the event guidelines. Amenities include rations (authentic), water, and provision of the bivouac sites.

Contact Information

www.battleofolustee.org

> "War, n. A by-product of the arts of peace." —Ambrose Bierce, *The Devil's Dictionary*

The Battle of Olustee (1864)

Olustee Battlefield Historic State Park, Baker County

Historical Background

It should come as no surprise that the site of the largest Civil War battle in Florida is also the site of one of Florida's largest living history events. Union forces had landed at and occupied Jacksonville. They then began moving westward across the Florida peninsula with a number of goals, including cutting the flow of food from central Florida to the rest of the Confederacy and the establishment of a new state government that would be loyal to the Union.

Unfortunately for the Union forces, the path to Tallahassee lay through Olustee, which sits on a narrow land bridge between a large lake on one side and a nearly impassable swamp on the other. It was here that a Confederate force of nearly equal size chose to make their stand. The battle ended in a Union defeat and over thirty years of reenactments (in conjunction with many other events) as part of the Olustee Festival in nearby Lake City, held annually on the third weekend of February.

"Both read the same Bible, and pray to the same God; and each invokes His aid against the other. It may seem strange that any men should dare to ask a just God's assistance in wringing their bread from the sweat of other men's faces; but let us judge not that we be not judged. The prayers of both could not be answered; that of neither has been answered fully." —President Abraham Lincoln

What You'll Find
- Two full-scale narrated Civil War battles involving nearly two thousand combatants
- Over three thousand reenactors portraying military and civilians of 1864
- Period crafts and music
- Sutlers selling items appropriate to 1864
- Medical demonstrations
- Authentic Civil War–era military and civilian camps

Planning Your Visit
Whom to bring: Although the reenactment weekend is a family event, pets are not allowed on-site during the week of the battle reenactment from Wednesday through Sunday.

Dates and times: Friday is a school day from 9 AM to 2 PM. Although the Civil War campsites are open for public viewing from 9 AM to 2 PM on Saturday, most of the reenactors will be in the morning parade in Lake City. A battle reenactment is on Saturday afternoon. A period ball (for participants only) is held Saturday evening. Campsites are open to the public from 9 AM to 2 PM Sunday. Due to a shortage of atheists resulting from all the gunfire and cannon volleys the day before, period church services will be held throughout the site in the midmorning on Sunday. The reenactment of the Battle of Olustee is held on Sunday afternoon.

Getting there: Olustee Battlefield State Historic Site is on Highway 90, just off

Interstate 10, 15 miles east of Lake City and 50 miles west of Jacksonville. Park entrance GPS coordinates are N30° 12.7613', W082° 23.328'. Olustee's zip is 32072.

Parking: Unless one parks along Highway 90 early Saturday or Sunday morning, the best places to park are at the Lake City Airport on the east side of Lake City to the west of Olustee, or at the Baker County Correctional Facility (CCF) to the east of Olustee. Both sites are on State Route 90. There is sufficient parking at these sites and a shuttle is available for only $1 for adults and 50¢ for children under twelve (pre-school-age children are free). (The shuttle service is faster from the Baker CCF.) The shuttle service from the parking areas is available on Saturday from 1:30 PM until 6:00 PM. Sunday the shuttle service runs from 9 AM until 5 PM.

Handicapped parking is available across the street from the main gate. You must have a handicapped parking pass issued by one of the 50 states or a doctor's note. Florida State Troopers patrol the handicapped parking area.

Fees and tickets: $5 for adults and $2 for children.

Facilities

Restrooms: Conventional restrooms are located in the interpretive center. ADA-compliant portable units are provided during reenactment weekend.

Other ADA compliance information: Visitors will be moving about on large, open fields that are relatively flat and surrounded by tall pine forests with palmetto undergrowth. Footpaths are well-packed dirt and unpaved.

Places to eat: Food vendors are present.

Picnic facilities: There are none on-site.

Places to sit: Bleachers are provided for watching the battles.

Places to stay on-site: There are none for visitors.

Reenactors

Needed are infantry, artillery, and cavalry Union or Confederate troops, but only of the types documented to have been at the actual Battle of Olustee. Civil War–era camp followers and other civilians are also welcome. Amenities include firewood, water, and campsite space.

Educators

Friday is a school day from 9 AM to 2 PM. Field trips are available. Curriculum aids are available on the Citizen Support Group website.

Contact Information

www.battleofolustee.org (Citizen Support Group)
http://www.floridastateparks.org/olustee/default.cfm

Fort Clinch State Park, Fernandina Beach, Amelia Island, Nassau County

Historical Background

Construction began on Fort Clinch in 1847. Although it is still well preserved, the fort was only used by the military during two wars: the Civil War and the Spanish-American War. Southern troops evacuated Fort Clinch in 1862 by order of Robert E. Lee. Federal troops then took possession for the remainder of the war.

What You'll Find

- First-person living historians recreating life in Fort Clinch during the Civil War
- Opportunities to interact with soldiers and civilians as they go about their duties
- (During certain events) impressions of medics, launderers, cooks, and carpenters
- Firearms and artillery demonstrations
- Nighttime tours of life at the fort by torchlight

Planning Your Visit

Whom to bring: This event is for the family. Pets are not allowed on the boardwalk or in the fort, but guide animals are welcome anywhere.

Dates and times: Except during special events, there is virtually always at least one living historian at Fort Clinch taking the part of a Union soldier assigned to the fort's construction battalion. He will be glad to tell you about the fort and his life in 1864. For those willing to make the required reservation from early May through early September, a Union soldier can also give a candlelight tour of Fort Clinch after dark (with the exception noted below), while regaling visitors with true stories and authentic lies.

On the first full weekend of each month, Fort Clinch is occupied by a Union garrison that lives there and carries out daily duties as would have been done in 1864. Visitors who arrive in December 1864 (by coming in the first full weekend of December) will find that the homesick Yanks have set up a Christmas tree, among many other holiday decorations. Saturday events are from 9 AM to 5 PM; Sundays run from 9 AM to noon.

Candlelight tours of Fort Clinch after sundown are also available on the first full weekend of each month, but these begin at specific times. Reservations are not required. Check with the visitor center for departure times.

The Union encampment of the first weekend in May is a special spring encampment. The hours are the same as above. With respect to the variety of trades and professions represented, the largest and most complete garrisons are at the Spring Encampment and at the Holiday Encampment the first weekend in December.

Southerners who wish to hang out with the home team will find a Confederate garrison at Fort Clinch on the third weekend in March and the second weekend in October. Saturday hours are 9 AM to 5 PM and Sundays are 9 AM to noon. Candlelight tours of the Confederate garrison after sundown are available during the October event only.

Getting there: Fort Clinch is at 2601 Atlantic Avenue in Fernandina Beach, 32034, on Amelia Island north-northeast of Jacksonville. The park's entrance consists of a relatively small sign that blends into its surroundings and a narrow paved road that vanishes almost immediately into the surrounding woods. (There are also two cannons pointed almost directly at Prince of Peace Lutheran Church across the street; this probably occasions a lot of fervent prayer within the church.) The GPS coordinates for the park's entrance are N30° 40.0828', W081° 26.0638'.

Parking: Limited at the visitor center. It's more available in mornings. There is a generous number of ADA-accessible spaces close to the visitor center, and there is room for RVs and buses.

Fees and tickets: Small fee (a few dollars) for admission to the park itself. The event is an additional pittance.

Facilities

Restrooms: ADA-compliant restrooms are at the visitor center in front of the Fort.

Other ADA compliance information: Pathways into and within Fort Clinch are either paved or consist of hard-packed dirt, sometimes with small rocks. Off the paths, the parade grounds are also hard-packed dirt, but not as level. Check beforehand with the rangers if it has been raining recently as to whether users of canes or wheelchairs may have problems on the parade grounds. There is almost no shade on the parade grounds but there are places to sit in the covered breezeway that serves as the fort's entrance.

Places to eat: There are no concessions, but the visitor center near the fort has machines for snacks and drinks.

Picnic facilities: Uncovered picnic tables with freestanding grills are located elsewhere in the park.

Places to sit: Visitors should plan on being on their feet while inside Fort Clinch except when within the breezeway.

Places to stay: Full-facility and youth campsites are elsewhere within the park.

Reenactors

Needed are Federal (Union, Yankees) or Confederate military reenactors and civilians in period clothing. Contact the park for more information or to volunteer. Walk-ons are not permitted. Amenities include water and firewood. Three meals are provided on first weekends. Special events get different amenities—contact Park staff for details.

Educators

There are no school days, field trips, or curriculum materials yet available.

Contact Information

Fort Clinch State Park
2601 Atlantic Avenue
Fernandina Beach, FL 32034
904-277-7274
www.floridastateparks.org/fortclinch/default.cfm

> Do not let the chaplain see your fingernails if they are decorated.

Railraiding: The Parrish Civil War Event (1861–65)
Parrish, Manatee County

Historical Background

Parrish did not see any action during the Civil War, especially involving trains, but the Civil War in Florida did involve trains. As it was part of Union strategy to blockade Florida's ports, railway supply lines were also targeted.

What You'll Find

- Period-correct Union and Confederate camps full of soldiers eager for visitors
- A hectic fourteen-mile train ride beset by ambushes, firefights, and artillery fire
- Troops from one side trying to hold prisoners on cars secretly carrying sympathizers for the other side
- Soldiers, spies, traitors, prisoners, the wounded, innocent and not-so-innocent civilians, and shady ladies—all around you

- First-person reenactors
- Different scenarios on different trains and in different cars
- A great deal of interaction between reenactors and spectators off the train and involvement of the spectators in the action once they've boarded the train

Note that the authenticity of this event is in the weapons, clothing, and tactics of the reenactors. The engine is from the 1950s, the passenger cars are from the 1940s, and there are utility poles in plain sight, but once the train starts up and lurches into the woods it's easy to picture yourself back in Civil War days.

Planning Your Visit

Whom to bring: This is a family event. No pets are allowed, but guide animals are always welcome. Be aware that some small children may think the gunfire is real, especially if they are from tough neighborhoods.

Dates and times: Second weekend in April and first weekend in October. The park opens at 10 AM so that the public can visit the period-correct camps. Train departures are at 11 AM and 2 PM each day.

Getting there: The train museum in Parrish is next to the post office on Highway 301 near Ellenton and just north of Sarasota and Bradenton. The GPS coordinates for the museum are N27°35.11698, W082°11.9931.

Parking: Ample parking is available, but will be guided. A section is set aside for those with special needs and properly identified vehicles.

Fees and tickets: Tickets are available online (getting them beforehand is strongly encouraged) and less than $15 per adult.

Facilities

Restrooms: Adequate portable facilities are available, but are not ADA-accessible.

Other ADA compliance information: Since these passenger cars were built before the era of ADA-accessibility guidelines, only certain ones are usable by those in wheelchairs, and can only be boarded with some help. The museum staff will be glad to assist, but they request that those with special needs contact the museum staff beforehand.

Places to eat: There is a small concession with food and drinks.

Picnic tables: There are only a couple of picnic tables under a shelter, and at least one of those may be being used by the event staff. There is room to spread picnic blankets, but little shade.

Places to sit: Seating is aboard the train itself, although there is a bench and one or two sheltered picnic tables available near the boarding area, some of which may be being used for the event.

Places to stay on-site: There are none, but places are nearby in Ellenton.

Reenactors

Needed are Union and Confederate forces, including infantry, artillery, and cavalry. Civilians of the Civil War era are also invited. Amenities include free firewood and water; space is provided for period-correct camps and for modern camping. Anyone in period-correct clothing rides the train for free.

Educators

There are no school days, field trips, or curriculum aids yet available.

Contact Information

http://www.frrm.org

Brooksville Raid (July 1864)
Brooksville, Hernando County

Historical Background
Commemoration and reenactment of a Civil War event that took place in Brooksville in July of 1864.

What You'll Find

- One of the largest groups of Civil War sutlers of any event in the southeastern United States
- The largest Civil War reenactment in Florida, with thousands of reenactors and their families
- Two narrated battles
- Authentic Union and Confederate encampments to visit
- A ladies' tea and a Saturday-evening period ball
- An 1860s-vintage baseball game
- Rural Florida families of the 1860s at work, play, and war
- For those reenactors who overdo it at the Saturday night Blue-Gray Ball, there is ample opportunity to repent mightily at church on Sunday morning

Planning Your Visit

Whom to bring: This is a family event.

Dates and times: The third full weekend in January, including that Friday as a school day. Camps open at 9 AM each day. Camps close on Friday at 2 PM, Saturday at 5:30 PM, and Sunday at 4:30 PM. The Blue-Gray Ball is from 8 to 11 PM on Saturday evening.

Getting there: The GPS coordinates of the Boy Scout camp are N28° 31.952', W082° 32.2524'. The address of the Sand Hill Scout Reservation (site of the event) is 11210 Cortez Blvd. in Brooksville, 34613.

Parking: Ample. Trams roam the area and help transport those coming from distant parking spaces.

Fees and tickets: There is no fee for students on school day. Children under five get in free; less than $5 apiece for children six and over, and slightly more for twelve and over.

Facilities

Restrooms: ADA-compliant portable restrooms and handwashing stations are plentiful.

Other ADA compliance information: Trams help transport people from the parking area, although they get scarce near the end of the day. There are no paved paths throughout the sutler area and the camps. It's all hard-packed ground, which can be a problem if wet. The sutler area is flat; the camp areas are not. Shade can easily be found in the sutler and camp areas, but not in the battlefield spectator area.

Places to eat: Concessions are available. More importantly, a hospital is right across the street for those who are involuntarily reconsidering the wisdom and magnitude of their culinary choices.

Picnic facilities: Some covered seating is available at the concessions. There are no grills.

Places to sit: Chairs are available for rental for a nominal fee and grassy areas for one's own chairs or picnic blanket are plentiful. There are no bleachers.

Places to stay on-site: Campsites for reenactors and sutlers only.

Reenactors

Needed are military and civilian Civil War–era types. No walk-ons are permitted. Registration must be by postal service (not by e-mail). See website for details. Amenities include space for primitive camping within the Union or Confederate campsites and hay for bedding. Horses must come with their own hay. The first forty horses pre-registered for participating in a battle receive a $10 bounty if pre-registered with the name of a rider. The first twenty pre-registered artillery units will be reimbursed $125 each for their powder. A $2 donation will be taken from each reenactor toward a raffle ticket; there will be five drawings, each for a $100 gift certificate toward any of the registered sutlers.

"Dance, v.i. To leap about to the sound of tittering music, preferably with arms about your neighbor's wife or daughter." —Ambrose Bierce, *The Devil's Dictionary*

Educators

Friday is a school day from 9 AM to 2 PM. Field trips are available, but no curriculum aids are available yet.

Contact Information

www.brooksvillereenactment.com

School Day coordinator: 352-799-0129 or everett_j@popmail.firn.edu

General information line: 352-799-0129 (Hernando County Historical Museum)

Battle of Hogtown (August 1864)
High Springs, Alachua County

Historical Background

This Civil War event is based on the second of two clashes in Gainesville. The city was occupied by the Union in February of 1864 after a Union raiding party entered the city to capture two trains and defeated the Confederate resistance. Guerilla tactics were used to eventually drive out the Federals, who returned with several hundred troops as reinforcements. In August of 1864, the Confederates ambushed the occupying Union force in Gainesville's town square and sent them back again to Jacksonville.

What You'll Find

- A narrated battle each day between Union and Confederate forces
- Sutlers hawking their period wares
- Authentic Union and Confederate encampments with troops eager for company
- A ladies' tea
- A Blue-Gray Ball

Planning Your Visit

Whom to bring: This is a family event. Guide animals are welcome. Pets are not allowed in Poe Springs Park.

Dates and times: First weekend in December. Battles are on Saturday at 2:30 PM and Sunday at 2 PM. Friday is a school day, 10 AM to 3 PM; weekend days are 9 AM to 6 PM. Ladies tea is at 11 AM on Saturday. Period ball is on Saturday evening.

Getting there: The address of Poe Springs Park is 28800 NW 182nd Avenue in High Springs, 32643. GPS coordinates are N29° 49.3175', W082° 38.4278'.

Parking: More than enough, with overflow parking as well. ADA-compliant spaces are provided.

Fees and tickets: Free with admission to the park, which is $5 for adults and less for children 6–12 (five and under are free.) Reenactors have a fee of a few dollars but get a free pork dinner Friday night.

Facilities
Restrooms: Fixed facilities and porta-potties are available and ADA-accessible.

Other ADA compliance information: The grounds are hard-packed dirt, but somewhat uneven. People using canes should be able to get around easily, but wheelchair users may need help.

Places to eat: There is a concession at the park.

Picnic facilities: Tables, covered and uncovered, are in the park, as well as grills.

Places to sit: There are bleachers set up for viewing the battle but also room for one's own chairs or a blanket.

Places to stay on-site: None but sites for the reenactor camps.

Reenactors
Needed are Civil War military and civilians of both sides, including cavalry, infantry, and artillery. Amenities include firewood and hay. There is a free nighttime meal for those helping on school day, and a bounty for cavalry and the first four cannons.

Educators
No curriculum materials are available yet, but Friday is a school day (10 AM to 3 PM) and field trips are available. Check with your school board.

Contact Information
Organizer: McLeanJGator@yahoo.com
Poe Springs County Park
28800 NW 182nd Avenue
High Springs, FL 32643
904-454-1992

> "Yankee, n. In Europe, an American. In the Northern States of our Union, a New Englander. In the Southern States the word is unknown. (See 'Damyank.')" —Ambrose Bierce, *The Devil's Dictionary*

A Firefight at Heritage Village (1861–65)
Largo, Pinellas County

Historical Background
Heritage Village is a twenty-one-acre living history complex in Pinellas County, full of historic buildings from Florida's pioneer era. In this event, the village focuses on the days of the Civil War.

What You'll Find
- A textbook example of time travelers finding themselves in the wrong place at the wrong time, as a skirmish erupts within the village itself

- The chance for visitors to mingle and talk with Union or Confederate soldiers going about their business in town before they notice each other, draw their weapons, and begin the unpleasantness
- Demonstrations of industry supporting the war effort, including salt making, meat smoking, and flag making
- Vintage baseball (according to 1800s rules)
- A ladies' social
- Sutlers looking to flee with their money, goods, and hides intact

Planning Your Visit

Whom to bring: This event is for the whole family.

Dates and times: Held the third Saturday in May from 10 AM to 4 PM.

Getting there: The GPS coordinates for Heritage Village are N27° 52.873', W082° 48.7013'. The address is 11909 125th Street North in Largo, 33774.

Parking: Adequate, with ADA-compliant spaces. A shuttle is available.

Fees and tickets: Free. Donations adored.

Facilities

Restrooms: Restrooms are ADA-accessible.

Other ADA compliance information: Due to paving and hard-packed, level dirt, wheelchair access is easy. Certain buildings, because of the need for preservation, are not ADA-accessible.

Places to eat: Many concessions will be available on-site.

Picnic facilities: Tables are present (some shaded), but there are no grills.

Places to sit: There is no need to bring chairs or a blanket.

Places to stay on-site: None, but many fine establishments are nearby.

Reenactors
Needed are Civil War infantry and artillery of both sides. Contact event organizers beforehand to let them know you are coming. An artillery-powder subsidy will be given to the first two field pieces of each side. There are no other amenities.

Educators
There are no school days, field trips, or curriculum aids as yet for this event, although Heritage Village itself has its own extensive educational resources.

"I was armed to the teeth with a pitiful little Smith & Wesson's seven-shooter, which carried a ball like a homeopathic pill, and it took the whole seven to make a dose for an adult. But I thought it was grand. It appeared to me to be a dangerous weapon. It had only one fault—you could not hit anything with it. One of our 'conductors' practiced awhile on a cow with it, and as long as she stood still and behaved herself she was safe; but as soon as she went to moving about, and he got to shooting at other things, she came to grief." —Mark Twain, *Roughing It*

Contact Information
Heritage Village
11909 125th Street N.
Largo, FL 33774
727-582-2123
www.county.pinellas.org/heritage

Ocklawaha River Raid (1865)
Weirsdale, Marion County

Historical Background
This popular event commemorates the only Civil War battle fought in Marion County. In March of 1865, a Union force from occupied Jacksonville marched into Marion

County and crossed the Ocklawaha River. From there they looted and then destroyed Marshall's Plantation, which had supplied the Confederacy with syrup and sugar. As the Home Guard responded, the Federals withdrew back across the Ocklawaha River and burned the bridge behind them. Except for a single horse killed during the raid, everything was then returned to Marion County.

What You'll Find
- Authentic encampments of both Union and Confederate armies
- Interaction with soldiers going about their daily duties or relaxing
- A slice of 1860s life at a civilian homestead
- Sutlers, many of whom are reenactors themselves, with wares to sell
- A "Call to Arms" at a Civil War recruitment station
- A battle reenactment at 2:00 PM each day
- Period music concerts
- Special children's activities
- A ladies' tea
- A Saturday-evening Blue-Gray Ball
- Sunday AM worship service

Planning Your Visit
Whom to bring: This is a whole-family event.

Dates and times: First or second weekend in November. Check with the website beforehand. The site will open for reenactor and sutler setup at noon on the Thursday before. Event hours are from 9 AM to 4 PM.

Getting there: The event is at the grounds of the Florida Carriage Museum, at 3000 Marion County Road, Weirsdale 32195. GPS coordinates are N28° 56.8299', W081° 54.3935'.

Parking: Ample guided, ADA-compliant parking is provided.

Fees and tickets: This event has many proud local sponsors, so the tickets are surprisingly cheap—only a few dollars per carload.

Facilities
Restrooms: Portable facilities are provided, some of which are ADA-accessible.

Other ADA compliance information: The grounds are gently rolling, hard-packed dirt, negotiable by users of wheelchairs or canes unless the grounds are soaked. Check the weather forecast beforehand. Horse-drawn haywagons help bring visitors in and out of the parking area.

Places to eat: Food and drink concessions are on-site.

Picnic facilities: Uncovered picnic tables are present without grills.

Places to sit: Bring your own chairs or blankets to watch the battles.

Places to stay on-site: None except for the reenactors' camps.

Reenactors

Needed are Civil War–era reenactors of all ages, including civilians, musicians, sutlers, and Federal and Confederate military (including infantry, artillery, cavalry, and medical units). Sutlers, cavalry, and artillery are asked to pre-register. Amenities include a powder ration for the first eight guns, hay rations for pre-registered horses, and primitive campsites.

Educators

School days, field trips, and curriculum aids are not yet available.

Contact Information

(Organizer) E-mail: LtCol2ndBattalion@gmail.com
www.ocklawahariverraid.com
Civil War Re-enactor/Living History Organization
11 Bahia Court
Ocala, FL 34472

Battle of Natural Bridge (1865)
Natural Bridge Battlefield Historic State Park, Leon County

Historical Background

The reenactment here is on the actual battlefield where Tallahassee's fate was decided. A Union force had landed at the St. Marks Lighthouse with the intent of marching to and taking Tallahassee. Warned of their coming, the sparse Confederate defenders were joined by a ragtag volunteer civilian militia of wounded soldiers who had been sent home to recuperate, men as old as seventy years, and boys as young as fourteen years from the military academy that would later become Florida State University. Three separate charges by the Federals over the natural bridge across the St. Marks River were repulsed before they gave up and scuttled back to their ships, having learned that that even back then, FSU was too tough for them to take on.

What You'll Find

- A skirmish on Saturday at 2:30 PM
- Reenactment of the Battle of Natural Bridge on the original battlefield at 2:30 PM Sunday
- Demonstrations of period skills such as sewing, spinning, knitting, needlework, and candlemaking
- A rare opportunity to observe and interact with the Soldier Aid Society, and for children to see what they did 150 years ago
- Medical demonstrations

- Period camps of Civil War–era civilians, Federals, and Confederates to visit and learn from
- Sutlers looking to buffalo your nickels
- A formal midmorning ladies' tea on Saturday

Planning Your Visit

Whom to bring: This is a family event.

Dates and times: First weekend in March. Sunday opening ceremonies are at 1:30 PM. Battles begin at 2:30 PM. Camps are open from 10 AM to 4 PM.

Getting there: The event takes place on the actual battlefield at Natural Bridge Battlefield Historic State Park, 32305, located six miles east of Woodville, off SR 363 (Woodville Highway), on Natural Bridge Road. Woodville is just south of Tallahassee. The GPS coordinates of the park entrance are N30° 17.0945', W084° 9.1817'.

Parking: Adequate. ADA-accessible parking is provided.

Fees and tickets: Free!

Facilities

Restrooms: Fixed restroom facilities are present and ADA-compliant; porta-potties are also provided; some of them are ADA-compliant.

Other ADA compliance information: The grounds are hard-packed dirt and negotiable by people using wheelchairs or canes unless the ground is soaked. Watch the weather or speak to the park staff beforehand.

Places to eat: Food concessions are on-site.

Picnic facilities: Picnic tables are available, some of which are covered and some of which are ADA-compliant, but there are not many of them. There is room for spreading a picnic blanket. Grills are available.

Places to sit: Bringing one's own chairs or blanket to see the battle is encouraged.

Places to stay on-site: Campsites (period only, for reenactors).

Reenactors

Needed are period civilians and Civil War military, both sides. This event is traditionally short on Yankees, so Yanks or galvanizers willing to take a good sound whipping are especially welcome. Because of the small battlefield, they cannot have mounted cavalry. Sutlers and artillery are by invitation only. Amenities include hay, wood, and a potluck dinner for reenactors on Saturday night.

Educators

School day is the Friday of the event weekend from 9 AM to noon. Field trips are available. Check with your school board. No curriculum aids are yet available.

Contact Information
Military: cellrich@hotmail.com
Sutlers: 386-963-3654
Other inquiries: theboudreaux@netzero.com
www.floridastateparks.org/naturalbridge/default.cfm

Natural Bridge Battlefield Historic State Park
7502 Natural Bridge Road
Tallahassee, FL 32305
850-922-6007

━━◆•▶◀•◆━━

The Pioneers
(1866–1900)

Paxton's Heritage Festival (1861–1900)
Paxton, Walton County

Historical Background
It's only a mile south of the Alabama state line, but it's still in Florida. The annual Paxton Heritage Festival features many reminders of the Florida Panhandle's past as well as some more modern events.

What You'll Find
- An authentic Civil War encampment with battle-weary soldiers willing to discuss how they live, what they are fighting for, and how they want to be remembered
- Period crafts and skills including blacksmithing, flintknapping, making musical instruments, making lye soap, and many others
- An active sugar cane mill for small children to taste cane juice for the first time, and for grown-up kids to remind themselves what that first taste was like

Planning your Visit
Whom to bring: This is for the family.
Dates and times: The festival is from 10 AM to 2 PM on the fourth Saturday in October.
Getting there: The merriment is next to the sheriff's substation one mile south

of the Alabama state line on Hwy 331. GPS coordinates are N30°58.0831', W086°18.0913'. Paxton's zip code is 32538.

Parking: Abundant.

Fees and tickets: Free!

Facilities

Restrooms: Portable restroom facilities are provided that are ADA accessible.

Other ADA compliance information: The grounds are of hard-packed, level dirt; users of canes or wheelchairs should have little trouble getting around.

Places to eat: Food concessions are on-site.

Picnic facilities: There are none on-site.

Places to sit: Bringing one's own lawn chairs or picnic blanket is advised.

Places to stay on-site: None.

Reenactors

Needed are appropriately costumed people from the 1700s and 1800s, especially those with a skill to demonstrate, and Civil War–era military. Volunteers should notify the event organizers ahead of time.

> Be sure to have a picnic or to just enjoy the view at the highest point in Florida, which is only two and a half miles away from Paxton. It's pretty up there.

Educators

There are no school days, field trips, or curriculum aids yet.

Contact information

This event is sponsored by the local Ruritan Club, which can be reached at topaxton@gtcom.net.

A Cracker Christmas (early 1860s to early 1870s)

Christmas, Orange County

Historical Background

Fort Christmas was abandoned in 1838 because it was no longer needed by the military. The pioneer settlement around it continued to grow.

What You'll Find

Over one hundred and fifty booths in a crafts fair, and a booth from the Christmas Post Office doing hand stamping of your Christmas cards. The living history portions of this event include:

- Cow hunters in camp telling about life on the trail hunting cows
- A Civil War encampment with soldiers
- Demonstrations of industry skills such as blacksmithing, rope making, and flint knapping
- Wood carving and chair caning
- Demonstrators in period clothing involved in domestic skills such as spinning, weaving, quilting, soapmaking, basket weaving, broom making, and bobbin-lace making

Planning Your Visit

Whom to bring: This is for the family.

Dates and times: The first weekend in December, from 10 AM to 4 PM.

Getting there: Fort Christmas is at 1300 Fort Christmas Road in Christmas, 32709. It is just off SR 50, twenty miles east of Orlando. GPS coordinates are N28° 33.6401', W081° 1.2821'.

Parking: Ample, with ADA-compliant spaces.

Fees and tickets: Free!

Facilities

Restrooms: ADA-accessible restrooms are provided.

Other ADA compliance information: The grounds are hard-packed dirt and, unless soaked, can be negotiated by those using wheelchairs, canes, or strollers.

Places to eat: Food concessions are on-site for this event.

Picnic facilities: Picnic tables and pavilions are not available during this event.

Places to sit: There is no need to bring chairs or a blanket.
Places to stay on-site: None.

Reenactors
Not needed.

Educators
There are no school days, field trips, or curriculum aids.

Contact Information
Fort Christmas Park
1300 Fort Christmas Road
Christmas, FL 32709
407-568-4149
www.nbbd.com/godo/FortChristmas

Remember to bring your Christmas cards for the Christmas postmark.

Heritage Day Festival (1863)
Forest Capital Museum State Park, Perry, Taylor County

Historical Background
This event at Forest Capital Museum State Park honors Florida's early settlers and their way of life, with a unique and special emphasis on the state's timberland and forest-related industries. Heritage Day is followed the next day by the area's Florida Forest Festival.

What You'll Find
- A preserved 1863 Cracker homestead with living historians in period dress
- A Civil War–era military encampment to visit and learn from men who carried their homes on their backs
- Cracker cow hunters ready to brag about how tough it was to find those critters hiding in the forest
- Weaving demonstrations using pine straw for baskets and palmetto fronds for shelter
- Demonstrations of needle arts such as quilting, crocheting, knitting, and tatting
- Lessons in using a Cracker whip
- A blacksmith
- Cane grinding and Cracker cooking

- Wood carving, split-rail fence building, and many other things that Florida pioneers did to pass the time while waiting for television to be invented
- Pioneer merchants offering the experience of pioneer shopping

The number and type of living history programs done on Heritage Day versus those done at the Florida Forest Festival (which is on the following day) varies each year. Check the website for more information.

Planning Your Visit

Whom to bring: The whole family will like this event. No pets; only working companion animals allowed.

Dates and times: It's held on the fourth Friday in October. Hours are 9 AM to 2 PM on Friday. Saturday's festival is from 9 AM to 4 PM.

Getting there: The GPS coordinates of the park entrance are N30° 4.8082', W083° 33.9716'. The park's address is 204 Forest Park Drive, Perry, 32348.

Parking: Places can get scarce on Saturday, the busier day. Carpooling is advised.

Fees and tickets: $1 for Friday; Saturday is free. Free parking.

Facilities

Restrooms: ADA-compliant restrooms are located at the museum.

Other ADA compliance information: A shuttle is provided on the Saturday, which is the much busier day. ADA-compliant parking is present. Sidewalks are present except around the Cracker homestead; the soil around the homestead is sandy and not negotiable by wheelchair users without help.

Places to eat: Concessions are numerous during the festivities.

Picnic facilities: There are no grills. There are three pavilions, which can be reserved.

Places to sit: It is not necessary to bring chairs or a blanket, but there are places to spread a blanket if picnicking.

Places to stay on-site: No, but lodging is available in Perry.

Reenactors

Needed are Civil War soldiers (Federal or Confederate) and civilians from 1864, including Florida Crackers and other rural Floridians, especially those who can demonstrate an old-time skill or craft. There are no amenities.

Educators

The Friday event is a school day, from 9 AM to 2 PM. Consult your local school board about field trips. There are no curriculum aids available yet.

Be sure to find out what "froggin" is, and "polecat candy."

Contact Information
Forest Capital Museum State Park
204 Forest Park Drive
Perry, FL 32348
850-584-3227
www.floridastateparks.org/forestcapital/default.cfm

The Good Ol' Days Festival at Homeland (late 1800s)
Homeland, Polk County

Historical Background
Built around a schoolhouse constructed on its present location in 1878, and filled with other historic buildings moved there from around Polk County, Homeland Heritage Park is an open-air preservation of the early settlement of what is now Polk County. Once a year the park dresses up a little and invites everyone over.

What You'll Find
The living history portions of this event include:
- A frontier family encampment with people eager to share about the hardships and small victories of starting a home with only what could be carried in
- A Civil War encampment with soldiers showing how they carried their living quarters with them
- Teaching stations demonstrating pioneer skills and crafts used to build communities from materials at hand
- Storytellers
- Fine Southern cooking
- Merchants willing to swap nineteenth-century goods for twenty-first-century cash

Planning Your Visit
Whom to bring: Anyone in the family who wants to have a good time.
Dates and times: It's held the first Saturday of April from 9 AM to 4 PM.
Getting there: The GPS coordinates are N27°49.2312, W081°49.52364. The street address is 249 Church Street in Homeland, which is just south of Bartow off Highway 17. Zip is 33830.
Parking: Adequate and guided, with overflow parking space provided. ADA-compliant spaces are also provided.
Fees and tickets: Free!

Facilities

Restrooms: ADA-accessible restrooms are immediately across the main parking lot from the entrance to the park itself.

Other ADA compliance information: The grounds are paved or are level, hard-packed dirt. Those using wheelchairs, canes, or strollers should have little difficulty unless the area is wet. Some of the buildings have ramps.

Places to eat: Food concessions are on-site during this event.

Picnic facilities: There are no facilities available during this event, except for places to spread a picnic blanket.

Places to sit: It is not necessary to bring one's own chairs or blanket.

Places to stay on-site: None, but lodging is available in nearby Bartow.

Reenactors

Needed are Civil War infantry of the Confederacy in appropriate uniform, authentically dressed civilians from the nineteenth century, especially civilians who can demonstrate a craft or skill. There are no amenities.

Educators

There are no school days or field trips. Curriculum aids for the park itself are at www.polk-county.net.

Contact Information

Homeland Heritage Park
515 East Boulevard Street
Homeland, FL 33830
863-534-3766
www.bartowchamber.com/homeland.htm

Christmas Notes at Homeland Heritage Park (late 1860s–1870s)

Homeland, Polk County

What You'll Find
A celebration of a Florida Christmas, pioneer-style. The living history portions of this event include:

- First-person interaction with encamped Union and Confederate soldiers sharing what they and their families do about being apart for the holidays
- An afternoon party with lessons on dances of the pioneer era
- Period crafts and lessons on pioneer skills
- A Victorian Santa Claus
- Christmas storytelling in the log cabin
- An encampment showing how Christmas was celebrated on the Florida frontier
- A (civilian) pioneer encampment from 1870s Florida
- Pioneer children's games

Planning Your Visit
Whom to bring: Everyone. The older or younger the better.
Dates and times: The second Saturday in December, from 10 AM to 8 PM.
Parking: Adequate, with overflow parking available.
Fees and tickets: Free!

Facilities
Places to eat: Free light refreshments are available to all.
Picnic facilities: None available during this event.
Places to sit: There is no need to bring chairs or blankets.

Reenactors
Needed are Union or Confederate soldiers for authentic camps. There are no facilities for horses. Also welcome are civilian impressions from mid-to-late-nineteenth-century rural Florida, especially if a period craft or skill can be demonstrated. Volunteers should contact the event officials beforehand.

Educators
There are no school days, field trips, or curriculum aids yet.

Contact Information
www.bartowchamber.com/homeland.htm

Dudley Farm Historic State Park (1850s–1940s)
Newberry, Alachua County

Historical Background

As technology advanced, Florida's urban areas changed, and so did Florida farms. Mule-driven plows gave way to tractors. The water power of the running stream was replaced by the gasoline-powered internal combustion engine when it came to running the gristmill. Despite the changes, there were still crops to be planted, nurtured, and harvested, and livestock to be fed. Certain seemingly endless chores were taken over by newfangled machines, freeing farm families for the endless chores of maintaining and repairing the newfangled machines.

What You'll Find

- A working farm that shows the changes in the Florida farm from the 1850s to the mid-1940s
- Original buildings including a dairy shed, a canning house, stables, a post office, and the family farmhouse with its separate kitchen (an example of pioneer fire safety)
- Crops such as corn, sugar cane, and sweet potatoes
- Livestock for children to help feed, including Cracker cows, Cracker horses, chickens, and free-ranging turkeys
- Authentically dressed staff going about their chores
- Many opportunities for visitors to get some hands-on experience in nineteenth-century farming
- Varying farm activities depending on the season, from spring planting to autumn harvest
- Demonstrations and teaching of pioneer skills and crafts

Planning Your Visit

Whom to bring: The whole family will enjoy this. No smoking or pets allowed on the farmstead. Service animals are always welcome.

Dates and times: The park is open Wednesday–Sunday from 9 AM to 5 PM. The farm portion closes at 4 PM.

Getting there: The park is seven miles east of Newberry and west of I-75 on SR 26 between Newberry and Gainesville. GPS coordinates of the park entrance are N29° 39.2726', W082° 32.6751'. Address is 18730 W. Newberry Rd. in Newberry, 32669.

Parking: Adequate for normal days; overflow areas are established for special events. Special access is enabled for visitors with mobility challenges; call the park beforehand to make arrangements.

Fees and tickets: Small admission fee by the carload (up to 8 passengers).

Facilities

Restrooms: ADA-compliant restrooms are at the visitor center.

Other ADA compliance information: There is an ADA lift into the farmhouse on the exterior. The grounds are level, hard-packed dirt. Wheelchairs or strollers may have problems in areas that have been recently soaked by heavy rains.

Places to eat: Despite all the crops, there is no place serving them on-site.

Picnic facilities: The picnic area has six uncovered tables and three grills.

Places to sit: It is not necessary to bring one's own chairs or blanket.

Places to stay on-site: None. A motel is close by in Newberry. Alarm clocks are provided in each room for city folks. Inquire at desk should you prefer a rooster.

Reenactors

Living history is handled by park staff and volunteers. For volunteer opportunities and amenities, check with the park staff, citizen support organization, or their respective websites.

Educators

There are no specific school days. Field trips are available, in groups of no more than 40; reservations must be at least a month in advance. Curriculum aids are not yet available.

Contact Information

www.floridastateparks.org/DudleyFarm
Dudley Farm Historic State Park
18730 W. Newberry Rd.
Newberry, FL 32669
352-472-1142

> "The farmer has to be an optimist or he wouldn't still be a farmer." —Will Rogers

---

Cane Day at Dudley Farm (1850–1940)
Newberry, Alachua County

Historical Background

This is an annual fundraiser for Dudley Farm Historic State Park. Originally a celebration of the birthday of Miss Myrtle Dudley (the last Dudley to live on the farm, and who willed it to the State of Florida), Cane Day has grown to be an old-time community gathering.

What You'll Find

- A working cane press

- Lessons on how to make syrup from sugar cane, from the grinding of the harvested stalks to the boiling of cane juice
- Live traditional music
- Food vendors with menus incorporating all four basic food groups: salt, sugar, cholesterol, and caffeine
- Children's games such as sack races
- Horse-drawn wagon rides
- Demonstrations of crafts and skills of the late nineteenth century

Planning Your Visit

Whom to bring: The whole family will enjoy this, unless they're dentists. No smoking or pets allowed on the farmstead. Service animals are always welcome.

Dates and times: It's the first Saturday in December, from 9 AM to 3 PM.

Parking: Can fill up, but overflow areas are established. Special access (including a designated parking area and a tram to the farmstead) is enabled for visitors with mobility challenges; call the park beforehand to make arrangements.

Fees and tickets: $4 a carload (up to eight people a carload).

Facilities

Restrooms: ADA-accessible facilities are at the visitor center. Portable facilities (may not be ADA-accessible) are added during this event.

Places to eat: Concessions will be available.

Reenactors

Those with a skill to demonstrate or those interested in volunteering in other capacities should check with the park staff, citizen support organization, or their respective websites (preferably) at least two months prior to Cane Day.

Educators

There are no school days, field trips, or curriculum aids yet. However, sugar cane is processed for about a week prior to Cane Day, if classes wish to schedule a field trip on one of those days.

Contact Information

www.floridastateparks.org/DudleyFarm
352-472-1142

Farm Plow Days at Dudley Farm
(1850s–early twentieth century)
Newberry, Alachua County
Historical Background
This is how it was done before the invention of the tractor and after the tractor either ran out of gas or broke down. Like the Energizer Bunny, those mules just keep going.

What You'll Find
- Plowing done by teams of mules, oxen, or draft horses
- Fewer backbreaking chores performed with simple hand tools
- Demonstrations of how Florida farmed before mechanization, as people and animals worked together to raise and harvest crops so that all could eat

Planning Your Visit
Dates and times: Plowing is demonstrated from 10 AM to 2 PM on the first or second Friday-Saturday pair in February.
Fees: This event is free with park admission (less than five dollars/carload, up to eight passengers).

Educators
The event's Friday is a school day. Field trips are available (consult your local school board), but reservations must be made two months in advance. There are no curriculum aids yet.

———————

Morningside Farm (1870)
Gainesville, Alachua County
Historical Background
Morningside Farm is part of Morningside Nature Center in the Gainesville park system. Besides being a working farm, it is also home to a number of historic buildings brought in from around Florida.

What You'll Find
- A working, single-family north Florida farm from Florida's Reconstruction era (1870) showing Cracker family life
- Costumed park staff and volunteers going about their farm chores such as feeding the animals
- Opportunities to help feed the livestock during their 3 PM meal
- Original turn-of-the-century buildings and historic-breed farm animals in the barnyard for visitors to enjoy
- Hot biscuits with freshly made butter

Planning Your Visit

Whom to bring: This is for the whole family. No pets (they'll chase the chickens!). Service animals are always welcome.

Dates and times: Open Labor Day through Memorial Day. Living history events are on Saturdays only. Closed on Christmas Eve, Christmas Day, Thanksgiving, and New Year's Day. Hours are 9 AM to 4:30 PM.

Getting there: The farm is three miles east of downtown Gainesville on the north side of SR 26 (East University Avenue). The GPS coordinates are N29° 39.1207', W082° 16.9842'. Zip is 32641.

Parking: There are plenty of spaces, including room for RVs, and there are some ADA-compliant spaces.

Fees and tickets: There are small fees for the two big annual events. On other days admission is free.

Facilities

Restrooms: Restrooms are ADA-accessible.

Other ADA compliance information: The grounds of the farm, including the approach from the parking lot, are hard-packed dirt with patches of bark chips. It is uneven in places, and those using wheelchairs or canes may need help. Some buildings have ramps; some others can have temporary ramps placed if farm officials know beforehand that they will be needed. Accommodations are gladly made if those with special needs will contact the farm before their visit.

Places to eat: There are none on-site except during some special events.

Picnic facilities: There is a picnic area without grills.

Places to sit: There is no need to bring chairs or a blanket.

Places to stay on-site: None, but the Gainesville area has a wide range of lodging establishments. These can fill up at times as it is rumored that there is a university in town with a football team, but no one in Tallahassee claims to know anything about it.

Reenactors

The farm has its own staff and volunteers. Those interested in volunteering should contact the farm's administration or view the website.

Educators

There are no designated school days except for the two days prior to the Farm and Forest Festival (see next entry). For field trips, contact your local school board. There are enough curriculum aids on the farm's website to fill a barn.

Contact Information

352-393-8756 or 352-334-3326
Morningside Living History Farm
3540 E. University Avenue

Be sure to see the Dorkings before they're all gone!

Gainesville, FL 32641
www.cityofgainesville.org (Search with keyword "Morningside")

Farm and Forest Festival (mid-nineteenth to early twentieth century)

Gainesville, Alachua County

Historical Background
This event at Morningside Farm is a celebration of nineteenth-century living in rural Florida, from the Panhandle's pine forests to the farm itself.

What You'll Find
- A visit to the Living History Farm, with its period-dressed farmhands who work, but who are also always ready to talk about what they are doing and why
- An array of pioneer skills at work and demonstration, such as rope making, basketry, spinning, and weaving
- A blacksmith clanging at the forge
- Traditional children's activities such as using tin-can stilts and tug-o-war
- Sheep shearing
- Horse-drawn wagon rides
- A Civil War encampment where soldiers answer questions about protecting Florida's farms from Northern marauders
- An inexpensive children's menu of foods on the school days
- Live music of the era all day

Planning Your Visit
Whom to bring: This event is for the family that wants to get down on the farm and see what life was like for Gramps and Gram when they were little. Unfortunately, pets must stay home less'n they scoot after the chickens and give the poor turkeys a fright. Guide animals are always welcome.
Dates and times: It is held the fourth weekend in April, with the previous Thursday and Friday being school days. Hours on school days are 9 AM to 1 PM. On weekend days they are 10 AM to 4 PM.
Fees and tickets: Admission for school days is $1.50 for pre-registered children and $2.50 for preregistered adults. Bus drivers in uniform get in free. The school days admission is good for the weekend festival days when with a paying adult. During weekend days, admission is $5 per adult and $3 for children three to twelve years, with children under three free.

Facilities
Places to eat: Food concessions will be on-site during the festival, with a low-priced menu for the children on school days.

141

Reenactors
Needed are period-dressed pioneers of the mid-to-late 1800s with a skill or who are willing to do farm chores. Volunteers should contact the administration beforehand.

Educators
School days are the Thursday and Friday of the festival. Contact your school board about field trips. Curriculum aids are posted on the farm's section of the City of Gainesville website.

A Cane Boil at Morningside Farm (1870)
Gainesville, Alachua County

Historical Background
Sugar cane was introduced to the Americas from the Orient, and in frontier Florida the only sweetener in the pioneer family's diet was cane syrup. The syrup was made after the annual harvest of sugar cane. The stalks were crushed in a mule-powered press in order to extract the juice. Hours of boiling reduced ten gallons of cane juice to a gallon of cane syrup.

What You'll Find
- The way cane syrup was made in 1870
- Living historians in period dress offering samples of the freshly made syrup ladled onto fresh homemade biscuits or cornbread
- A fiddling contest within earshot
- A blacksmith working the forge
- Pioneer crafts and skills on display, such as soapmaking
- Fine Southern cooking

Planning Your Visit
Whom to bring: The whole family and anyone else with a sweet tooth. Guide animals are welcome; pets cannot be allowed because of the other animals on the farm.

Dates and times: The event is held the Saturday after Thanksgiving from 9 AM to 5 PM.

Fees and tickets: Eight bits per adult and half-price for ages three through twelve years. Under three is free.

Facilities
Places to eat: There are no concessions on-site.

Picnic facilities: A picnic area is on-site, but there's a lot of competition for it.

Places to sit: There is no need to bring one's own chairs or blankets.

Reenactors

Those interested in volunteering should contact the farm's administration office or view the website.

Educators

There is no designated school day; field trips are not available. Curriculum aids are found on the City of Gainesville website in the "Nature Operations" subsection.

A Cow Hunter Camp (1876)

Lake Kissimmee State Park, Lake Wales, Polk County

Historical Overview

The image of the lonesome cowboy driving a herd of lowing cattle doesn't often conjure up a map of Florida, but there were cattle ranches in Florida a hundred years before any cattle set their hooves into the soil of the American West. As Spanish influence in Florida waned, their cattle wandered freely throughout the territory feeding, growing, and multiplying—a sort of mobile crop to be harvested by Native Americans, farmers, and cattle barons. Rather than cowboys, Florida had cow hunters. Instead of driving cattle from a ranch to a market, cow hunters first crossed the peninsula to hunt, capture, and brand freely wandering cattle. Along the way the claimed cattle were left in camps to be cared for by one or two cow hunters who would stay behind until the group came back through to drive all the captured cattle to market.

What You'll Find

- A trail from the parking lot leading to a fully operational 1876 cow camp with a corral full of Cracker cattle, watched over by at least one cow hunter
- The cow hunter, a first-person reenactor, who leads a lonely life and will be glad to show you around the camp and to answer questions about his life
- First-hand lessons about why the American West has cowboys and Florida has cow hunters

Planning Your Visit

Whom to bring: The cow camp can be enjoyed by the whole family; even infants will probably be fascinated by the Cracker cattle in the corral. Pets are not allowed. Service animals are always welcome.

Dates and times: The cow camp is open from 9:30 AM to 4:30 PM weekends and holidays except for Christmas and New Year's Day. From May 1 to October 1 it is only open on holiday weekends.

Getting there: The cow hunter camp is a part of Lake Kissimmee State Park just east of Lake Wales and off Highway 60 at 14248 Camp Mack Road, Lake Wales, 33853. The GPS coordinates for the park entrance are N27° 58.145', W081° 22.81'.

Parking: Ample parking is available at the trailhead leading to the cow camp. The lot is just an elliptical patch of packed dirt. There is adequate room for RVs. The footpath to the cow hunter camp is about six or more feet wide but consists of several inches of sand in many places. Wheelchair users should speak beforehand to park personnel to arrange for transportation by motorized cart.

Fees and tickets: There is a small fee to get into the park, but once inside, admission to the cow camp is free.

Facilities

Restrooms: There are no restrooms at the cow camp or at the parking lot that serves it. There are ADA-compliant restrooms very close by the parking lot at the marina.

Other ADA information: The parking lot at the marina has special ADA spaces.

Places to eat: A limited concession area is located just outside the park. A wide variety of establishments can be found in nearby Lake Wales. The park has picnic areas with grills, tables, and four pavilions.

Places to sit: There are log benches at the cow camp.

Places to stay on-site: Modern and primitive campsites are located elsewhere in the park.

> Be sure to ask the cow hunter about swamp water and gator milk, and how cow-hunter dogs handle cattle stampedes.

Reenactors

The park has its own staff of volunteers. Those interested in volunteering should contact the ranger staff.

Educators

The cow hunter camp can accommodate school groups of at least fifteen on a field trip, even during the off-season when it is not open otherwise. No prepared lesson plans are yet available.

Contact Information

Lake Kissimmee State Park
14248 Camp Mack Road
Lake Wales, FL 33853
863-696-1112
http://www.floridastateparks.org/lakekissimmee/default.cfm

Homeland's Schoolmarms and Schoolmasters (1880s)

Homeland, Polk County

Historical Background

The schoolhouse at Homeland Heritage Park is the only building that is still sitting where it was built; the others were brought in from elsewhere in Polk County. Built in 1878, the school was in use till 1956. There are people living in Homeland today who received part of their education in that school.

What You'll Find

- An immersion experience in which students experience education within a one-room schoolhouse in the year 1880
- Teaching done by a period-dressed schoolmarm or schoolmaster
- Lessons from the McGuffey Eclectic Reader
- Writing and ciphering with slates and slate pencils
- The teaching of manners as well as obligations before, during, and after school

- Ample opportunity for the discerning student to observe the differences between their experience and the conditions under which their older relatives received their educations, such as:
- The walking distance between Grampa's house and the school is no longer five miles
- There is no longer three feet of snow on the ground between hurricanes
- Those walking to school nowadays are not required to carry fifty pounds of books and a little brother or sister on their backs
- Recent grading of the grounds has removed the steep inclines encountered when walking both to and from school

Planning Your Visit

Whom to bring: This is a semi-private event for third-, fourth-, or fifth-grade students, arranged through the local school board or with the staff at Homeland Heritage Park.

Dates and times: This event can be arranged for any school day. Students are transported from their own schools early in the morning and are divided into two groups. One tours the Heritage Park while the other is in the schoolhouse. At mid-morning they switch. They are returned to their own school by the end of the school day.

Getting there: Transportation is by school bus both to and from the park.

Fees and tickets: The program itself is free, although costs may be associated with transportation to and from the park.

Facilities

ADA compliance information: There is a ramp into the schoolhouse. The doorway is wide enough to accommodate wheelchairs.

Places to eat: There are no concessions at the park. Lunch has to be arranged by the students' school.

Picnic facilities: There is a pavilion on-site, but no grill.

"Academe, n. An ancient school where morality and philosophy were taught."
—Ambrose Bierce, *The Devil's Dictionary*

"Academy, n. (from academe). A modern school where football is taught." —Ambrose Bierce, *The Devil's Dictionary*

Reenactors

Volunteers for schoolmarms or schoolmasters should contact the Polk County government.

Educators

After their immersion experience, each student will be given a copy of the "Book of Lessons," which reviews what they have learned.

Contact Information
Homeland Heritage Park
515 East Boulevard Street
Homeland, FL 33830
863-534-3766
www.bartowchamber.com/homeland.htm

Panhandle Folk Life Days (late 1800s)
Blountstown, Calhoun County

Historical Background

The Panhandle Pioneer Settlement in Blountstown is a living history museum consisting of a farmstead and an early Florida agricultural community, with sixteen historic or recreated buildings on forty-seven acres. Staffed mostly by volunteers dedicated to preserving Florida's pioneer heritage and open four days a week, the settlement is most active during its annual events, the biggest and most educational of which is Panhandle Folk Life Days.

What You'll Find

- An active rural Florida village from the nineteenth century
- Pioneer domestic skills on display such as soapmaking, laundry methods, crocheting, and quiltmaking
- A blacksmith at work
- Pioneer food production methods such as churning butter, making cracklings, and beekeeping
- Wood-carving demonstrations

Planning Your Visit

Whom to bring: This is for the whole family.

Dates and times: This event is held the first Thursday–Saturday in April, with the first two days being school days; the third day (Saturday) is open to the public. Hours are 9 AM to 3 PM.

Getting there: The Panhandle Pioneer Settlement is in Sam Atkins Park in Blountstown, about fifty miles west of Tallahassee. GPS coordinates are N30° 27.3749', W085° 4.2082'. The address is 17869 NW Pioneer Settlement Rd. in Blountstown, 32424.

Parking: There is ample and ADA-accessible parking.

Fees and tickets: Under $5 for ages four years and older.

Facilities

Restrooms: ADA-accessible restrooms are available.

Other ADA compliance information: With the system of boardwalks and the hard-packed soil of the park's grounds, those using wheelchairs or strollers should be able to get around unless the grounds are very wet.

Places to eat: There is a concession area on-site and staffed during large-scale events. Refreshments, snacks, and candy are available in the General Store.

Picnic facilities: Covered and open-air picnic tables are on-site.

Places to sit: There is no need to bring one's own chair or blanket.

Places to stay on-site: None, but there are two small motels in Blountstown, and chain motels in Marianna.

Reenactors

Needed are appropriately dressed impressions of Florida civilians of the nineteenth century, especially those with a skill to demonstrate and teach. Interested volunteers should contact the settlement staff before the event. There are no amenities.

Educators

The first two days of the event are school days. Pre-registration and reservations are encouraged. Consult your school board regarding field trips. A Student-Teacher's Guide is available containing lessons correlated with Sunshine State Standards.

Contact Information

850-674-2777
Panhandle Pioneer Settlement
Sam Atkins Park
Blountstown, FL 32424
www.ppmuseum.org

Goat Day/Pioneer Day (1800s)
Blountstown, Calhoun County

Historical Background

This celebration started out as "Goat Day," sponsored by the Blountstown Rotary Club to call attention to the place of goats in the food industry. Since it was held at the Panhandle Pioneer Settlement, it wasn't long before the pioneers got involved and Goat Day also became known as "Pioneer Day."

What You'll Find

Besides the usual trappings of a country festival and lots of goats for the children to pet, there are some aspects of the good old days:

- Tours of the settlement by guides in period dress
- A greased-pig chase with several slippery swine, or ham on the lam
- A penny dig (trying to find coins buried in a sandpile)
- A hay ride
- Live heritage music from different cabins' porches
- Butter being churned to be put onto those fresh, hot biscuits and crackling bread being made in front of you
- A blacksmith clinking away, making handy household items to order
- Demonstrations of many other essential skills, such as how pioneer mothers laundered the children and their britches after a day of hayrides

Planning Your Visit

Whom to bring: As many family members as you dare. Pets are not allowed because of the goats, but guide animals are welcome.

Dates and times: The third Saturday in October, from 9 AM till 3 PM.

Fees and tickets: Children four and under are free; see website or contact office for fee details, specials, and more.

Facilities

Places to eat: There are food concessions on-site. See the previous entry for other facilities.

Reenactors

Interested volunteers should contact the settlement staff before the event.

Educators

There are no school days or field trips, but curriculum aids are available upon contacting the settlement staff.

Contact Information

Panhandle Pioneer Settlement
Sam Atkins Park
Blountstown, FL 32424
www.ppmuseum.org
850-674-2777
www.blountstownrotary.com/goatday.htm

"Riding aloft on a mountain of fragrant hay. This is the earliest form of the human pleasure excursion, and for utter joy and perfect contentment it stands alone in a man's threescore years and ten; all that come after it have flaws, but this has none." —Mark Twain, *Down to the Rhone*

Rocky Bayou's Pioneer Day (late 1800s)
Fred Gannon Rocky Bayou State Park, Okaloosa County

Historical Background

This is the only living history event in Florida with a restored and functioning chuckwagon, providing opportunities to show children how Florida's pioneers used this method to supply meals while traveling. The wagons were normally pulled by mules, but teams of horses were used if the jackasses were unavailable, as when they were pulling plows or serving in Congress.

What You'll Find

- Hands-on activities, including candle dipping and rag-doll making
- Heritage music
- A restored pioneer chuck wagon demonstrating the nineteenth-century equivalent of roadside fast food, as it is made-to-order over an open fire
- Storytellers
- A first-hand look at how to start a fire with flint and steel
- Demonstrations of domestic skills such as quilting and weaving
- A blacksmith pounding away on the anvil

Planning Your Visit

Whom to bring: Anyone in the family who likes to eat.

Dates and times: First Saturday in November from 10 AM to 2 PM.

Getting there: This event is held at Fred Gannon Rocky Bayou State Park, the address of which is 4281 Hwy 20 in Niceville, 32578. GPS coordinates are N30° 29.7793', W086° 25.9519'

Parking: Adequate.

Fees and tickets: Free! Park admission fees are waived for this event.

Facilities

Restrooms: ADA-accessible restrooms are located near the playground and the boat dock.

Other ADA compliance information: Unless soaking wet, the grounds are firm enough to accommodate those using wheelchairs, canes, or strollers.

Places to eat: The chuck-wagon staff is ready to serve any culinary preferences that involve large black pots or open fires.

Picnic facilities: Pavilions for rental and tables are elsewhere in the park. Visitors are encouraged to bring a picnic lunch to enjoy while they relax and listen to the music.

Places to sit: Visitors are encouraged to bring a blanket or lawn chairs.

Places to stay on-site: There are campgrounds elsewhere in the park.

Reenactors

Needed are impressions of nineteenth-century Florida civilians, especially if a trade or skill can be demonstrated. Volunteers should contact the park staff beforehand.

> Be sure to inquire as to how pioneer chuck wagons restocked when on the trail.

Educators

There are no school days, field trips, or curriculum aids yet.

Contact Information

Fred Gannon Rocky Bayou State Park
850-833-9144
www.floridastateparks.org/rockybayou/default.cfm

———◆◆◆———

A Cracker Weekend (1851–1900)
Rainbow Springs State Park, Marion County

Historical Background

The word "cracker" dates from the time of Shakespeare, during which the word was used to mean a braggart. Today it is unclear what the term means, especially a "Florida Cracker." To some it is an insult, to others a point of pride. A common usage is for a self-sufficient rural pioneer in the late 1700s, 1800s, or early 1900s who had been born and raised in Florida, especially one who cracked whips to help control cattle.

What You'll Find

The living history portions of this event include:
- A proud introduction to Florida Cracker history and culture
- Demonstrations of Cracker arts and skills such as yarn spinning, corn grinding, butter churning, and firestarting with flint
- A Cracker cow camp to visit and from which to learn about the cattle and cowhands who were here long before the first cattle came to the American West
- An encampment of trappers showing how they made their living in early frontier Florida territory and ready to share their secrets
- Merchants looking to corral some of your coins
- Demonstrations of how items for the home were fashioned from local materials

In addition, there are talks on Cracker culture, plus music throughout the day.

Planning Your Visit

Whom to bring: This is for the whole family.

Dates and times: The third weekend in February from 10 AM to 4 PM.

Getting there: This event is at Rainbow Springs State Park, on Highway 41 north of Dunnellon. GPS coordinates are N29° 6.2114', W082° 26.3477'. The address is 19158 SW 81st Place Road in Dunnellon, 34432.

Parking: Ample, with volunteers as guides.

Fees and tickets: Free with park admission of $1.

Facilities

Restrooms: Modern, ADA-accessible restrooms are found at the ranger station.

Other ADA compliance information: The grounds are hard-packed dirt and are uneven in some places, causing problems for those using wheelchairs or strollers. Those with mobility challenges should call ahead to arrange for assistance if needed.

Places to eat: There is a food concession at the park.

Picnic facilities: There are picnic tables, grills, and pavilions at the park; these are all at the end of a long walkway.

Places to sit: There are a number of shady spots in which to spread a blanket.

Places to stay on-site: The park's campground is about six miles away.

Reenactors

Needed are those in period clothing representing Florida pioneers from the late 1700s to early 1900s, especially if a skill or craft can be demonstrated. Cracker cowboys or trappers are also welcome. Amenities provided are firewood and water.

Educators

There are no school days, field trips, or curriculum aids yet.

Contact Information

Rainbow Springs State Park
19158 S.W. 81st Pl. Rd.
Dunnellon, FL 34432
352-465-8555
Campground: 352-465-8550
www.floridastateparks.org/rainbowsprings/default.cfm

Be sure to find out why the waterfalls can't be heard at night.

Ocali Country Days (1851–1900)
Silver River State Park, Silver Springs, Marion County

Historical Background
This three-day event offers a living history timeline of 1800s Florida, mostly the latter half.

What You'll Find
- Union and Confederate Civil War encampments getting along with each other for the sake of the locals
- A cow hunter camp with lonely cow hunters anxious to talk about life on the trail
- A pioneer Cracker village
- An 1890s homestead showing life before plastic and video games
- Seminole chickees
- Bluegrass and folk music all day
- Demonstrations of butter churning, corn cracking, and making syrup from sugar cane
- Merchants with period wares graciously accepting modern money

Planning Your Visit
Whom to bring: This is for the whole family.
Dates and times: Held the first full week of November. The weekdays are reserved for school groups. The general public is invited on the weekend days from 9 AM to 4 PM.
Getting there: The festival is inside Silver River State Park. From the north: Take I-75 to the CR 326 exit; go east on 326 to CR 35; south on CR 35 to the state park entrance. From the south: I-75 to SR 40; east on 40 to CR 35; turn right or south on 35 to the state park entrance. From the west on SR 40: continue east on 40 to CR 35; turn right or south and proceed to state park entrance. GPS coordinates for the park's main entrance are N29° 12.0617', W082° 3.1678'. Address is 1425 NE 58th Avenue in Ocala, 34470.
Parking: Carpooling is recommended.
Fees and tickets: A few dollars per person on school days; about $5 per person on the public days.

Facilities
Restrooms: The park's visitor center has ADA-compliant restrooms. Portable facilities are also provided during this event, but they may not be ADA-accessible.
Other ADA compliance information: There is an ADA-compliant bathhouse for campers. One of the cabins has a ramp to a firepit. Two campsites are wheelchair accessible. The grounds are hard-packed, level dirt and easily negotiated by wheelchairs, canes, and strollers.

Places to eat: Numerous concessions for food and drink are on-site during the event.

Picnic facilities: The park has three pavilions with grills for rental.

Places to sit: There is space for spreading picnic blankets.

Places to stay on-site: Camping is available elsewhere within Silver River State Park. There are ten cabins and a full-facility campground within the park as well, and primitive youth camping.

Reenactors
Needed are Floridians of the 1800s, including townspeople, artists, craftspeople, farmers, cow hunters, Civil War military of both sides, and Seminoles and other Native Americans of Florida. All reenactors must pre-register and be approved beforehand; last-minute walk-ons may not participate. There are no amenities.

Educators
The weekdays are for school groups only, including homeschoolers. Field trips are available on the school days. Check with your school board. No curriculum aids are yet available.

Contact Information
Silver River State Park
1425 NE 58th Avenue
Ocala, FL 34470
352-236-7148
www.floridastateparks.org/Silverriver

Citizen Support Organization: www.thefriendsofsilverriver.org/
www.silverrivermuseum.com

Baker's Heritage Day and Folk Festival (late 1800s)
Baker, Okaloosa County

Historical Background
Reminiscent of the fictional town of Brigadoon, the nineteenth-century version of Okaloosa County pops up in the midst of Baker once a year, for a single day.

What You'll Find
The living history portions of this elaborate festival include
- Civil War soldiers stopping to rest for the day between campaigns
- The art of open-hearth cooking in a log cabin
- Pioneer skills such as flintknapping, blacksmithing, shingle making, and wood splitting without an axe
- Domestic pioneer crafts and skills such as butter churning, spinning, crocheting, quilting, corn grinding, and broom making from corn shucks

Planning Your Visit
Whom to bring: This is a family event.
Dates and times: The festival is the first Saturday in November, from 10 AM to 8 PM; some activities will stop earlier in the day.
Getting there: The Baker Block Museum is at 1307 Georgia Avenue, Baker, 32531. GPS coordinates are N30° 47.8448', W086° 40.9379'.
Parking: Ample, with ADA-compliant spaces available.
Fees and tickets: Free!

Facilities
Restrooms: ADA-accessible facilities are located within the museum.
Other ADA compliance information: The grounds are either paved or hard-packed, and unless the soil is soaked there should be no problem with canes, strollers, or wheelchairs.
Places to eat: Food concessions are at the event.
Picnic facilities: There are tables in the Heritage Park adjacent to the museum.
Places to sit: Bringing a lawn chair is advised for those who would like to "set for a spell" and enjoy the music.
Places to stay on-site: None.

Reenactors
Civil War–era military and civilians or pioneer impressions of late nineteenth-

century Florida are needed, especially if a skill or craft can be demonstrated. Volunteers should contact the museum staff before the event.

Educators
There are no school days or field trips, but the museum has abundant curriculum aids available. Contact their education staff for details.

Contact Information
Baker Block Museum
P.O. Box 186
Baker, FL 32531
850-537-5714
www.bakerblockmuseum.org
E-mail: bakermuseum@aol.com

Davenport's Quilts and Tea Festival (late 1800s)
Davenport, Polk County

Historical Background
While brothers, fathers, and husbands were off grabbing all the publicity by waving weapons at each other, history's ladies kept a lower profile. Household chores and maintenance were less confining if done together, and especially with a little class. Teas provided some class; quilting provided a way to visit and to have something to show for it. As for weapons, there were always wit and gossip.

What You'll Find
A celebration of a different period in history each year, spread over a square mile in historic Davenport. Living history parts include:
- First- and third-person impressions by reenactors of the year's era mingling with the guests
- Venues both inside and outside of historic Davenport homes
- Quilting and tea sessions as done in the featured period
- Sutlers still trying to unload goods from 1860 or whenever

Planning Your Visit

Whom to bring: This is a family event. Although guide animals are welcome and pets are allowed at the outside venues, pets cannot come into the private homes.

Dates and times: The event is held the second Friday and Saturday of November, from 9 AM to 3 PM.

Getting there: Davenport's Historic District is at the intersection of CR 547 & Hwy 17-92, east of 27 and south of I-4.

Parking: Adequate parking is scattered about the event sites, which are serviced by tram or horse and buggy.

Fees and tickets: Free! But donations gratefully accepted, especially by the horses, who are getting tired of the same old hay, day in and day out.

Facilities

Restrooms: All venue sites have ADA-compliant restrooms available. Because the sites change annually, information regarding changing tables is inconsistent.

Other ADA compliance information: The Historic District provides ADA-compliant sidewalks and crossings.

Places to eat: Concessions are on-site.

Picnic facilities: This is unpredictable because of the changing locations from year to year.

Places to sit: Benches are available within the Historic District.

Places to stay on-site: None, but lodging is available along Hwy 27.

Reenactors

Impressions are needed from 1800 to the early twentieth century, since the featured year will always be within that time frame. Amenities include limited free camping with modern showers, use of restrooms, water, and space for reenactor camps.

Educators

School days, field trips, and curriculum aids are not yet available.

Contact Information

www.davenportfl.org

Organizers: quiltsandtea@msn.com; davenporthissociety@msn.com

863-422-2267

Legends and Lore of Bagdad (1890s to 1940s)

Bagdad, Santa Rosa County

Historical Background

Although a center of commerce and Florida's lumber industry for over a hundred years, the fortunes of Bagdad Village sharply declined with the onset of the Great Depression and the depletion of the forests. Its cemetery's headstones contain the names of Bagdad's most remarkable families as well as birthplaces ranging from Norway to Africa to Nova Scotia. The "Legends and Lore" event brings that storied past to life.

What You'll Find

- Reenactors in period dress at the gravesites telling the stories of those buried there, including veterans, in the style of eyewitness accounts to Bagdad's past
- Many volunteers doing impressions of their own ancestors
- Artists present to record the event

Planning Your Visit

Whom to bring: Everyone except pets. This is an event for the family.

Dates and times: The second Saturday in October from 10 AM to 1 PM.

Getting there: Bagdad is just south of Milton and a few miles northeast of Pensacola. The cemetery is on the west side of Bagdad Village. GPS coordinates are N30° 36.0073', W087° 1.9217'. Zip is 32530.

Parking: Adequate. ADA-compliant spaces are provided.

Fees and tickets: Free!

Facilities
Restrooms: There are no facilities at the cemetery.

Other ADA compliance information: The grounds are hard-packed, level soil with an occasional tree root, easily negotiable by canes, strollers, or wheelchairs unless soaked. Shade is abundant because of all the live oaks.

Places to eat: There are no concessions.

Picnic facilities: No facilities are available.

Places to sit: Plan on being on your feet.

Places to stay on-site: None.

Reenactors
Needed are volunteers in period dress ranging from the 1840s to 1940s, especially those who can do an impression of an ancestor within the cemetery. Contact the Bagdad Cemetery Association if interested. There are no amenities.

> "In order to know a community, one must observe the style of its funerals and know what manner of men they bury with most ceremony." —Mark Twain, *Roughing It*

Educators
There are no school days, field trips, or curriculum aids yet.

Contact Information
www.bagdadcemetery.com
Bagdad Cemetery Association
P.O. Box 134
Bagdad, FL 32530

Fourth of July at the Barnacle (1890s)
The Barnacle State Park, Coconut Grove, Miami-Dade County

Historical Background
Built in 1891 on the shore of Biscayne Bay, the Barnacle was the home of Commodore Ralph Munroe, one of Coconut Grove's most influential early citizens. The property, home, and its contents have survived over a century of time and hurricanes, and are still preserved as they were at the turn of the twentieth century.

What You'll Find
- An old-fashioned Fourth of July picnic as would have been celebrated in Commodore Munroe's day

- The house and grounds all gussied up in traditional Independence Day bunting
- The staff and volunteers inviting the public to join them in period dress
- Nineteenth-century lawn games
- Lessons on and demonstrations of kite making and nautical knot-tying
- Plenty of room to spread a blanket and have a picnic
- Tours of the Barnacle itself

Planning Your Visit

Whom to bring: This is a family event. Guide animals are welcome, but pets are not allowed in the house. On the grounds they must be well behaved, cleaned up after, on a leash no longer than six feet, and never left alone.

Dates and times: July 4, from 11 AM to 3:30 PM.

Getting there: The Barnacle is on 3485 Main Highway in Coconut Grove, 33133. GPS coordinates are N25° 43.5782', W080° 14.6404'.

Parking: Within the park itself there is only ADA-compliant parking. Ample parking is located on the streets a very short walk from the park, but during this event parking is much more convenient for early arrivals.

Fees and tickets: $5 for ages twelve and older, $2 for ages six through eleven. Children under six years old get in free.

Facilities

Restrooms: ADA-compliant restrooms are located at the entry gate.

Other ADA compliance information: Paved pathways lead from the park entrance all the way to the bay. The Barnacle itself is accessible by wheelchair on the first floor; viewing of the upper floor is provided by DVD for those not able to use the stairs. The park staff is glad to make arrangements for those with special needs if they are contacted at least a day before the visit. The grounds are hard-packed dirt and, unless soaked, are negotiable by those using wheelchairs, canes, or strollers.

Places to eat: There are no concessions within the park. You bring the picnic lunch; they provide a great spot in which to eat it.

Picnic facilities: There is a pavilion with a grill on-site, along with several hundred other people who want to use it.

Places to sit: Acres of beautifully landscaped grounds with benches.

Places to stay on-site: None, but lodging is available in nearby Miami.

Reenactors

Not needed.

Educators

There are no school days, field trips, or curriculum aids.

Decide in advance where you want to go for fireworks. This is a daytime event.

Contact Information
305-442-6866
www.floridastateparks.org/thebarnacle/default.cfm

Cracker Country (1890s)
Tampa, Hillsborough County

Historical Background

The maps of Florida changed as the nineteenth century wore on. The unconquered Seminoles still had their homeland, though it was smaller than before. The main population centers were on the coasts, with the rare exception of places like Tallahassee and Gainesville. The rural interior was a patchwork of farms and ranches, crisscrossed by trappers and cow hunters and dotted with small rural towns.

What You'll Find

- A living history museum located on the Florida State Fairgrounds at the eastern edge of Tampa, recreating a small rural Florida town of the 1890s
- Thirteen preserved buildings
- Authentically costumed interpreters portraying daily living as Florida pioneers, sharing the stories of early Floridians' experiences
- During different seasons of the year, special programs or events that are self-contained living history experiences
- A gift shop offering a wide selection of low-priced items so that children can take home a keepsake at minimal expense

Planning Your Visit

Whom to bring: This is a family event, except pets are not allowed (because of the farm animals). Guide animals are always welcome.

Dates and times: Hands-on history tours are offered the third Saturday of every month from 10 AM. to noon. Every Wednesday, Thursday, and Friday between 1:30 PM and 4 PM visitors can explore Cracker Country's public buildings, farm structures, and homes from the turn of the nineteenth century. For other public-access hours, please check individual programs by phone or on the website.

Getting there: For all you GPS users, the coordinates are N 27°59.258', W 082°22.373'. There is more than one entrance, but the one most consistently open is the Orient Road entrance off I-4, west of I-75. Address is 4800 Orient Rd. in Tampa, 33610.

Parking: Abundant. ADA-compliant parking is available close to the museum entrance.

Fees and tickets: Varies according to the program you're coming for, but generally only a few dollars except for afternoon tea time, which is $20.

Facilities

Restrooms: ADA-accessible.

Other ADA compliance information: A limited number of wheelchairs are available on a first-come, first-served basis at no charge. Approximately half of the historic buildings are accessible by wheelchair. The grounds are hard-packed, level dirt, with rare uneven patches and occasional tree roots in the historic area that may interfere with wheelchair travel. Those with special needs are welcome at Cracker Country, and accommodations can be made by calling the administrative offices beforehand.

Places to eat: No.

Picnic facilities: There is a large bank of uncovered picnic tables just outside the entrance (perfect for school groups), but there are no grills.

Places to sit: Many shaded sitting areas are scattered throughout.

Places to stay on-site: No, but several motels are across the street.

Reenactors

They use their own volunteers. Those interested in volunteering should contact the administrative offices or review the website.

> Remember that educational programs are season-appropriate. An activity that is appropriate for autumn in Florida would not be presented in March.

Educators

School days, field trips, and extensive curriculum materials are available.

Contact Information

813-627-4225 or (toll-free) 800-345-3247
www.crackercountry.org
Cracker Country
4800 Orient Rd
Tampa, FL 33610

The Barefoot Mailman Hike (1885–1892)
Pompano Beach to Miami Beach, Broward and Miami-Dade counties

Historical Background

Until 1892, when a road was completed from Jupiter to Miami, a letter mailed from Palm Beach to

Miami (a distance of 68 miles) would have to get to its destination by a roundabout route through New York City and then by boat from Havana, Cuba—a journey of over 3000 miles and at least six weeks. In 1885 the Post Office decided that it might be faster to walk, and hired men to do so. Much of the route was along the firm sand where the surf met the beach. It was better to walk those stretches barefoot because the salt water ruined shoes. Nearly the entire route was through wilderness, so the mailmen had to carry everything they needed for the trip with them, including fresh water. The round trip from Palm Beach to Miami and back took six days.

Of the 68 miles, 40 were by land and 28 by water (down rivers, across inlets, and across Biscayne Bay).

Each year in early February the Barefoot Mailmen are remembered by groups of Boy, Girl or adult Scouts by a two-day "Barefoot Mailman Historical Hike" from Pompano Beach to Miami Beach.

Younger or less experienced Scouts have the option of doing the second day's leg only. This is a twelve-mile stretch from Haulover Beach Park to South Point Park in Miami Beach. This leg is called the "Big-Toe Hike of the Barefoot Mailman."

What You'll Find

- Hikers who may be carrying troop flags, wearing their Scout uniforms, and having someone supply their fresh water, but who otherwise have to be as self-sufficient as the Barefoot Mailmen themselves
- A hike that goes on, rain or shine, just like the Postal Service
- The most realistic part: the stretch on the beach itself through John U. Lloyd Beach State Park
- Hikers carrying letters or cards in a personal mailbag to be given a special postmark at the end of the hike

Planning Your Visit

Whom to bring: This is a private event. Participants must be a Boy Scout (Second Class or higher), Girl Scout, Venture Scout, Varsity Scout, Venture Guest, or a registered adult Scouter. Hikers must be at least 12 years of age by the New Year's Eve before the hike.

Dates and times: This is normally done the first full weekend in February. Start times depend on the number of participants.

Getting there: The hike normally begins at the Pompano Beach pier.

Parking: There is parking at either end of the planned route for family members or members of the public who want to watch.

Fees and tickets: Registration fee is about twenty dollars.

Facilities

Except for locally available restrooms, hikers will make no use of any facilities along the designated path except for sidewalks where needed, and the campground designated for the overnight campsite.

Reenactors
There is no need for reenactors in this event.

Contact Information
www.sfcbsa.org
Organizer: s_pblair@bellsouth.net

------◆◆◆◆◆------

A Spanish-American War Event (1898)
Fort Clinch Historical State Park, Fernandina Beach, Amelia Island, Nassau County

Historical Background
Begun in 1847, Fort Clinch was active during the Civil War, then abandoned till it was briefly reactivated during the Spanish-American War.

What You'll Find
- Reenactors portraying some of the war's participants, talking to visitors about their reasons for fighting in the war and why Florida is so important to the war effort
- Displays of artifacts relating to the Spanish-American War

Planning Your Visit
Whom to bring: This is a family event. Only working animals such as guide dogs are allowed on the boardwalk or in Fort Clinch.
Dates and times: Third weekend in September. Saturday hours are from 9 AM to 5 PM; Sunday hours are from 9 AM to noon.
Getting there: The state park's entrance is relatively inconspicuous except for two large cannons pointed across Atlantic Avenue in the general direction of Prince of Peace Lutheran Church, providing a visual example of the separation of church and state. Fort Clinch is at 2601 Atlantic Avenue in Fernandina Beach, 32034, on Amelia Island, north-northeast of Jacksonville. The GPS coordinates for the park's entrance are N30° 40.0828', W081° 26.0638'.
Parking: Parking is available next to the visitor center in front of Fort Clinch. There are a generous number of ADA-compliant spaces and room for RVs as well as buses. Parking is more likely to be available in the mornings.
Fees and tickets: There is a small fee (a few dollars) for admission to the park itself. The event is an additional pittance.

Facilities

Restrooms: ADA-compliant restrooms are at the visitor center in front of Fort Clinch.

Other ADA compliance information: Pathways into and within Fort Clinch are either paved or consist of hard-packed dirt, sometimes with small rocks. Off the paths, the parade grounds are also hard-packed dirt, but not as level. Check beforehand with the rangers if it has been raining recently as to whether users of canes, strollers, or wheelchairs might have problems on the parade grounds. There is almost no shade on the parade grounds, but there are places to sit in the covered breezeway that serves as the fort's entrance.

Places to eat: There are no concessions, but the visitor center near the fort has machines for snacks and drinks.

Picnic facilities: Uncovered picnic tables with freestanding grills are located elsewhere in the park.

Places to sit: Visitors should plan on being on their feet while inside Fort Clinch except for within the breezeway.

Places to stay: Full-facility and youth campsites are elsewhere within the park.

Reenactors

Needed are civilians, Rough Riders, and other military personnel during the Spanish-American War period. Participation is by invitation only; walk-ons are not permitted. Volunteers should contact park personnel beforehand. Amenities include display and encampment space, water, firewood, free admission to the park for the weekend, and some meals. Contact park personnel for details.

Be sure to be aware of and to obey the traffic laws of Amelia Island, even when they seem unnecessarily restrictive or if it is late at night and the streets are empty. I could not tell if they were occupied, but at night police cars can turn up in the most unexpected places there. Judging from the density of exhaust fumes and number of empty doughnut boxes they left behind, I am convinced that there were at least two squad cars hiding in the trunk of my car the entire time I was on the island.

Educators

No school days, field trips, or curriculum aids are yet available.

Contact Information

Fort Clinch State Park
2601 Atlantic Avenue
Fernandina Beach, FL 32034
904-277-7274
www.floridastateparks.org/fortclinch

Fort Lauderdale's Class of 1899
Fort Lauderdale, Broward County

Historical Background
Fort Lauderdale's first school began in October of 1899 as eighteen-year-old Miss Ivy Julia Cromartie led her group of nine students through a mile and a half of palmettos and woods to the newly constructed schoolhouse. Despite the need to watch out for snakes when walking to and from the one-room building, the student body had grown to fourteen by the end of the school year. (Students who were fond of arithmetic eagerly watched for adders.)

What You'll Find
Students participating in Pioneer School Day will:
- Be encouraged to wear clothes appropriate for the very late nineteenth century
- Learn grade-appropriate lessons of the times in geography, history, arithmetic, and recitations from their own Miss Cromartie
- Recite the Pledge of Allegiance as it was done in 1899
- Follow 1899 class rules and write their lessons on slate boards
- Do laundry by hand at the historic King-Cromartie House
- Learn children's games of the era at the New River Inn
- Discover the challenges of school life before today's advances in education such as metal detectors, drug screens, and armed guards in the hallways

Planning Your Visit
Whom to bring: This program is for first through sixth graders.

Dates and times: Reservations must be made.

Getting there: The event is held at the Fort Lauderdale Historical Society at 219 SW Second Avenue (a one-way street) in downtown Fort Lauderdale, where the Flagler Railroad crosses the New River. GPS coordinates are N26°7.2134, W080°8.7482.

Parking: Parking is sufficient, ranging from free spaces at the Society complex itself to a nearby city parking garage and metered spots on the streets.

Fees and tickets: The program's cost is less than $10 per student.

Facilities
Restrooms: Some are ADA compliant.

Other ADA compliance information: Anyone with special needs (ranging from food allergies to the need for wheelchair access) is asked to notify the staff in advance so that accommodations can be made. The Society staff wants visitors to feel welcome.

Places to eat: Drinks are available from vending machines.

Picnic facilities: There are picnic tables along the river that borders the property and a raised pavilion on the property itself. There are no grills.

Places to sit: It is not necessary to bring one's own blanket or chairs.

Places to stay on-site: None.

Reenactors

The Society has its own set of volunteers, but those interested in joining such a group are welcome to contact the staff.

> "Adder, n. A species of snake. So called from its habit of adding funeral outlays to the other expenses of living." —Ambrose Bierce, *The Devils' Dictionary*

Educators

Field trips can be arranged by contacting your local school board. Curriculum aids are not yet available.

Contact Information

Fort Lauderdale Historical Society
219 SW Second Avenue
Fort Lauderdale, FL 33301
954-463-4431
www.oldfortlauderdale.org

Spring Heritage Day at the Junior Museum (late 1800s)
Panama City, Bay County

Historical Background

This event, designed for future anthropologists, historians, and archaeologists, also includes special activities for grownups.

What You'll Find

The living history components of this event include:

- Gardening, cow milking, and other ways our ancestors filled the larder, as well as dutch-oven cooking to make pioneer mouths water
- Blacksmithing, leather working, potterymaking, and other industries of the past
- Domestic skills such as spinning, quilting, candlemaking, and weaving pine-needle baskets
- Native American crafts and dancers
- Historians and storytellers

Planning Your Visit

Whom to bring: This is a family event. Guide animals are welcome, but the presence of a petting zoo precludes bringing pets.

Dates and times: Second Saturday in March, from 10 AM to 3 PM.

Getting there: This is held at the Junior Museum of Bay County at 1731 Jenks Avenue in Panama City, 32405. The GPS coordinates are N30° 10.8134', W085° 39.759'.

Parking: Abundant, as it is spread over several lots adjacent to the museum.

Fees and tickets: Less than $10 per person.

Facilities

Restrooms: ADA-accessible restrooms are in the museum.

Other ADA compliance information: The museum is fully ADA accessible.

Places to eat: Food concessions are on-site.

Picnic facilities: There are no picnic tables or grills.

Places to sit: There are a few benches within the museum, but not outside.

Places to stay on-site: None, but unless spring break has started early there is lodging available all over Panama City.

Reenactors

Needed are impressions of seventeenth- through nineteenth-century Florida pioneers, especially if a craft or skill can be demonstrated. Volunteers should contact the museum staff beforehand. There are no amenities.

Educators

There are no school days, field trips, or curriculum aids yet.

Contact information

exhibitsjrm@knology.net
850-769-6128
www.jrmuseum.org/events.htm

The Munson Community Heritage Festival (1851–1900)

Munson, Santa Rosa County

Historical Background

This annual festival, partly sponsored by the staff at Blackwater River State Forest, has such a large and varied agenda of old-time ways that one cannot help but wonder how many of them are still being practiced today. For such a small community, a remarkable job of heritage preservation is being done.

What You'll Find

The living history portions of the event include:

- Cow milking, cane-syrup making with a sugar cane mill, bee keeping, a chicken house, pioneer-style animal trapping, plowing with a mule, and other ways of obtaining food for family and community
- Wood-stove cooking, preserve making, corn shelling, meat smoking, a water-powered gristmill, Dutch-oven cooking, and other ways of processing and preparing food two centuries ago
- Representing the very pinnacle of pioneer agricultural technology, and rarely seen elsewhere in the world of Florida living history: a working moonshine still!
- Thread spinning, quilting, chair caning, basket making, tatting, wood carving, corn-shuck doll making and other pioneer domestic skills
- Pioneer industries such as whip making, shoe cobbling, cross-cut sawing and blacksmithing
- An authentic Civil War encampment with soldiers who will tell you all about their experiences

In addition, there are Native American displays, continuous heritage Southern string music, and guided ecology tours. Live forest animals and live forest rangers will be on display.

Planning Your Visit

Whom to bring: This is a family event. Although guide animals are welcome, pets should not come because of the wildlife displays.

Dates and times: The second weekend in October, from 9 AM to 5 PM.

Getting there: Munson is about seven miles south of the Alabama line and is northeast of Pensacola, at the intersection of State Routes 4 and 191.

Parking: There is abundant parking, and an ADA-compliant section.

Fees and tickets: Free!

Facilities

Restrooms: Portable restrooms are provided.

Other ADA compliance information: The grounds are hard-packed dirt, but uneven. Those using wheelchairs may need help, especially if the grounds are soaked.

Places to eat: Food concessions are on-site.

Picnic facilities: None. There is plenty of room to spread a blanket.

Places to sit: Bringing one's own chairs or blankets on which to relax and enjoy the music is recommended.

Places to stay on-site: None.

Reenactors

Appropriately garbed Native Americans or pioneers from the last several centuries are needed, especially if a period skill or craft can be demonstrated.

> Despite the moonshine still's importance to the community, it has to look legal. That clear stuff coming out of it is distilled water, not corn squeezin's.

Educators

There are no school days, field trips, or curriculum aids yet.

Contact Information

850-957-6140
www.fl-dof.com/state_forests/blackwater/heritage_festival.html

---

The Turpentine Event at Topsail Hill (1900)
Topsail Hill Preserve State Park, Walton County

Historical Background

During the late nineteenth and early twentieth centuries Florida was an important source of turpentine and pitch. Obtaining these products was hard and miserable work, so much so that a lot of it was done by groups of prisoners whose services were "sold" to the timber barons of the day. The prisoners in each group were chained together at the ankle, yet forced to hurry from tree to tree, dragging their chain through the palmetto underbrush.

What You'll Find

- Groups of visitors brought by tram to a jumping-off point for a short hike into the woods to a very simple turpentine camp
- At the camp the children find that they have been pressed into service and are shown how to dip sap and to chip boxes
- For their work they receive "babbits" (tokens for the outrageously overpriced items at the company store) and then spend them
- The humor runs light and dark but non-threatening, and the adult impressions (foreman, other workers) are first-person

Planning Your Visit

Whom to bring: This event is for children. Pets are not allowed on the tram, so visitors are discouraged from trying to bring them to the event. (The turpentine camp is a half-mile walk from the visitor center parking lot.) Dress warmly if it's cold.

Dates and times: One of the first three Saturdays in January and in June (check the park website as to which Saturday.) Starts at 10:00 AM.

Getting there: Located in Santa Rosa Beach ten miles east of Destin. The address is 7525 W. Scenic Highway 30A in Santa Rosa Beach, 32459. GPS coordinates are N30° 22.2073', W086° 16.2988'.

Parking: Ample. A tram takes visitors to the event. ADA spaces are provided.

Fees and tickets: There is a small fee (a few dollars) for park admission. Once inside the park, the event is free.

Facilities

Restrooms: ADA bathrooms are at (among other places) the tram station and the end of the tramline. There are no restrooms nearby once the tram leaves the visitor center for the dropoff at the turpentine camp.

Other ADA compliance information: The walk to the turpentine camp is over a sandy path. It would be fairly difficult for someone on crutches or a wheelchair to get to the camp from the tram. Strollers would also have problems.

Places to eat: There is a small concession at the park office.

Picnic facilities: There are pavilions elsewhere in the park, but not at the event site. The park has no grills.

Places to sit: The turpentine camp has two benches; consider bringing chairs.

Places to stay on-site: Bungalows and RV campsites are available in the park. Tent camping will be available soon.

Reenactors

Volunteers and staff handle this part. Interested volunteers should contact the park office.

Educators

There are no school days, field trips, or curriculum aids yet.

Prisoners serving on turpentine crews had often been arrested on trumped-up charges in order to furnish a labor supply. An occasional prisoner amputated his own hand or foot so as to be declared unfit for work and to escape the wretched working conditions at the turpentine camps.

Contact Information

Topsail Hill Preserve State Park
850-267-0299
www.floridastateparks.org/topsailhill/default.cfm

Koreshan State Historic Site, Estero, Lee County

Historical Background

Here is an example of an event that promotes tolerance of a group whose beliefs sometimes differed greatly from our own, yet who were industrious men and women with similar wants and needs.

What You'll Find

- An unusual immersion experience, in that visitors are taken on a guided nighttime walk through the settlement, which is like a small village
- Encounters with reenactors doing first-person impressions of Koreshans speaking with one another, conversations heard indirectly, as the reenactors do not interact with the tour groups; the effect is that of eavesdropping on conversations between others

Planning Your Visit

Whom to bring: This is a family event, although small children may not appreciate it fully. Reservations are required. Pets are allowed on ghost walks within usual park restrictions, but only service animals are allowed inside buildings.

Dates and times: The last weekend in January and the first weekend in February. There are four walks a night beginning every 15 minutes starting at 7 PM.

Directions: Exit 123 from I-75 onto Corkscrew Road. Go west 2 miles before crossing Hwy 41. Continue on Corkscrew another 1000 yards to the park's entrance. GPS coordinates: N26° 25.8729', W081° 48.8847'. The Park is in Estero, zip 33928.

Parking: Ample.

Fees and tickets: There is a small fee for park admission, which includes a self-guided tour book or audiotape. There is an additional fee for the ghost walk (cash or check only).

Facilities

Restrooms: All restrooms are ADA compliant.

Other ADA compliance information: The paths in the settlement are hard-packed shell and considered ADA accessible. Five of the buildings within the site are ADA accessible. One of the picnic areas is entirely ADA compliant, including the grills.

Places to eat: There are no concessions on-site, but many are close by.

Picnic facilities: There are uncovered picnic tables with grills.

Places to sit: Not needed for the ghost walks.

Places to stay on-site: Elsewhere within the park are full-facility campgrounds by reservation; some are designated for tent camping.

Reenactors

Needed are impressions of late nineteenth and early twentieth century members of the Koreshan Unity. Volunteers should contact park officials or view the official park website. There are no amenities.

Educators

There are no school days, field trips, or curriculum aids yet.

Contact Information

Koreshan State Historic Site
P.O. Box 7
Estero, FL 33928
239-992-0311
www.floridastateparks.org/koreshan/default.cfm

The Early Twentieth Century (1901–1938)

Open House at the Lighthouse (early twentieth century)
St. Marks National Wildlife Refuge, St. Marks, Wakulla County

Historical Background

With twelve hundred miles of coastline and over thirty lighthouses in the state, one would think that there would be many living history events involving lighthouses and their keepers. At this writing, there is only one, and it is during the Wildlife Heritage and Outdoors Festival at St. Marks National Wildlife Refuge.

What You'll Find

Among many other attractions, the living history portion of this event includes:

- An open house at the lighthouse keeper's quarters, hosted by a reenactor in an authentic lighthouse keeper's uniform
- Demonstrations of tying and casting a cast net
- Teaching stations on tomahawk-throwing, primitive archery, and shooting a black-powder musket
- An eighteenth-century hunter-trapper's encampment, where you can learn about living in the Florida wilderness of centuries ago
- Demonstrations of traditional salt making and mullet smoking

Planning Your Visit

Whom to bring: Everyone except Fido. Because of the wildlife displays, pets are not allowed. However, guide animals are always welcome.

Dates and times: Held the first Saturday in February from 10 AM to 3 PM.

Getting there: The St. Marks Lighthouse is 25 miles south-southeast of Tallahassee at 1255 Lighthouse Road in St. Marks, 32355. The GPS coordinates are N30° 4.4304', W084° 10.7808'.

Parking: Adequate.

Fees and tickets: Free!

> "Lighthouse, n. A tall building on the seashore in which the government maintains a lamp and the friend of a politician."
> —Ambrose Bierce, *The Devil's Dictionary*

Facilities

Restrooms: ADA-accessible restrooms are available at the visitor center.

Other ADA compliance information: Unless soaked, the festival grounds are easily negotiable by users of wheelchairs, canes, or strollers. The lighthouse keeper's open house is also accessible by wheelchair.

Places to eat: Food vendors are on-site at the festival.

Picnic facilities: Picnic tables are available elsewhere in the refuge.

Places to sit: One's own lawn chairs may be handy during certain long events, such as the turkey calling contest.

Places to stay on-site: There are none.

Reenactors

Authentically dressed civilian impressions from Florida of the late nineteenth and early twentieth centuries or earlier are welcome, especially if a skill or craft can be demonstrated. Interested volunteers should contact the refuge staff beforehand.

Educators

There are no school days or field trips available, but curriculum aids are posted online at www.fws.gov/saintmarks.

Contact Information

www.fws.gov/saintmarks
St. Marks National Wildlife Refuge
P.O. Box 68
St. Marks, FL 32355
850-925-6121

> Be sure to ask the lighthouse keeper how his daughters got husbands.

Dunedin's Dearly Departed (1899–1940s)
Dunedin, Pinellas County

Historical Background
Originally settled in 1899 by Scottish families, Dunedin is the winter home of the Toronto Blue Jays and continues to be one of the most attractive communities on Florida's west coast.

What You'll Find
- First-person impressions of late Dunedin residents
- A guided walk from graveside to graveside in which visitors hear what these residents' lives were like before they found themselves on the other side of the grass.

The conversations are supplemented by old photos and other historic materials from the museum.

Planning Your Visit
Whom to bring: This is a family (public) event. No pets, but guide animals are welcome.
Dates and times: Held on the first Saturday in October from 10 AM to 4 PM.
Getting there: The Dunedin Cemetery is at 2400 N. Keene Road in Dunedin, 34698. GPS coordinates are N28° 0.3791', W082° 45.7939'.
Parking: Adequate, with ADA-compliant spaces available.
Fees and tickets: Adults are asked to donate up to $5 each, while children under 12 are free.

Facilities
Restrooms: ADA-compliant restrooms are available during the event.
Other ADA compliance information: The cemetery grounds are easily negotiable by those using wheelchairs, canes or strollers.
Places to eat: Cookies and lemonade are available during the event.
Picnic facilities: There are none in this cemetery.
Places to sit: None, but there are places to lie down for a long time.
Places to stay on-site: I won't touch this one.

Reenactors
Needed are reenactors taking on roles of people buried in the cemetery who have contributed to the history of Dunedin. The time period covered is 1890s–1940s. To volunteer, contact the Dunedin Museum staff beforehand. There are no amenities.

Educators
As yet there are no school days, field trips, or curriculum aids available.

Contact Information
Dunedin Historical Museum
P.O. Box 2393
Dunedin, FL 34697-2393
http://dunedinmuseum.org

◆◦×◦◆

Christmas at Lignumvitae Key (1910s)

Lignumvitae Key, Florida Keys, Monroe County

Historical Background

Owned by the Matheson family from 1919 to 1953 before being purchased by private investors, Lignumvitae Key was bought by the State of Florida in 1971. The island, the Matheson House, and the caretakers' house all became Lignumvitae Key Botanical State Park.

What You'll Find

- Christmas in the Keys of a century ago as the Matheson House and caretakers' home are decorated as they were in the early 1900s
- A Spanish stopper tree with handmade ornaments
- Handcrafted art from native vegetation
- Tours of the island and buildings

Planning Your Visit

Whom to bring: This is for the family.

Dates and times: This event is held the first weekend in December. The tour boats that serve the island start at 9 AM and stop at 3:30 PM.

Getting there: Lignumvitae Key is reachable only by watercraft. Visitors are advised to use the shuttle from Robbie's Marina at Islamorada because of the shallows around the island that make the approach tricky. GPS coordinates of the island are N24° 54.1196', W080° 41.9593'. The marina is at mile marker 77.5 bayside.

Parking: At the marina, adequate.

Fees and tickets: Visitors eighteen years and over are less than $10; those under eighteen years old are free.

Facilities

Restrooms: ADA-accessible restrooms are at the departure point (Robbie's Marina).

Other ADA compliance information: The island is accessible by wheelchair, but getting out of the boat can be made more difficult by changing tides.

A golf cart is available for touring the trail system. Visitors with special needs should contact the park staff beforehand.

Places to eat: Holiday snacks are provided. There are no concessions.

Picnic facilities: None.

Places to sit: Only within the homes.

Places to stay on-site: None.

Educators

There are no school days, field trips, or curriculum aids.

Contact Information

Lignumvitae Key Botanical State Park

P.O. Box 1052

Islamorada, FL 33036

305-664-2540

www.floridastateparks.org/lignumvitaekey/default.cfm

Marjorie Kinnan Rawlings Has Left the Building (1930s)
Cross Creek, Alachua County

Historical Background

This ongoing living history event takes place in what was the quiet and nearly idyllic setting for many literary works by Marjorie Kinnan Rawlings, winner of a long list of awards, including the Pulitzer Prize. Her best-known book is *The Yearling*.

What You'll Find

- The preserved home and citrus farm where Marjorie Kinnan Rawlings lived and wrote from 1928 to 1943
- The chance to see where she sat as she wrote, and to see the views that inspired her
- Ms. Rawlings' world in the 1930s
- Workers in period attire explaining that she is away for the day as they offer tours of the house and property
- Her day-to-day life described, with a little gossip added
- Maybe a glimpse of the "ghost deer"

Planning Your Visit

Whom to bring: This is for the whole family. Pets are allowed, but must be well behaved and on a leash no longer than six feet. They must be carried when inside a building. Guide animals are always welcome.

Dates and times: Open daily from 9 AM to 5 PM. Guided tours from rangers and volunteers in period clothing begin on Thursdays through Sundays at 10 AM, 11 AM, 1 PM, 2 PM, 3 PM, and 4 PM from October through July. Group tours can be done on Tuesdays and Wednesdays but must be scheduled a month in advance. Exceptions are Christmas Day and Thanksgiving, when the house is closed.

Getting there: Between Ocala and Gainesville in Cross Creek, at 18700 S. CR 325. GPS coordinates for the park entrance are N29° 28.79', W082° 9.5761'. Zip is 32640.

Parking: Adequate, with a single ADA-compliant space.

Fees and tickets: Small fee to get into the park, additional small fee for the guided tour.

Facilities

Restrooms: Restrooms with ADA-accessible stalls are at the park next door.

Other ADA compliance information: The grounds are hard-packed dirt and negotiable by those using wheelchairs, strollers, or canes. The house is wheelchair accessible.

Places to eat: No.

Picnic tables: Picnic tables are at the adjacent park.

Places to sit: There is no need to bring one's own chairs or blankets.

Places to stay on-site: None.

Reenactors

Handled by staff and volunteers. Interested volunteers should contact the park staff.

Educators

There are no school days. Field trips can be arranged through your local school board. No curriculum aids are yet available.

Contact Information

Marjorie Kinnan Rawlings Historic State Park
18700 S. CR 325
Cross Creek, FL 32640
352-466-3672
www.floridastateparks.org/marjoriekinnanrawlings/default.cfm

The World War II Years
(1939–1945)

Warbirds (1939–45)

Kissimmee, Osceola County

Historical Background

During the years of World War II, over seventy percent of Allied pilots did fighter training in a North American T-6 Texan. This two-seater propeller-driven aircraft allows the student pilot to fly the plane from the front seat with the instructor (and a duplicate set of controls) in the back seat.

What You'll Find

- An opportunity to fly the same trainer for fighter pilots as the old folks told you about when you asked what they did in the war
- The chance to take to the air and then take the controls
- Under the guidance of your instructor (and backseater), your shot at doing aerobatics that impress Grandpa and horrify Grandma
- The thrill of flying in formation with one or two others
- Pictures for when your friends refuse to believe you

Planning Your Visit

Whom to bring: Any aspiring fighter jockey who can accept flight instruction, is at least four feet tall, and has parental permission if under the age of eighteen.

Dates and times: Warbirds fly from 9 AM till 5 PM every day except Thanksgiving, Christmas, and New Year's Day.

Getting there: Home base is the Kissimmee Gateway Airport at 233 Hoagland Blvd. in Kissimmee, 34741. This is seven miles east of I-4, exiting at 64A. GPS coordinates are N28° 17.6202', W081° 26.9307'.

Parking: More than enough, with ADA-compliant spaces.

Fees and tickets: This varies according to the length of the flights and the options, such as aerobatics or photography. Prices range from $220 to $745.

Facilities

Restrooms: Once in the plane, you're out of luck. You will need to supply your own set of Depends if you're going to try any aerobatics.

Other ADA compliance information: Those with special needs should contact the Warbirds office to determine whether they will be able to physically perform the maneuvers needed to fly.

Places to eat: Not in the plane.

Picnic facilities: None.

Places to sit: The cockpit.

Places to stay on-site: None, but the Kissimmee area has a wide range of choices.

Reenactors

Not needed.

Educators

No curriculum aids are available.

Contact Information

Warbird Adventures, Inc.
Kissimmee Gateway Airport
233 N. Hoagland Blvd.
Kissimmee, FL 34741
407-870-7366 or 800-386-1593
www.warbirdadventures.com
E-mail: fly@warbirdadventures.com

Dade Battlefield State Park, Bushnell, Sumter County

Historical Background

The Dade Battlefield area is no stranger to WW II troops. The military used the area for training during the war years.

What You'll Find

- Third-person impressions of WW II Allied or Axis soldiers
- Authentic encampments showing how the combatants lived
- Period military vehicles, weapons, and uniforms on display
- Music of the 1940s
- Vendors nervously watching the skies for V-2 rockets and enemy bombers

Planning Your Visit

Whom to bring: This is a family event, one that grandparents may especially, enjoy.

Dates and times: First Saturday in August, from 10 AM to 4 PM.

Getting there: The park is located south of Bushnell between I-75 and US 301, off County Road 476 on South Battlefield Drive. Take Exit 314 east from I-75. GPS coordinates are N28° 39.2242', W082° 7.5098'. Zip is 33513.

Parking: Ample, with volunteers guiding vehicles.

Fees and tickets: Admission is less than $5 per carload.

Facilities

Restrooms: ADA-accessible restrooms are available.

Other ADA compliance information: The grounds are level, hard-packed dirt and should be easily negotiable by wheelchair unless soaked.

Places to eat: There is a concession on-site serving lunch.

Picnic facilities: Pavilions and grills are available elsewhere in the park.

Places to sit: There is no need for seating at this event, but there are many good spots for spreading a picnic blanket.

Places to stay on-site: No.

Reenactors

Needed are citizens and military of WW II era, including both Axis or Allied troops. Past nationalities represented have included British, Canadian, French, and German soldiers. Amenities include firewood, water, and encampment space.

> Be sure to remind children that the German reenactors are just that, and are not promoting the politics of the Third Reich.

Educators

There are no school days, field trips, or curriculum aids yet.

Contact Information

Dade Battlefield Historic State Park
7200 CR 603 South Battlefield Drive
Bushnell, FL 33513
352-793-4781
www.floridastateparks.org/dadebattlefield/default.cfm
www.dadebattlefield.com

Bivouac and Barracks (1939–45)
Zephyrhills, Pasco County

Historical Background
This annual event benefits the World War II Barracks Museum in Zephyrhills.

What You'll Find
Authentic World War II encampments, where you can find out if Grandpa's stories are really true

- A battle reenactment
- Weapons demonstrations (using blanks)
- Vintage aircraft on display

Planning Your Visit
Whom to bring: This is a family event.

Dates and times: The third weekend in February from 10 AM to 4 PM on Saturday and 10 AM to 2 PM on Sunday.

Getting there: The location is the Zephyrhills Municipal Airport at 39450 South Avenue, 33542. GPS coordinates are N28° 13.952', W082° 9.5837'.
Parking: Enough for a fleet of vintage aircraft and your vehicle.
Fees and tickets: Free!

Facilities
Restrooms: ADA-accessible facilities are on-site.
Other ADA compliance information: The grounds are open, level, and mostly paved. There is little shade.
Places to eat: A concession is on-site.
Picnic facilities: There are none.
Places to sit: There are seats in the terminal building.
Places to stay on-site: There is no lodging for the public except for camping.

Reenactors
Military appropriate to the WW II years in uniform are needed. Contact the event organizers beforehand. There are no amenities.

Educators
No school days, field trips, or curriculum aids are available.

Contact Information
Zephyrhills Municipal Airport
39450 South Avenue
Zephyrhills, FL
813-788-5969
Event organizer: jjbolender@aol.com

World War II Living History Weekend (1939–45)
Winter Park, Orange County

Historical Background
This event is sponsored by the Central Florida World War II Museum.

What You'll Find
- Authentic encampments from Allied and Axis armies
- Demonstrations of different weapons used in World War II
- A battle reenactment each day
- Displays of fully operational World War II–era military vehicles
- A Saturday-night USO dance

Planning Your Visit

Whom to bring: This is for the whole family.

Dates and times: The last weekend in April from 9 AM to 5 PM on Saturday and 9 AM to 3 PM on Sunday. Setup is Friday.

Getting there: This is held at the Scottish Rite Masonic Center at 1485 Grand Road in Winter Park, 32792. GPS coordinates are N28° 37.9978', W081° 17.2202'.

Parking: Adequate.

Fees and tickets: Free!

Facilities

Restrooms: ADA-accessible restrooms are provided.

Other ADA compliance information: The grounds are either paved or consist of hard-packed level soil. Unless soaked, they should be easily negotiable by wheelchair. There is little shade.

Places to eat: Concessions are on-site.

Picnic facilities: There are none on-site.

Places to sit: Seating is available in the center.

Places to stay on-site: None, but many establishments are nearby.

Reenactors

All impressions of the World War II years are welcome. Amenities include encampment space.

Educators

No school days, field trips, or curriculum aids are available.

Contact Information

info@cfloridaww2museum.org

813-504-3826

From Battlefields to Big Bands: USO Show at the Depot (1941–45)

Naples, Collier County

Historical Background

Formed in 1941 at the urging of President Franklin Roosevelt, the United Services Organizations took on the responsibility of boosting the morale of American military members and their families. Train depots across the country were normally closed during the war years to save fuel, but opened every Saturday night for USO shows and dances for the troops stationed locally.

What You'll Find

- An opening ceremony and address honoring veterans of all wars
- An afternoon of Big Bands, singers, '40s music, and period dancing

Planning Your Visit

Whom to bring: This is a perfect time to drag Gramps and Grandma from their easy chairs and to film them teaching the jitterbug to the youngest members of the family. Dancin' fools and wallflowers from U.S. Armed Forces throughout history are welcome, even if their uniforms are a little snug (they made them smaller back then).

Dates and times: Veterans Day (November 11), from 11:30 AM to 2 PM.

Getting there: Held at the Naples Depot at 1051 Fifth Avenue South; zip is 34102. GPS coordinates are N26°8.53806, W081°47.5632.

Parking: Adequate, with ADA-compliant spaces.

Fees and tickets: Free!

Facilities

Restrooms: ADA-accessible restrooms are available in the depot.

Other ADA compliance information: The grounds are level, hard-packed dirt where not paved, and should be easily negotiable unless soaked. Some shade is available outside.

Places to eat: None on-site.

Picnic facilities: There are none on-site.

Places to sit: There is plenty of seating inside the depot, but music is being played outside as well. Visitors are advised to bring their own lawn chairs.

Places to stay on-site: None, but Naples has many places to rest up after cutting all those rugs.

Reenactors

Singers and musicians from the 1940s are needed. Contact event organizers beforehand.

Educators

No school days, field trips, or curriculum aids are available.

Contact Information

Collier County Museum
239-774-8476
www.colliermuseums.com

Fort Clinch Historical State Park, Fernandina Beach, Amelia Island, Nassau County

Historical Background

Although Fort Clinch was not active during either of the World Wars, its history (used during the Civil War and the Spanish-American War) and excellent state of preservation make it an appropriate location for this event honoring men and women who served during WW II. In this way Fort Clinch, whose construction began over 150 years ago in 1847, still stands ready to serve.

What You'll Find

- Encampments and living historians, not all of them American soldiers and civilians
- Impressions of other nationalities such as Russian or German troops
- Military displays and memorabilia of the Allies, Axis, and Home Front

Planning Your Visit

Whom to bring: This is a family (public) event. Only working animals such as guide dogs are allowed on the boardwalk and inside the fort. No pets.

Dates and times: Saturday of Memorial Day weekend, 9 AM to 5 PM, and Sunday, 9 AM to 12 PM.

Getting there: The two cannons of Fort Clinch State Park are across the street from the spacious and beautifully landscaped grounds of Prince of Peace

Lutheran Church. Fort Clinch is at 2601 Atlantic Avenue in Fernandina Beach, on Amelia Island, north-northeast of Jacksonville, 32034. GPS coordinates for the park's entrance are N30° 40.0828', W081° 26.0638'.

Parking: Not always adequate. It is more likely to be available in the morning. There are a generous number of handicapped spaces close to the visitor center, and there is room for RVs and buses.

Fee and tickets: There is a small fee (a few dollars) for admission to the park itself. The event is an additional small fee.

Facilities

Restrooms: ADA-compliant restrooms are at the visitor center in front of Fort Clinch.

Other ADA compliance information: Pathways into and within Fort Clinch are either paved or consist of hard-packed dirt, sometimes with small rocks. Off the paths, the parade grounds are also hard-packed dirt, but not as level. If it has been raining recently, check with the rangers as to whether wheelchair users may have problems on the wet parade grounds. There is almost no shade on the parade grounds, but there are places to sit in the covered breezeway that serves as the fort's entrance.

Places to eat: There are no concessions, but snack and drink machines are located in the visitor center near the fort.

Picnic facilities: Uncovered picnic tables with freestanding grills are located elsewhere in the park.

Places to sit: Plan on being on your feet once inside Fort Clinch. There are places to sit outside the visitor center in front of the fort.

Places to stay on-site: Full facility and youth campsites are located elsewhere in the park.

Reenactors

Needed are impressions of soldiers of any nationality who served during WW II, as well as civilian support personnel and resistance fighters. Volunteers should contact the park staff. Walk-ons are not permitted. Amenities include water, firewood, space for encampments and displays, free admission to park, and some meals.

Educators

School days, field trips, and curriculum aids are not available.

Contact Information

Fort Clinch Historical State Park
2601 Atlantic Avenue
Fernandina Beach, FL 32034
904-277-7274

Ocala, Marion County

Historical Background

As the Allies advanced up the boot of Italy toward Rome, their progress was impeded not only by Axis resistance and military strategy, but also by flooded marshes and mountain routes made impassable by blizzards.

One possible route lay through the Liri Valley, the head of which was a formidable natural mountain fortress from which the German troops could not only watch every Allied movement, but also rain as much hostile fire upon them as they pleased.

What You'll Find

- Two tactical battles and multiple missions
- An area reminiscent of the Liri Valley, with rocky cliffs, two lakes, a suspension bridge, and no place to hide
- Period military vendors ready to turn your dollars into lire

Planning Your Visit

Whom to bring: This is a private event for reenactors and WW II vendors only.

Dates and times: The second weekend in January (perfectly timed to take advantage of Florida's two-day winter). Registration begins at 10 AM on Friday; event closes at 1 PM on Sunday.

Getting there: This is held at the Hard Rock Cycle Park northwest of Ocala at 6849 Old Gainesville Rd., 34475. GPS coordinates are N29° 15.4745', W082° 10.6513'.

Parking: Abundant.

Fees and tickets: Reenactor fees are $30 if preregistered, or $5 more at the gate. Sutlers are $35 dollars if preregistered, or $5 more at the gate.

Facilities

Restrooms: Modern restrooms are available.

Places to eat: None on-site. Dinner is provided on Saturday. There is no lunch break either day. (After all, this is war.)

Picnic facilities: All destroyed by German artillery fire.

Places to sit: If you find one, don't use it for long. The enemy is watching.

Places to stay on-site: Camping is primitive.

Reenactors

All WW II units are welcome even if that unit was never in Italy. Individual reenactors will be placed with an existing unit. No one under fourteen years old will be allowed; those fourteen to sixteen may not carry a weapon. Those under the age of eighteen must be supervised by a

> "Never let the enemy pick the battle site."
> —Gen. George Patton

188

parent or guardian or be with an established Scouting Venturing group.

Educators
No curriculum aids are available.

Contact Information
www.geocities.com/liriflorida/

———◆✕◆———

*The Southern Outpost Military Vehicle Winter
Rally and Swap Meet (1939–45)*

Belleview, Marion County

Historical Background
These aren't the little die-cast reproductions of military vehicles. They're the real thing—life-size and fully operational.

What You'll Find
- A firefight between Allied and Axis reenactors on Saturday
- Weapons demonstrations both days
- Operational vehicles from the WW II years on display

Planning Your Visit
Whom to bring: This is a family event. Older relatives should especially enjoy it.
Dates and times: Second weekend in February, from 8 AM to 5 PM.
Getting there: This is held at the Market of Marion, located at 12888 SE U.S. Hwy 441 in Belleview. GPS coordinates are N29° 2.0507', W082° 1.5518'.
Parking: Plentiful.
Fees and tickets: Any donation will get you in (and will be appreciated!)

Facilities
Restrooms: ADA-accessible restrooms are available.
Other ADA compliance information: The grounds are either paved or level, hard-packed soil. Unless the ground is soaked, people with wheelchairs, canes, or strollers should have no problem.
Places to eat: A concession is on-site.
Picnic facilities: They're thought to be under one of the tanks. We'll know as soon as enough people volunteer to help push it away.

Places to sit: Within the vehicles themselves. There are no benches, but there is a fence to lean against with some shady spots.

Places to stay on-site: None.

Reenactors

Military and civilian impressions from both Axis and Allies are welcome, especially if accompanied by a vintage military vehicle. Amenities include display space availability and a dinner on Friday night for participants.

> "Just drive down that road until you get blown up." —Gen. George Patton's instructions to reconnaissance troops

Educators

There are no school days, field trips, or curriculum aids available.

Contact Information

www.flmvpa.org

Von Kessinger's Express (1944)

Parrish, Manatee County

Historical Background

This "what-if" World War II scenario takes place every year a few days after the anniversary of the June 6, 1944, Allied invasion of Normandy, popularly known as D-Day. The German defenders were caught off guard by the actual location and timing of the assault. Allied troops who had been parachuted behind enemy lines were cutting communications lines and adding to the confusion.

What You'll Find

- You and over a hundred other paying passengers on a moving train accompanied by spies, saboteurs, French resistance fighters, German troops, Gestapo agents, assassins, and one general (von Kessinger himself, trying to get to Paris and eventually Berlin, carrying documents that must not fall into enemy hands)
- Allied troops lurking somewhere along the way
- All the passengers, including you, caught up in action that differs from train to train and even between different cars
- Authentic German and Allied camps and military vehicles for your viewing

Planning Your Visit

Whom to bring: Everyone. Be aware that some small children may think the gunfire is real. No pets are allowed, but service animals are welcome.

Dates and times: Second weekend in November. The park opens at 10 AM so that the public can visit the period-correct camps. Train departures are at 11 AM and 2 PM on Saturday and noon on Sunday.

Directions: Parrish is near Ellenton and just north of Bradenton. The address is 12210 83rd St. East, Parrish, 34219. GPS coordinates are N27° 35.406', W082° 25.5236'.

Parking: Free and ample parking is available, including for those with special needs. Attendants will guide you in.

Fees and tickets: Tickets are available online and reasonably priced, between $15–20 per adult. Prices are lower for children. Getting tickets beforehand is strongly recommended.

Facilities

Restrooms: Both fixed and portable facilities are available. As yet there are no ADA-compliant facilities.

Other ADA compliance information: Those with special needs are encouraged to call the museum a few days beforehand in order to make suitable arrangements for getting onto and off the train. The grounds are hard-packed dirt, but uneven. Those using wheelchairs may need assistance.

Places to eat: A small concession is present.

Picnic facilities: There are a couple of covered picnic tables and two sheltered benches, but at least one table will be in use by the reenactors themselves. There are no grills.

Places to sit: Seating is aboard the train itself. You'll stand while waiting to board.

Places to stay on-site: No, but motels are a few minutes away by car.

Reenactors

Needed are WW II troops: American, British, and European Theater. Civilians are also welcome in period-correct clothing. Walk-ons are not permitted. Volunteers should contact the railroad museum beforehand. Amenities include free firewood and water and space for period-correct camps. Reenactors in period dress ride the train free.

Educators

There are no school days. Field trips and curriculum aids are available.

Contact Information

877-869-0800 (toll-free)
http://www.frrm.org

Be sure to *trust no one.*

Operation Omega: The Falaise Pocket (1944)
New Smyrna Beach, Volusia County

Historical Background

As Allied forces pushed farther into France after D-Day, Adolf Hitler ordered a German counterattack, but did not provide adequate support. The German forces found themselves deeper in Allied territory and in imminent danger of being surrounded. The Germans fought desperately to maintain a corridor for escape.

What You'll Find

- An excellent location of twelve hundred wooded acres
- Realistic-looking props such as 88-mm flak guns, PAK guns, a sentry post, and road signs

- An ongoing construction of the French village of Chamois

Planning Your Visit

Whom to bring: This is a private event for reenactors only. Period trackless military vehicles are welcome. No one under sixteen years of age may participate; restrictions for minors are on the website under "Regulations."

Dates and times: This event will be on the first full weekend in December. Registration is on Friday from 1300 to 2000. Hostilities begin at 0900 on Saturday and end at 1600, with a tactical battle on Sunday (depending on participation) from 0900 to 1200.

Getting there: Address is 790 Omega Ranch Rd., New Smyrna Beach, 32170.

From Interstate 4: Take the exit 118-A for SR 44 Volusia County, toward New Smyrna Beach. Travel east approximately 5.2 miles. Look for a large cellular tower on your right. Entrance to the event site is 150 feet before the cell tower on the right.

From Interstate 95: Take exit 249 to SR 44 west toward DeLand. Travel west approximately 9.5 miles. Once you pass Pioneer Trail on your right, look for a large cellular tower on your left. Entrance to the event site is 150 feet past the cell tower on the left.

Parking: Adequate.

Fees and tickets: Fee is $25 at the gate.

Facilities

Restrooms: None.

Places to eat: None on-site.

Picnic facilities: Unfortunately, they were destroyed in a recent Luftwaffe bombing raid.

Places to stay on-site: Primitive camping for participants only.

Reenactors

Impressions of the Axis and Allied units involved in Operation Overlord are welcome. Period and authentic uniforms are required. There are no amenities except use of the site.

Educators

There are no school days, field trips, or curriculum aids.

Contact Information

www.2ndrangerbattalion.org/events.html

"May God have mercy upon my enemies, because I won't." —Gen. George Patton

VE Day in Florida (1945)
The Villages, Lake County

Historical Background
This is a commemoration of the day the Axis forces surrendered in the European Theater of World War II. This event, was formerly held in St. Augustine.

What You'll Find
- Authentic World War II camps of both Allied and Axis troops
- A USO party on Saturday night to the sounds of Big Band music
- Fully operational WW II–era military vehicles on display

Planning Your Visit
Whom to bring: The whole family. No pets on the dance floor, though.
Dates and times: Second weekend in May from 10 AM to 5 PM.
Getting there: The event is in The Villages at 1014 Canal Street, 32162. GPS coordinates are N28° 54.4804', W081° 58.4873'.
Parking: Adequate, with ADA-compliant spaces.
Fees and tickets: Free!

Facilities
Restrooms: ADA-accessible facilities are present.
Other ADA compliance information: The grounds are paved and level. The building is ADA-compliant.
Places to eat: A concession is on-site.
Picnic facilities: None.
Places to sit: There's plenty of seating in the building.
Places to stay on-site: None, but lodging is close by for those who have to regroup after a day of dancing in the streets.

Reenactors
Impressions from the World War II years (civilian and military) are welcome.

Educators
There are no school days, field trips, or curriculum aids.

Contact Information
www.cfloridaww2museum.org

Tico Warbird Airshow (mid–twentieth century to today)
Space Coast Regional Airport, Brevard County

Historical Background
For those who are used to experiencing living history on the ground or at sea, this event, which displays it in the air, will be especially neat.

What You'll Find
The living history components of this well-regarded airshow include:
- WW II–era authentic Allied and Axis encampments
- Dogfights between vintage aircraft
- WWII–era and Korean War–era aircraft doing strafing and bombing runs with pyrotechnics

These are among a long list of events that the entire family will enjoy.

Planning Your Visit
Whom to bring: The whole family will appreciate this airshow; there are specific activities on board for children. No pets, though.

Dates and times: This event takes place on the second weekend in March (including Friday). Gates open at 8:30 AM. The flightline is open from 9 AM to noon. Aerial demonstrations start at 1 PM; the airshow closing is at 5 PM each day.

Getting there: The event is held at the Space Coast Regional Airport, at 6600 Tico Road in Titusville, 32780. GPS coordinates are N28° 31.135', W080° 47.5873'.

Parking: Abundant and free.

Fees and tickets: Adults are $20 a day; children four to twelve years old are $15 a day; children under three are free. Advance tickets are cheaper, and a three-day pass is the best deal.

Facilities
Restrooms: ADA-accessible portable facilities are provided.

Other ADA compliance information: The grounds are level and paved, but there is little shade.

Places to eat: Concessions are on-site.

Picnic facilities: There are none, and coolers are not allowed on-site.

Places to sit: Bringing one's own lawn chairs is recommended, especially since much time will be spent looking up.

Places to stay on-site: None.

Reenactors
Needed are military in uniform, especially from the twentieth century. No walk-ons. Volunteers should contact the event organizers beforehand.

Educators
There are no school days, field trips, or curriculum aids.

Contact Information
www.nbbd.com/festivals/warbird
321-268-1941
E-mail: vacwarbirds@bellsouth.net

The Post-War Twentieth Century
(1946–2000)

Train Engineer for a Day (1950s)
Parrish, Manatee County

Historical Background
The Parrish Railroad Museum has a collection of operational engines, cars, and such with miles of track to run them on. A new program offers the opportunity to take over the controls of an engine dating from the 1950s.

What You'll Find
- A chance to become a train engineer of the early to mid-1950s
- Under the supervision of a qualified engineer, you take over the controls of a locomotive for an hour of commanding fifteen-hundred horsepower and over a hundred tons of moving steel, starting and stopping a locomotive down the track
- Learn and use an engineer's hand signals, ring the bell as often as you like and even toot the horn (but not excessively—the museum has neighbors)
- If you come during the annual Month of Steam (either February or March), you will get a locomotive pulling three freight cars and a red caboose at no additional expense

Planning Your Visit
Whom to bring: No pets, but guide animals are always welcome. Engineer candidates must be at least eighteen years old with a valid driver's license and physically capable of climbing up into and down from the engine itself. For a small additional fee, another person can ride on the locomotive with you to witness and record your day of glory.
Dates and times: Weekends only. Be there by 12:15 PM for an orientation to your engine. Your departure is at 12:45 PM.

Getting there: Parrish is near Ellenton and just north of Bradenton. The event is at 12210 83rd St. East, Parrish, 34219. GPS coordinates are N27° 35.406', W082° 25.5236'.

Parking: Ample parking is available on hard-packed ground.

Fees and tickets: Engineer tickets are available online (getting them beforehand is strongly encouraged). Prices vary, but average around $200.

Facilities

Restrooms: There is a restroom in the museum itself that is small but clean. It is not wheelchair accessible, being a preserved railroad car several decades old. (Ask what the engineers of old used to do!)

Other ADA compliance information: The grounds are hard-packed dirt and not easily traveled when wet. The locomotive itself is boarded by a series of steep, narrow steps.

Places to eat: Not on board the locomotive.

Picnic facilities: There are only a couple of picnic tables under a shelter, and at least one of those may be being used by the staff of any event that going on. There is room for picnic blankets to be spread.

Places to sit: Seating is aboard the engine itself, although there is a bench and one or two sheltered picnic tables available near the boarding area. The locomotive's seats are solid metal. There are no cushions for tender fannies.

Places to stay on-site: None.

Don't worry about running over anything except maybe a snail. Florida laws allow the train to go no faster than ten miles an hour. Should there be a turtle rocketing down the track ahead of you, be careful of its backwash so that you don't get derailed.

Contact Information
941- 776-0906
http://www.frrm.org

━━━◆◆◆━━━

An Afternoon with Marjory Stoneman Douglas (1947–1998)
Everglades City, Collier County

Historical Background
Where developers saw a swamp to be drained and replaced with endless city blocks, Marjory Stoneman Douglas saw a place of beauty like no other in the world, whose lifeblood was the water that was being drained away. The most famous of her numerous books is *The Everglades: River of Grass*.

What You'll Find
The living history portion of this several-day festival is a luncheon presided over by an actress/reenactor portraying Marjory Stoneman Douglas herself in a first-person impression.

Planning Your Visit
Whom to bring: This event is best appreciated by adults and interested teenagers.

Dates and times: The festival is held over a four-day period during the last week in February, immediately followed by the annual Everglades City Swamp Country Fair. The luncheon itself is on the first day of the festival at noon, with the living history session starting at 1 PM and ending about 3 PM. There are worthwhile functions prior to the luncheon starting at 10:30 AM. See festival schedule for details.

Getting there: The luncheon is at the Seafood Depot at 369 Collier in Everglades City, 34139. GPS coordinates are N25° 51.6658', W081° 22.9815'.

Parking: Adequate, with ADA-compliant spaces.

Fees and tickets: $20 apiece.

Facilities
Restrooms: ADA-accessible restrooms are available in the restaurant.
Other ADA compliance information: The Seafood Depot has an entrance ramp.
Places to sit: If you have a ticket, you have a seat.
Places to stay on-site: There are motels and lodges down the street.

Reenactors
Not needed.

Educators
There are no school days, field trips, or curriculum aids.

Contact Information
Museum of the Everglades
105 East Broadway
Everglades City, FL 34139
239-695-0008

Wolfpacks in the Gulf: The S.S. American Victory (1940s–1960s)

Tampa, Hillsborough County

Historical Background
The Merchant Marine is a civilian auxiliary of the U.S. Navy, carrying cargo and passengers for the government. During World War II, forty-five Merchant Marine vessels were sunk by German submarines in the Gulf of Mexico. One of the surviving vessels, the S.S. *American Victory,* served in World War II, the Korean War, and the Vietnam War.

What You'll Find
The ship is open for tours every day except Monday. Living history components of past programs and events have included:
- Putting out to sea on the bridge of a restored Victory-class Merchant Marine ship of the World War II era, then passing under the Sunshine Skyway bridge
- Low and slow passes overhead by vintage aircraft
- Tours of the ship, including the engine room
- Weaponry demonstrations, such as the ship's artillery
- Learning to interpret signal flags
- Transmitting messages to landlubber friends using Morse Code

- Immersion in the past with help from the period music and the World War II reenactors on board
- Learning to mark time with the ship's bell
- Mastering essential marlinspike skills and wondering the rest of your life how you got along without them

Planning Your Visit

Whom to bring: Touring the ship is for the whole family, but pets are discouraged because places other than the main deck are accessible only by ladder. Special events may be targeted to a limited age range (such as elementary school students).

Dates and times: Check the ship's website for details regarding these during special events and programs.

Getting there: The ship docks at 705 Channelside Drive, 33602, behind the Florida Aquarium. GPS coordinates are N27° 56.6658', W082° 26.7485'.

Parking: The Florida Aquarium parking lot and the Port Authority parking lot (both clearly marked) are available; the Port Authority lot's fee is much cheaper than the Aquarium's parking fee.

Fees and tickets: These vary according to the program or special event and are available on the website.

Facilities

Restrooms: Because it is a preserved Merchant Marine vessel from the 1940s, the restrooms aboard are not ADA compliant.

Other ADA compliance information: There is a ramp to board the ship, but it has occasional small steps in its course and a wheelchair user would need assistance.

Places to eat: There are vending machines aboard. There is no need to fear that the food products have been in them since the 1940s.

Picnic facilities: Picnic tables and seating have been installed under an overhang and can accommodate about thirty seasick people.

Places to sit: There are numerous places to rest one's sea legs.

Places to stay on-site: None, but shore leave can be enjoyed at many nearby places of lodging within Tampa.

Reenactors

Volunteers are welcome for a variety of impressions from the mid-twentieth century, especially the war years. (Since the Merchant Marine was the only service that allowed women to serve in combat roles during World War II, women reenactors are welcome.) Contact the staff about volunteering and amenities.

Educators

There are no school days, but the season's educational programs are described on the official website. Field trips can be arranged through your local school board. Curriculum aids are posted on the website.

Contact Information

S.S. American Victory
705 Channelside Drive
Tampa, FL 33602
813-228-8766
E-mail: amvic@americanvictory.org
www.americanvictory.org

The Future, If the Good Lord Is Willing and the Creek Don't Rise

Bridging Yesterday and Tomorrow: The Kennedy Space Center

ATX: The Astronaut Training Experience (now and beyond)
Kennedy Space Center, Titusville, Brevard County

Where We're Headed

Future moonwalkers, starship crewmembers, and volunteers for a continuing mission to explore strange new worlds can start their training right here.

What You'll Find

- First-hand coaching from veteran astronauts
- A variety of training programs for individuals, families, or teams
- Mission simulations on full-scale orbiter mockups and a life-sized, fully detailed mission control setup
- Realistic simulators for a variety of astronaut activities and experiences, such as driving a car on the surface of the Moon or feeling multiple g-forces

Planning Your Visit

Whom to bring: ATX Family is for eight years and older. ATX Core is for sixteen years and over. ATX Team varies, of course, with the composition of the team.

Dates and times: ATX Core is a half-day; there are morning or afternoon programs. ATX Family is a two-day program. ATX Team is variable. For scheduling, see the Kennedy Space Center website.

Getting there: This is located at the Astronaut Hall of Fame at 6225 Vectorspace Boulevard in Titusville, 32780. GPS coordinates are N28° 31.5257', W080° 46.975'.

Parking: Abundant.

Fees and tickets: Prices range from about $150 to over $600, depending on the program one enrolls in. Advance reservations are required.

Facilities

Restrooms: ADA-accessible facilities with changing tables are available on-site.

Other ADA compliance information: Those with physical challenges should contact the ATX administrators beforehand about accommodations.

Places to eat: A concession is on-site.

Picnic facilities: None are on-site.

Places to sit: The majority of time is spent sitting. Seating is not a problem here.

Places to stay on-site: There are none, but lodging is close by. One motel even has a room with a starfield on the ceiling and a bed inside a simple mockup of the space shuttle.

Reenactors
Not needed.

Educators
There are no school days, but field trips can be arranged through your local school board. The amount of educational resources and curriculum aids on the Kennedy Space Center and NASA websites stretches to infinity and beyond.

> "Future, n. That period of time in which our affairs prosper, our friends are true and our happiness is assured."
> —Ambrose Bierce, *The Devil's Dictionary*

Contact Information
For reservations and tickets: 321-449-4830
www.kennedyspacecenter.com/astronaut-training-experience.aspx

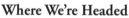

SLX: The Shuttle Launch Experience (foreseeable future)
Kennedy Space Center, Titusville, Brevard County
Where We're Headed
Although the space shuttle is soon to be replaced by a more advanced orbiter, there will still be blastoffs, increased g-forces, weightlessness, and mesmerizing sights.

What You'll Find

- A $65-million re-creation of the sensations of being on a shuttle launch
- Briefings over monitors and other screens as you approach your cabin
- The roar of liftoff as you shake, rattle, roll, and feel increased g-forces
- A transient sense of floating as the bay doors open and you see how the Earth looks from space
- A leisurely spiral descent through a field of stars back towards your home world

Planning Your Visit

Whom to bring: There is a minimum height requirement for the Shuttle Launch Experience of forty-eight inches. Except for service animals, pets are not allowed inside the KSCVC complex. A free kennel is available for those visitors who are traveling with their pet porcupine or whatever.

Dates and times: Kennedy Space Center Visitor Complex is open every day of the year, except December 25 and certain launch days. Current operating hours are from 9 AM to 6 PM.

Getting there: The visitor center is at the end of SR 405, as far down on this road as the public is allowed to go. The complex is east of Titusville and of Orlando. Visitors from other planets should detour to the usual facility at Area 51 and catch the government transport from there.

Parking: Vast. The lots seem to stretch to the horizons and can probably be seen all the way from Mars. The central walkway to the ticket booths of the visitor center has curbs that are hard to see but easy to trip over. A tram

If you are old and crabby like me and have lost your sense of wonder, this is where you'll find it.

is provided, but not every day and not nearly often enough. There is a loop for dropping people off close to the visitor center complex and plenty of ADA-compliant parking.

Fees and tickets: The Shuttle Launch Experience is free with admission to the KSC Visitor Center complex. Tickets for adults are about $40 and children under twelve are about $30.

Facilities

Restrooms: Most restrooms throughout the KSCVC are ADA accessible. Companion/family restrooms are indicated on the visitor guide. Changing tables are available within restrooms.

Other ADA compliance information: Those with physical challenges should contact the ATX administrators beforehand about accommodations.

Places to eat: Within the visitor complex, yes.

Picnic facilities: There are many uncovered picnic tables, but no grills. There is plenty of inside eating space as well.

Places to sit: There is no need for one's own chairs or blankets.

Places to stay: None on-site, but many motels/hotels are nearby.

Educators

Field trips can be arranged through your local school board. There is a special day for homeschoolers. See the website for details. Curriculum aids are online at the Kennedy Space Center official website and at NASA's Educator Resource Center.

Contact Information

For ticket reservations: 321-449-4400

For general information and inquiries: 321-449-4444

For NASA's Educator Resource Center: 321-867-4090

(Note how the phone numbers to this area begin with a countdown: 3-2-1-Blastoff!)

http://www.kennedyspacecenter.com/shuttle_launch_Experience/index.asp

> Be sure to find and touch the Moon Rock while at the visitor center. It doesn't look like much, but it will be hard to forget the moment you touched a piece of another world.

Getting to Know the Neighbors: The Shark Dive (2020)
Sea World, Orlando, Osceola County

Where We're Headed

As Florida gets more crowded with people, inevitably the interactions between humans and animals will increase, whether on land or sea. If cooperation and tolerance are chosen over competition, the need for education to better appreciate our neighbors and our shared environments will only increase.

What You'll Find

A true immersion experience: Forty-five minutes in a giant aquarium teeming with fish and a variety of sharks, some of them bigger than you. Here's the rundown:

- After a briefing, you'll be fitted with a wet suit and a helmet that allows breathing and talking underwater without scuba gear
- To protect the sharks from you, you'll be in a Plexiglas cage with steel bars that runs slowly along a 125-foot track under water
- A radio inside the helmets allows you to speak with the instructor for your dive
- Your family, friends, and enemies can watch from outside the tank (with different reasons for watching you being dangled in front of the sharks)
- As part of the event package, Sea World's professional photographers will record your last moments as you get outfitted and enter the submerged cage

Planning Your Visit

Whom to bring: Ages ten years and up may participate. Only two ~~meals~~ people may go at a time.

Dates and times: When Sea World is open, the dives are scheduled for 10 AM, 11 AM, 12 PM, 2 PM, 3 PM, and 4 PM.

Getting there: This is at Sea World Orlando, on the Central Florida Parkway off Interstate 4. GPS coordinates are N28°24.8974, W081°27.7142.

Parking: Adequate, but the more convenient parking is more expensive. There are ADA-compliant spaces. A tram serves some distant areas.

Fees and tickets: The cost is about $150 per person. Discounts are available for certain passholders. Parking and an entry pass to Sea World are extra (and needed) to get to the Shark Dive.

Facilities

Restrooms: These are available only before and after your time in the water. Please don't pee on the sharks!

Other ADA compliance information: Those with special needs should contact the reservations specialist as to whether they can be accommodated. Sea World is very friendly toward those with special needs, but the equipment has its limitations.

Places to eat: The shark tank is along one side of a full-service restaurant. An interesting juxtaposition.

Picnic facilities: There are none.

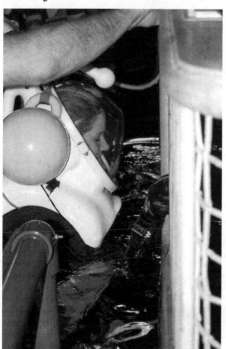

Places to sit: There is no seating in the cage. However, you are buoyed up by the salt water. The cage is large enough for you to sit on its floor if you like.

Places to stay: Many places of lodging are close by.

Educators

This program does not lend itself to school days or field trips.

Contact Information

www.seaworld.com/orlando/default.aspx (click on "Animal Connections")
888-800-5447

DisneyQuest: Worlds Within Worlds of Virtual Reality (2020)
Disney World, Orlando, Osceola and Orange counties

Where We're Headed

Artificial reality has gained a toehold in the real world at DisneyQuest, a five-story self-contained world where anything that can be seen and/or heard is possible. The Disney imagineers have provided a journey into the future that is more than passive entertainment—much, much more, and in unexpected directions that serve to stimulate imaginations, not suppress them.

What You'll Find

The most cutting-edge components of DisneyQuest are:
- Virtual-reality experiences such as being the gunner or the pilot on a rescue ship gathering stranded colonists from a doomed planet under attack
- Being a self-propelled ball in a life-sized pinball machine
- Surviving arena after arena of opponents (some of whom can fly) armed only with your speed, wits, and virtual sword
- Flying on a magic carpet through a 360-degree castle on a mission to save Aladdin's genie
- Paddling a rubber raft down a prehistoric river either to find adventure or to have adventure find you
- Standing on deck while sailing the Caribbean with your trusty cannon and the rest of your scurvy pirate crew

Planning Your Visit

Whom to bring: Anyone two and up, including elderly retired pinball wizards from days long past. There's something for everyone. Certain activities have height restrictions; see the website for details.

Dates and times: Despite protests from guests who insist that it's really not necessary, DisneyQuest closes from about 11:30 PM to 11 AM the next day so that families can get some rest while debriefing each other on their day at the video wars.

Getting there: DisneyQuest is near the west end of Downtown Disney, the free portion of Disney World in Orlando.

Parking: Enough to park a fleet of Galaxy-class starships, with a generous number of ADA-compliant spaces and a loop drive for dropping people off close by.

Fees and tickets: Ages ten years and over is $40; from three years to nine years is $34. The pass is good for the entire day and evening, so that one can leave and re-enter during the day. Additional purchases can be made within the building (meals, burning one's own CD full of music, etc.) One dream come true is that the standalone arcade games are all free—no more need for pocketfuls of quarters!

Facilities
Restrooms: ADA-compliant restrooms with changing tables are on each floor.

Other ADA compliance information: The entire complex is ADA compliant. A printed guide is given on admission that clearly labels which features can be enjoyed while in a wheelchair and which require transfer out of a wheelchair into another seat.

Places to eat: A food court concession is on the fourth and fifth floors, appearing to have enough seating to accommodate everyone in the building at once.

Picnic facilities: None.

Places to sit: Benches are plentiful and convenient, allowing older visitors to rest comfortably while watching the younger ones and reflecting that youth is wasted on the young.

Places to stay on-site: Disney World has enough lodging available on-site and immediately adjacent to accommodate the entire population of any state in this country. Free transportation such as buses and water taxis deliver to points within easy walking distance of DisneyQuest.

Educators
There are no school days as such or curriculum aids, but field trips are possible. Consult your school board.

Contact Information
http://disneyworld.disney.go.com/ destinations (click on "Downtown Disney" then the "Entertainment" button.)

For ticket information: 407- 939-1289

Don't worry about the hygiene of the virtual reality helmets. I spent some time unobtrusively watching the hosts on different floors as they wiped down the helmets with disinfectant towelettes between users. They didn't miss anything, no matter how busy they were otherwise.

❖

Jules Undersea Lodge (2025)
Key Largo Undersea Park, Key Largo, Monroe County

Where We're Headed
The Jules Undersea Lodge began in the 1970s as "La Chalupa," a research facility on the ocean floor off Puerto Rico. It was designed for the workers to be able to live inside and work outside, exploring the continental shelf. Once its

mission was over, it was hauled to the bottom of the Emerald Lagoon off Key Largo, still perfectly habitable, and opened to the public. Living under the seas is no longer just for researchers.

What You'll Find
- The world's only underwater hotel
- An entry area with bathroom facilities and a hot/cold freshwater shower (the lodge is dry and air-filled inside, like any lodge up on land)
- An 8-by-20-foot common room with a dining area, entertainment center, and kitchen with a microwave, sink, refrigerator, and viewport window
- Two 8-by-10-foot bedrooms, each with a double bed and a 42-inch viewport through which the local fish can observe whatever is going on in the double beds
- Each bedroom also has a phone, intercom, stereo entertainment center, sink, refrigerator, and a pull-down berth

Planning Your Visit
Whom to bring: No pets, except maybe a fish. If you have a saltwater fish and are planning on taking it for a swim, your fish must be well behaved, on a leash no longer than six feet, and never left alone while leashed. Please clean up after your fish.

Dates and times: Open every day of the year except for two weeks at Christmas and during a variable period in the summer for summer break. Those wishing a day visit should arrive by 10:30 AM; overnighters should arrive by 12:30 PM. Checkout time is between 8:30 AM and 9:30 AM.

Getting there: Jules Undersea Lodge is located at the bottom of the Emerald Lagoon in Key Largo Undersea Park, Key Largo, Florida. The GPS coordinates of 51 Shoreland Drive are N25°8.00166, W080°23.9112. Although the only way to get into the lodge is by diving, a program is available for novices; they will be fitted with scuba gear, shown how to use it, and escorted all the way both ways by a trained professional.

Parking: A small parking lot shared with a local restaurant is available topside. A set of four spaces is clustered in front of the gates to the park. Because the four spaces are so close to the entrance, there is no need for handicapped parking. Parking next to the Underwater Lodge itself is strongly discouraged unless you are arriving in a submarine.

Fees and tickets: These vary according to which package you're buying, whether it's for a few hours' visit to explore the lodge (about a hundred dollars) or an overnight stay (several hundred dollars, well worth the envy and admiration of everyone around you for years to come). See the website for a list of all that there is to do.

Facilities

Restrooms: There is a restroom and shower facility in the lodge.

Other ADA compliance information: The topside grounds have plenty of shade and are either paved or are hard-packed soil with a thin veneer of fine gravel. All entrances have ramp access. Steps, especially those that can get

slippery or wet, are wide and have associated rails. Underwater platforms within shallow water also have structures to hold on to for security.

Places to eat: There is a well-stocked kitchen within the lodge. Fresh, hot pizza can be ordered for delivery to the lodge by a diver. There are vending machines with drinks in the topside cluster.

Picnic facilities: There are picnic tables topside that are shaded but not covered; there are no grills and too many oxygen tanks around to even think about putting a grill in. There are no grills immediately outside the lodge.

Places to sit: There are many places to sit and relax.

Places to stay: The underwater lodge itself, of course. Bunks are available topside. A hotel is close by.

Educators

There are no education days except for schools of fish. Field trips are available for humans through the local school board. Curriculum aids are available but not online.

Contact Information

Jules' Undersea Lodge
at Key Largo Undersea Park
51 Shoreland Drive
Key Largo, FL 33037
305-451-2353
www.jul.com
info@jul.com

Because of its sturdy construction, protected location, 24-hour topside monitoring station, and redundant systems, the lodge is far safer than some might think. There are no fewer than five different ways to communicate easily with the outside world. Even if all the redundant systems failed, there is enough air inside for six hours of comfortable breathing before the extra resources inside might have to be tapped. The Keys paramedics train at the lodge, so they are familiar with it. Should there be simultaneous disasters—a tsunami, plague, pestilence, a category-five hurricane, a nuclear blast in nearby Miami—the lodge would be the safest place in the Florida Keys to ride them out.

MarineLab (mid-twenty-first century)
Key Largo Undersea Park, Key Largo, Monroe County

Where We're Headed

MarineLab started out as a long-term teaching project at the U.S. Naval Academy on how to build an undersea laboratory. Completed in 1976, it was never used as such until it was moved to Florida in 1984 and then to its current location at the bottom of the Emerald Lagoon in 1985. Since then it has been a base for marine research, underwater habitat research, and teaching. It is available to groups of high school and university students, as well as the general public through Jules Undersea Lodge. This is one of the jumping-off points for exploring our oceans.

What You'll Find

- An air-filled (perfectly dry inside) cylinder that is sixteen feet long and eight feet wide, attached to a framework on the lagoon floor
- Suspended from the bottom of the cylinder is an acrylic sphere, 66 inches in diameter, that allows a person to sit in it and get a 360-degree look at what's going on in the lagoon
- Bunks that convert into workbenches, and a plethora of scientific equipment for sampling and analysis
- A home base for remotely controlled explorer robots—you can hang out in the lab, munching on snacks and steering a cute little robot all over the Emerald Lagoon!

Planning Your Visit

Whom to bring: No pets allowed, except possibly a saltwater fish (preferably housebroken). No one under 10 years of age can go to the underwater facility since scuba diving requires a minimum age of ten years.

Dates and times: This is determined by the "mission," or activity that is being planned at the lab and its adjacent facilities. If a MarineLab activity is combined with a day trip at the Jules Undersea Lodge, then visitors and non-divers should arrive at the topside portion of the park by 10:30 AM. If coming for an overnight stay at the lodge, certified divers should arrive by 12:30 PM.

Getting there: MarineLab is located at the bottom of the Emerald Lagoon in Key Largo Undersea Park, Key Largo, Florida. The topside facilities are alongside the lagoon at the end of Transylvania Avenue. GPS coordinates are N25.133361, W80.398520.

Parking: A small parking lot shared with a local restaurant is available topside. There are also four small spaces just in front of the wooden gates of the topside facilities' entrance. The four spaces are arranged so close to the gates that there is no need for handicapped parking spaces.

Fees and tickets: Reservations to enter the MarineLab Habitat require booking at least two months in advance. It can be accessed by the general public as an additional activity during stays in Jules Undersea Lodge, which requires reservations as well. Student groups or researchers can make reservations through Marine Resources Development Foundation. The price range for a visit to MarineLab via the Jules Undersea Lodge depends on the package, but starts at about $100 and includes many amenities.

Facilities

Restrooms: MarineLab has a shower and portable marine toilet, but there are better ones at the nearby lodge.

Other ADA compliance information: Most of the topside facility restrooms are ADA compliant. The grounds are either paved or hard-packed earth with a fine gravel, easily negotiated by a wheelchair or a cane. All topside buildings have ramp access.

Places to eat: Topside, there is a cafeteria for resident students and a small kitchen in one of the dorm rooms. There is a small kitchen with a sink, a microwave, and a refrigerator in the Jules Undersea Lodge and in the lab. Meals are provided to aquanauts participating in 24-hour or longer missions in the lab, and are served in the lodge to those guests accessing the lab from there. Fresh, hot pizza can also be delivered to the lodge. (For real! I recommend their Meat Lover's Special—it's delicious, although you'll be hungry again a week later.)

Picnic facilities: Picnic tables are topside around the lagoon.

Places to sit: Benches and chairs are also in place around the lagoon.

Places to stay on-site: It's possible to stay overnight in the lab itself, depending on the mission. Students have topside dorms with restrooms and a cafeteria. Recreational visitors can stay in the nearby Jules Undersea Lodge or in a local place of lodging.

Educators

Science teachers are encouraged to bring students into both habitats (lab and lodge). Habitat programs are typically four, twenty-four, or seventy-two hours in duration, and can be arranged through Marine Resources Development Foundation.

Contact Information
305-451-1139
P.O. Box 787
Key Largo, FL 33037
www.mrdf.org/MRDF_MarineLabHabitat.html
E-mail: mrdf@mrdf.org

An example of research in interspecies communication gone awry: this poor dolphin will have to go back to his pod and not only explain why he has lipstick all over his fins, but also what it is like to be tickled.

Losing Weight Without Diet or Exercise:
The Zero-G Flights (2025)

Cape Canaveral, Brevard County

Where We're Headed
Space travel for commercial passengers is becoming more commonplace. One doesn't have to go all the way into space to become weightless, however.

What You'll Find
- An immersion experience in which you are a passenger on a modified 727 airliner whose up-and-down flight path allows you to float weightlessly for twenty to thirty seconds at a time. Here's the rundown:
- In addition to the flight-path weightlessness, you will feel the reduced gravity of Mars and of the Moon
- If you normally weigh one hundred fifty pounds, you will find yourself weighing only fifty pounds, then twenty-five pounds, then nothing at all
- Your normal weight will be returned to you in perfect condition as the flight ends
- As part of the package, your experience will be recorded on DVD and in still pictures

Planning Your Visit
Whom to bring: Those under eight years of age, or those who are pregnant, may not go on the flight. Children ages eight through fourteen require

215

an adult chaperone or companion. Certain medical problems require a doctor's permission.

Dates and times: Flights are normally on Saturdays. A day should be set aside for the event; there are briefings and some preparation in the morning, flying time is midday and takes several hours, and then a post-flight "re-gravitation" is necessary after landing. See the official website for the scheduled dates.

Getting there: The morning preparations' location will be announced when the flight is confirmed, which is two weeks before takeoff. Transportation to and from the plane is provided.

Parking: Adequate.

Fees and tickets: This varies with the price of jet fuel, but is usually in the neighborhood of $3500–$5000 apiece.

Facilities

Restrooms: Modern, ADA-compliant facilities are available before and after the flight. The restrooms on board are not ADA-accessible.

Other ADA compliance information: Those with physical challenges should contact the Zero-G staff beforehand about accommodation.

Places to eat: Snacks are available before and after the flight, but not on the plane.

Picnic facilities: Not available.

Places to sit: Seating is available on the plane, but once airborne and weightless, passengers will not only be allowed to move about the cabin, but fly around the cabin if they like.

Places to stay on-site: (You wish.) Pre-flight preparations are usually in a local hotel.

216

Educators
Group trips for educators and/or students can be arranged, as well as research flights in which experiments can be carried out.

Contact Information
Zero Gravity Corporation
8000 Towers Crescent Drive, Suite 1000
Vienna, VA 22182
888-664-7284 or 703-524-7172
info@gozerog.com
www.gozerog.com

Timeline Events
These events cover multiple periods in history.

Arcadia Mill's Open House (pre-Columbian era through nineteenth century)
Milton, Santa Rosa County
Historical Background
This timeline-type festival is appropriately held during Florida Archaeology Month. Arcadia Mill was the site of one of the largest antebellum industrial parks in Florida. Their Open House is growing into a celebration of the history of the Santa Rosa County area, onward from the pre-Columbian era.

What You'll Find
The living history portions of this event include:
- A Civil War encampment with authentically uniformed reenactors briefing new visitors (like you) on how the war is going in the Mill area
- Demonstrations of domestic fiber skills such as spinning and weaving
- Activities for children such as quill writing and candlemaking
- Heritage crafts being practiced, such as woodcarving

Planning Your Visit
Whom to bring: This is a family event.
Dates and times: Held the first Saturday of March, from 10 AM to 4 PM.
Getting there: Arcadia Mill Archaeological Site is at 5701 Mill Pond Lane in Milton, 32583. GPS coordinates are N30° 36.7865', W087° 5.0263'.

Parking: Adequate, with ADA-compliant spaces.
Fees and tickets: Free!

Facilities
Restrooms: Modern, ADA-accessible restrooms are on-site.
Other ADA compliance information: The grounds are either paved or of level, hard-packed soil that is negotiable by wheelchair or cane unless soaked. Shade is plentiful.
Places to eat: None, but there are drink machines available.
Picnic facilities: Tables and grills are on-site.
Places to sit: There is no need to bring a picnic blanket or lawn chairs.
Places to stay on-site: None, but lodging is available in Milton.

Reenactors
Needed are civilian and military impressions from the history of western Florida, especially the Santa Rosa County area. Practitioners of heritage skills or crafts are also needed. Volunteers should contact the administrative staff regarding opportunities and amenities.

Educators
School days, field trips, and curriculum aids are not yet available.

Contact Information
Arcadia Mill Archaeological Site
5701 Mill Pond Lane
Milton, FL 32571
850-626-3084
www.historicpensacola.org/arcadia.cfm

The Southwest Florida Heritage Festival (1700s–1800s)
Crowley Museum and Nature Center, Sarasota, Sarasota County

Historical Background
It may look like little more than a swamp even on modern maps, but southwest Florida was a busy place even in the 1800s. Intruding on the Seminole homeland were pioneers, cow hunters driving their Cracker cattle to market, and Union troops trying to stop the flow of food and salt to the Confederate military.

What You'll Find

The living history aspects of this festival include:

- A Civil War military encampment and a small skirmish
- Reenactors in period dress doing third-person impressions of cow hunters, woodworkers, and blacksmiths
- 1800s-era pioneers busy making sugar cane syrup and cooking in Cracker ovens
- A smokehouse operation
- Merchants serving their needs and yours

Planning Your Visit

Whom to bring: Guide animals are always welcome, but pets are not allowed since they may become frightened by the artillery or the cracking of cow hunters' whips.

Dates and times: Second Saturday of January from 9:30 AM to 4 PM.

Getting there: The center is at 16405 Myakka Road, on the far eastern side of Sarasota, 34240. GPS coordinates are N27°18.1552, W082°15.3262.

Parking: Parking is ample and guided, with a special-needs section. A tram transports visitors to and from the event, and from one end of the event area to the other.

Fees and tickets: Less than $10 for adults, and even less for children five and over. Parking is $3 per car. Check the website for updates.

Facilities

Restrooms: Fixed and portable restrooms are available and ADA compliant.

Other ADA compliance information: In general, the grounds are hard-packed dirt and shell, and level except for an occasional tree root. Unless soaked, they are easily negotiated by wheelchair or cane users. The admission building, museum, and one other building are the only ones that are ADA accessible. Accommodations can be made for those with special needs, who are welcome and strongly encouraged to contact the museum before coming. Benches and other seating are plentiful and for the most part shaded. Raised boardwalks for nature exploration are in excellent condition and are wheelchair friendly. Paved pathways are still being added to the grounds at this time.

Places to eat: Food and drink concessions are present.

Picnic facilities: There are two sets of picnic tables. No grills are on-site.

Places to sit: There are no bleachers for the skirmish, but there is plenty of room to spread a blanket. The presence of the tram makes it easier to bring one's own chairs if desired.

Places to stay on-site: Not for visitors. Lodging is nearby in Sarasota.

Reenactors

Although the festival has previously featured an 1800s timeline, the entire timeline up through the twentieth century is welcome, including Florida pioneers and cow hunters. The only exception is that military cavalry is not needed because of space limitations. Reenactors are encouraged to contact the event's organizers beforehand. Amenities include ice, firewood, water, space for primitive campsites, and a limited number of modern campsites without hookups.

Educators

There are no school days or curriculum aids, but field trips are available. Contact your local school board.

Contact Information

Crowley Museum and Nature Center
16405 Myakka Road
Sarasota, FL 34240
941-322-1000
http://www.cmncfl.org

Historic Pensacola Village
Pensacola, Santa Rosa County

Historical Background

Historic Pensacola Village is a set of twenty-five properties in the city's historic district. Eleven are open to the public. Tours of the village span 450 years of the area's history, with some emphasis on Spanish frontier Pensacola, the Victorian era, and the early twentieth century.

What You'll Find
- Early Pensacola colonial life—ways shared by period-costumed guides
- The only living history programming in Florida that focuses on the Second Spanish Colonial period, including the War of 1812
- Other programs such as colonial cooking, laundry, and disease treatment

- Activities such as spinning, candle making, woodworking, basket making, and broom making are offered on a scheduled basis (visit the website for updated information)
- A wide variety of immersion programs for schoolchildren

Planning Your Visit

Whom to bring: The family. Guide animals are welcome, but pets are not allowed.

Dates and times: The village is open from Tuesday through Saturday from 10 AM to 4 PM.

Getting there: Tickets are sold at the Tivoli High House Gift Shop at 205 East Zaragoza Street in Pensacola, 32502. GPS coordinates are N30° 24.5154', W087° 12.695'.

Parking: Sufficient.

Fees and tickets: Less than $10 for adults; even less for seniors, children four through sixteen, AAA members, and active-duty military.

Facilities

Restrooms: ADA-accessible restrooms are available.

Other ADA compliance information: The grounds are paved or consist of level, hard-packed soil. Not all the buildings are ADA-accessible. Visitors with special needs should contact the village administration to make accommodations before coming.

Places to eat: Drinks and small concessions are available in the Tivoli High House Gift Shop. Local restaurants are within walking distance.

Picnic facilities: There are none on-site.

Places to sit: There are places within the village buildings and on the grounds.

Places to stay on-site: None, but lodging is plentiful in Pensacola.

Reenactors

Mainly needed are authentically garbed reenactors of the Colonial era, military and civilian, either British or Spanish, as well as American pioneers. Ability to demonstrate a heritage craft or skill is also welcome. Interested persons should contact the Village staff regarding volunteering and amenities.

Educators
There are no school days, but field trips are certainly available. Contact the village staff regarding curriculum aids. Lesson plans are available online.

Contact Information
Historic Pensacola Village
P.O. Box 12866
Pensacola, FL 32591
850-595-5985
www.historicpensacola.org

＊＋＞＜＋＜＋●

Heritage Village
Largo, Pinellas County

Historical Background
Heritage Village is a twenty-one acre open-air museum of over two dozen historic buildings, some of them going back to the nineteenth century. The buildings have period-appropriate exhibits, furnishings, and authentically dressed living historians busy with heritage crafts and tours. Special events showcase Pinellas County life up to the mid-twentieth century.

What You'll Find
Opportunities to observe and maybe even participate in:
- Pine-needle and palm-frond weaving
- Rope making
- Fiber arts such as spinning and weaving
- Pioneer-style laundering and cooking
- Blacksmithing
- EnterAction venues that touch the past in a new way

Planning Your Visit
Whom to bring: Don't be surprised if the whole family wants to come back.
Dates and times: Check the website—days and hours are seasonal.
Getting there: The GPS coordinates for Heritage Village are N27° 52.9533', W082° 49.6721'. The address is 11909 125th Street N. in Largo, 33774.
Parking: There is adequate parking, with ADA-compliant spaces.
Fees and tickets: Free. Donations adored.

Facilities

Restrooms: ADA-accessible restrooms are available throughout the village.

Other ADA compliance information: The grounds have paved walkways and hard-packed dirt. Unless soaked, the grounds are easily negotiated by those using wheelchairs, canes, or strollers. Five buildings are wheelchair accessible: the visitor center, the church, the H. C. Smith Store, the Harris School, and the gift shop.

Places to eat: A concession is often present during special events. Vending machines for snacks and drinks are on-site.

Picnic facilities: There is a pavilion with tables on-site. Other tables are scattered about the village. There are no grills.

Places to sit: Benches are conveniently provided, many in shady places.

Places to stay on-site: None, but there are many twenty-first-century establishments in the metropolitan area.

Reenactors

For the normal village operations, civilian impressions throughout the 1800s and early 1900s are needed. Additional impressions are needed for certain special events. Volunteers are welcome and should contact the staff regarding opportunities and amenities. Heritage Village also recruits volunteers from ages twelve to seventeen who are interested in living history.

Educators

There are no school days. Contact your local school board regarding field trips. Curriculum aids are available.

Contact Information
Heritage Village
11909 125th Street N.
Largo, FL 33774
727-582-2123
heritagevillage@pinellascounty.org
www.pinellascounty.org/Heritage

A Walk Back in Time: Life and Times on the Old Kings Road
Florida Agricultural Museum, Flagler County

Historical Background
This timeline event focuses more on the long and varied history of rural Florida than anything else, as might be expected of an agricultural museum.

What You'll Find
While walking down a three-quarter-mile trail, you will visit more than ten different camps or homes along the timeline of Florida's heritage, including:
- Timucuans and Seminoles
- Sixteenth-century Spanish colonials
- Eighteenth-century British
- Nineteenth-century Crackers
- Farmer/Rancher/Agribusiness types of the early twentieth century
- Trappers, traders, and women of the old rural South
- Colonial-era free blacks
- Cow hunters and moonshiners
- Even a few modern archaeologists at work (Hey, somebody has to dig up the dirt on everyone else in Florida)

Planning Your Visit
Whom to bring: This is public (family) event. Guide animals are always welcome.

Dates and times: Takes place the third or fourth weekend in March from 9 AM to 4 PM.

Getting there: The museum is at 1850 Princess Place Road, Palm Coast, 32137. The GPS coordinates are N29° 38.728', W081° 15.4062'.

Parking: Adequate, with ADA-compliant spaces.

Fees and tickets: $6 for adults, $4 for children, and $4 for museum members.

Facilities
Restrooms: Restroom facilities are on-site.

Other ADA compliance information: The event takes place along a three-quarter-mile trail through the woods on uneven ground. Although a stroller or a cane could be used with little problem, those using walkers or wheelchairs will need help.

Places to eat: There is a food concession.

Picnic facilities: There are none along the trail.

Places to sit: Except for natural features such as fallen trees or large rocks, there are no places to sit along the trail. Visitors should plan on being on their feet and in a sturdy pair of walking shoes.

Places to stay on-site: None.

Reenactors

To see what kind are needed, refer to "What You'll Find" above. Definitely contact the museum staff if interested, as they have an ambitious development plan.

Educators

School days, field trips, and curriculum aids are not yet available.

Contact Information

famuseum@pcfl.net or 386-446-7630
www.flaglerlibrary.org/history/agrimuseum/agri1.htm
Florida Agricultural Museum
1850 Princess Place Road
Palm Coast, FL 32137

Earth Day at Washington Oaks Gardens

Washington Oaks Gardens State Park, Palm Coast, Flagler County

Historical Background

As part of its annual Earth Day celebration, Washington Oaks Gardens State Park features a set of living history venues ranging from pre-Columbian times through Florida's British period.

What You'll Find

The living history portions of this event include impressions of:

- Spanish military and colonials worrying about the pesky British
- British soldiers and colonials wishing the Spanish would withdraw to Cuba
- Native Americans wishing that everyone else would go back to where they came from
- Demonstrations of heritage skills and crafts

Planning Your Visit

Whom to bring: This is a family event.

Dates and times: The park opens at 8 AM and program activities start at 10 AM, going till 4 PM.

Directions: The park is two miles south of Marineland off US Hwy A1A, at 6400 North Oceanshore Blvd. in Palm Coast, 32173. GPS coordinates of the park entrance are N29° 38.0866', W081° 12.3078'.

Parking: Adequate, with ADA-compliant spaces.

Fees and tickets: $8 dollars per vehicle (up to eight people). A two-day pass is available for $15 per vehicle.

Facilities

Restrooms: ADA restroom facilities are at the visitor center and picnic area.

Other ADA compliance information: The grounds are level, hard-packed soil with some shade. Unless the grounds are soaked, those using wheelchairs, canes, or strollers should have minimal, if any, problems.

Places to eat: A concession is on-site during this event. Baked goods are for sale.

Picnic facilities: There is a covered pavilion, with other tables and grills located throughout the picnic area.

Places to sit: A picnic blanket or lawn chairs would be useful for relaxing and enjoying the live music.

Places to stay on-site: None.

Reenactors

Needed are military and civilians from all along the timeline of Florida history. Amenities include limited space available for overnight encampments and a free lunch for the reenactors both days.

Educators

There are no school days, field trips, or curriculum aids yet.

Contact Information

Washington Oaks Gardens State Park
6400 North Oceanshore Blvd.
Palm Coast, FL 32173
386-446-6780
www.floridastateparks.org/washington-oaks

The Old Florida Festival
Collier County Museum, Naples, Collier County

Historical Background
This is the most complete timeline event in Florida, a showcase of six thousand years of south Florida history.

What You'll Find
Moving from one encampment to another, you'll see:

- The First Floridians (Paleoindians), Stone Age snowbirds who were so desperate to flee the brutal northern winters that they were willing to walk all the way here, and saw no reason to walk back
- Native Americans—Calusa, Creek, and Seminole, including Black Seminoles
- A sixteenth-century garrison of Spanish explorers, cleaning their armor and inspecting their weapons, preparing to go farther inland
- A sordid-looking gang of pirates amusing themselves
- Black freedmen from Fort Mose's militia, keeping a wary eye on the pirates
- Spanish colonists accommodating themselves to a strange new world
- Trappers and frontiersmen making their way through the wilderness
- Continental and British soldiers with differing opinions as to how the American Revolution is going
- Townspeople using their heritage skills to build thriving settlements
- Cracker cow hunters and a Civil War encampment
- World War II–era soldiers training in Naples before going overseas to fight
- A number of artisans and sutlers engaged in their patriotic duty to redistribute your wealth

Planning Your Visit
Whom to bring: Bring the family. Guide animals are welcome, but no pets are allowed.
Dates and times: Held on the third weekend in November from 10 AM to 5 PM both Saturday and Sunday, rain or shine.
Getting there: This event is at the Collier County Museum at the Collier County Government Center, 3101 Tamiami Trail East in Naples, 34112. GPS coordinates are N26° 7.7174', W081° 46.1162'.
Parking: Adequate.
Fees and tickets: $5 for adults, $2 for students, and free for children under eight.

Facilities
Restrooms: Modern, ADA-accessible restrooms are available in the museum.
Other ADA compliance information: The festival grounds are either paved or composed of level, hard-packed soil. Unless the grounds are soaked, users of wheelchairs, walkers, canes, or strollers should not need help.
Places to eat: A concession is on-site during this event.
Picnic facilities: None.
Places to sit: There is no need to bring blankets or lawn chairs.
Places to stay on-site: None, but there is encampment space for participants. After sloshing through six thousand years of history, you can clean and rest your weary legs at one of the fine establishments in Naples.

Reenactors
Needed are authentically costumed impressions (preferably first-person) from anywhere in the timeline of south Florida's history, including pre-Columbian. If a period craft or skill can be demonstrated, all the better. Volunteers should contact the museum staff beforehand regarding opportunities and amenities.

For educators
No school days, field trips, or curriculum aids are yet available.

Contact Information
Collier County Museum
3301 Tamiami Trail East

Naples, FL 34112
239-774-8476
www.colliermuseums.com/home.php

Clay Landing Days

Manatee Springs State Park, Levy County

Historical Background

Survival skills in modern-day Florida include timely applications of sunscreen, defensive driving, and the endless search for a convenient parking spot. For the early pioneers and Native Americans, things were very different. Shelter and many other necessities had to be made from materials on hand. What you were hunting for dinner might be hunting you for dinner. It was rough and primitive, but it was the Florida of our ancestors. The Florida riverbank area that those ancestors called Clay Landing is now part of Manatee Springs State Park.

What You'll Find

- You'll meander down the park's north trail system on a hayride or in a covered wagon
- On your journey you will encounter different groups of Native Americans and of early Florida settlers going about the daily business of securing food and shelter
- Since part of surviving is helping each other, you might even get to share a bit of their food
- You'll see different heritage skills in practice as they make homes for themselves using materials at hand

Planning Your Visit

Whom to bring: This event will be enjoyed by the whole family. Although guide animals are always welcome, pets are not allowed at this event.

Dates and times: The event is held the last two days of the long Thanksgiving weekend from 8 AM to 5 PM.

Getting there: This park is six miles west of Chiefland, at the end of SR 320 after it branches off U.S. Hwy 98. The GPS coordinates are N29° 29.7646', W082° 58.0035'. The address is 11650 NW 115th St., Chiefland, 32626.

Parking: Adequate.

Fees and tickets: Free with paid park admission, which is less than $5 per carload. Children under five years are admitted for free with a paid adult.

Facilities

Restrooms: There are no restrooms along the north trail system. ADA-accessible restrooms are available at the concession and the ranger station.

Other ADA compliance information: The vehicles used for the rides along the north trail system are designed so that those with special needs can use them with minimal or no assistance necessary.

Places to eat: You can eat and drink at the park concession while waiting to be merry on the hayride.

Picnic facilities: Not in the event area.

Places to sit: You'll be sitting while riding in one of the wagons.

Places to stay on-site: There are many modern and youth-group camping sites at the park.

Reenactors

Needed are impressions of pioneers of the early 1800s and Native Americans. Amenities provided are firewood and water.

Educators

No school days, field trips, or curriculum materials are yet available.

Contact Information

Manatee Springs State Park
11650 N.W. 115th St.
Chiefland, FL 32626
352-493-6072
www.floridastateparks.org/manatesprings/default.cfm

Yesterdays Festival

Mike Roess Gold Head State Park, Clay County

Historical Background

Here is the Florida of your grandparents and their grandparents.

What You'll Find

The living history portions of this celebration include:

- Reenactors, exhibits, and artifacts of the Florida timeline from Native Americans to cow hunters to World War II soldiers
- World War I representation, which is rare for events
- Demonstrations of open-fire and cast-iron cooking and other heritage skills

There are also live musicians, dancing and clogging, antique cars, and guided hikes.

Planning Your visit

Whom to bring: This is a family event.

Dates and times: Held on the last Saturday in January from 9 AM to 5 PM.

Directions: Six miles north of Keystone Heights on SR 21, between Keystone Heights and Middleburg. GPS coordinates are N29° 50.8888', W081° 57.6962'. Address is 6239 S.R. 21, Keystone Heights, 32656.

Parking: Sufficient.

Fees and tickets: Free with park admission, which is a few dollars per carload.

Facilities

Restrooms: The park has ADA-accessible restrooms available.

Other ADA compliance information: All the park's newest cabins are ADA accessible. The grounds are sometimes sandy, and a wheelchair or cane user may need help. If the park is contacted beforehand, the staff will gladly try to accommodate any visitor with special needs.

Places to eat: Food and drink concessions are present at the event.

Picnic facilities: The park has pavilions, tables, and grills.

Places to sit: Although benches are scattered about, visitors may wish to bring a blanket or lawn chairs to stay and enjoy the music and dancing.

Places to stay on-site: Although they can fill up quickly, the park has numerous places to stay, ranging from primitive campsites to air-conditioned cabins and RV campsites.

Reenactors

Authentically dressed impressions along the entire Florida timeline are welcome up through the mid-twentieth century. Those who can demonstrate heritage skills or crafts are also solicited. Volunteers should contact the park staff beforehand. Amenities include water, ice, firewood, and lodging if not camped on-site.

Educators

No school days, field trips, or curriculum aids are yet available.

Contact Information

Mike Roess Gold Head Branch State Park
6239 S.R. 21
Keystone Heights, FL 32656
Park staff: 352-473-4701
www.floridastateparks.org/goldhead/default.cfm

De Leon Springs State Park, Volusia County

Historical Background

Because this is a timeline event, the name should really be "The Life of Florida in a Day." Few people even in Florida are aware that Ponce de Leon (who was reputed in legend to have come across De Leon Springs while searching for the Fountain of Youth) landed in Florida in 1513, nearly 500 years ago. There's no hard evidence that he got this far inland, but a 6000-year-old canoe recently found at the bottom of the springs says that the local Native Americans had been enjoying the 72-degree water for at least that long.

What You'll Find

- A non-narrated reenactment of a skirmish among soldiers, settlers of the early 1800s, and Seminoles, using original weapons from the times
- A Seminole village, a Timucuan settlement, and soldiers' encampments of 1830s–era Federals as well as Civil War–era camps of both sides
- Cow hunters and their camp

There are also exhibits of Indian artifacts, period rifles, and other weapons. Visitors may join in on Native American dances. Artisans are present and accounted for.

Planning Your Visit

Whom to bring: This is a (public) family event. Pets are not allowed in the beach area. Guide animals are welcome.

Dates and times: Takes place on the first Saturday in August. Park hours are 8 AM to sunset. Event is from 9 AM to 4 PM. Introduction to the skirmish is at noon.

Getting there: Follow the state park signs for about six miles on U.S. Hwy 17 North out of DeLand. At Ponce DeLeon Blvd., turn left and go one mile to the park's entrance. The GPS coordinates for the entrance to DeLeon Springs State Park are N29° 7.9302', W081° 21.6442'. Zip is 32130.

Parking: Limited. Carpooling and carriving early are recommended. ADA-compliant spaces are available.

Fees and tickets: A small admission fee is charged to enter the park. Donations are welcome.

Facilities

Restrooms: ADA-compliant restrooms are available in the park.

Other ADA compliance information: Wheelchairs are available to help negotiate the park, including the nature trail. Paved paths and the relatively level, shell-packed ground make it fairly easy to get around with a cane, stroller, or wheelchair.

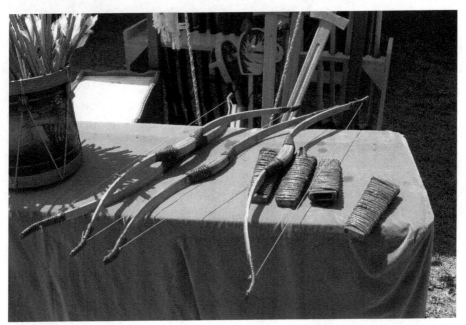

Places to eat: Old Spanish Sugar Mill Restaurant, open 9 AM–5 PM Monday–Friday and 8 AM–5 PM on Saturday and Sunday, serving till 4 PM.

Picnic facilities: Not available during this event.

Places to sit: Lawn chairs and picnic blankets are welcome and recommended. There are no bleachers for the skirmish.

Places to stay on-site: No, except at the encampments for the reenactors.

Reenactors

Needed are Native Americans, including Timucuans and Seminoles; Civil War military (Union or Confederate), and others along the timeline of Florida history from before European contact to modern times. Amenities include free firewood, food rations, water, and ice. Straw is available on request. A gift certificate is also provided to each reenactor.

Educators

There are no school days, field trips, or curriculum aids yet.

Fascinating Fact

The mill was always technologically up to date because it was often having to be rebuilt after people raided the area and demolished it, whether Seminoles or Union troops during the Civil War. There is no record of any armies invading this part of Florida in order to make improvements to the mill, although it would have been the more neighborly thing to do. But the reenactments would have been less exciting to watch.

Contact Information
DeLeon Springs State Park
601 Ponce DeLeon Blvd./P.O. Box 1338
De Leon Springs, FL 32130
386-985-4212
www.floridastateparks.org/deleonsprings/default.cfm

The Fort King Festival
Ocala, Marion County

Historical Background
This small festival commemorates the history, from its beginnings through the Civil War, of the Marion County area, where pioneers, cow hunters, and Native Americans crossed paths.

What You'll Find
- Living history encampments of Seminoles and of Federal soldiers
- Early settlers busy blacksmithing, spinning, weaving, and demonstrating other heritage skills

Planning Your Visit
Whom to bring: This is a family event. Guide animals are welcome.

Dates and times: Takes place the fourth Saturday of September from 10 AM–5 PM.

Getting there: GPS coordinates are N29°11.0627, W082°6.0199. The event is held at Ocala's McPherson Government Complex at 307 SE 26th Terrace, 34471.

Parking: Ample. ADA-compliant parking is provided.

Fees and tickets: Free admission and parking. Lunch is $7 and includes a museum visit. A museum visit without lunch is $2.

Facilities
Restrooms: ADA-accessible restrooms are available within the museum.

Other ADA compliance information: There are relatively few places to sit, but shade is plentiful. The grounds are level, hard-packed soil.

Places to eat: The recommended sources of sustenance are the chicken dinners sold for lunch. These are the museum's primary fundraiser—though still reasonably priced.

Picnic facilities: Tables and chairs are provided for those purchasing lunch.

Places to sit: Tables and chairs are provided for public use during the day.

Places to stay on-site: Participants may stay at their period camps. For others, motels or campgrounds are available nearby.

Reenactors

Living history interpreters from any of Florida's time periods are welcome. Those interested in attending or needing more information should contact the museum staff.

Educators

School groups are welcome, as are other groups. Field trips can be arranged through your local school board. Guides and curriculum aids are available on request.

Contact Information

Marion County History Museum
307 SE 26th Terrace
Ocala, FL 34471
352-629-2773

Wakulla Springs' Wildlife Festival
Wakulla Springs State Park, Wakulla County

Historical Background

It started out as a celebration of the return of local songbirds during the spring. The Wakulla Wildlife Festival now encompasses three days, four state parks, a national forest, a national wildlife refuge, the Wakulla River, and Apalachee Bay.

What You'll Find

The living history portions feature:

- Hearing the origin of the Pocahontas story from Juan Ortiz, a survivor of one of the first Spanish expeditions to Florida
- Visiting with soldiers who are fighting in the Seminole Wars
- Learning from a nineteenth-century farmer that the headaches of making moonshine don't all result from hangovers
- Seeing how Native Americans wove sturdy baskets from local plants
- Observing a pioneer woman spinning yarn from cotton, silk, wool, and other natural fibers
- Standing safely back as a blacksmith works his forge and anvil
- Listening in as an 1876 Florida Cracker shares secrets of living off the land
- Studying pioneer methods of working with wood and of making fishnets

In addition there is fine art, foot-stompin' music, guided tours, and much more.

Planning Your Visit

Whom to bring: The whole family will enjoy this one.

Dates and times: The living history segments are from 9 AM to 3 PM on the first Saturday in April.

Getting there: This event is at Wakulla Springs State Park, which is about twenty miles south of Tallahassee, at 550 Wakulla Park Drive in Wakulla Springs, 32327. GPS coordinates are N30° 13.7415', W084° 18.1235'.

Parking: Adequate parking is provided with ADA-compliant spaces.

Fees and tickets: Free with a $4 vehicle admission fee.

Facilities

Restrooms: Portable units are available; ADA-accessible restrooms are within the lodge on-site.

Other ADA compliance information: Paved walkways and hard-packed grounds allow easy access by those using wheelchairs, canes, or strollers.

Places to eat: Concessions will be on-site, and the lodge's restaurant is highly recommended. There are snacks in the lodge's gift shop.

Picnic facilities: There are tables and grills close to the lodge.

Places to sit: There is no need to bring one's own chairs or blankets.

Places to stay on-site: A legendary lodge is on-site, at which you can rest those feet you were stompin' all day to that excellent music.

Reenactors

Needed are impressions from along the entire timeline of history of the Wakulla County area, especially if a craft or skill can be demonstrated. Amenities include firewood and water. Other amenities can be requested from the event organizers.

Educators

There are no school days, field trips, or curriculum aids yet available for the living history portion of this event.

Contact Information

www.wakullawildlifefestival.org
850-561-7286

The Morikami Museum and Japanese Gardens
Delray Beach, Palm Beach County

Historical Background
In the early twentieth century a group of Japanese farmers established a community called Yamato (an ancient name for Japan) in what is now northern Boca Raton. Due to factors such as competition from Cuba and plant disease such as pineapple blight, the community did not survive. The only Japanese immigrant who remained was George Sukeji Morikami. He eventually bought a two hundred–acre site in Delray Beach, where he prospered as a fruit and vegetable wholesaler. Before his death he donated the land to Palm Beach County to be maintained as a park and a memorial to the Yamato Colony.

What You'll Find
Like no other place in Florida, this museum is an illustration of the variety of cultural influences that make up the state's history and heritage.

- See Florida rock, soil, and plants arranged into six distinct types of Japanese gardens on sixteen acres
- Stroll through all six of the gardens, each one representing a different Japanese historical period, and embark on a journey through more than a thousand years of history
- Contemplate cascading waterfalls, a pine forest, and a bamboo grove.
- See Florida plants in a new way at the bonsai exhibit, especially impressive when the bougainvillea are in bloom

Planning Your Visit
Whom to bring: The whole family will enjoy this, although pets are not allowed. Small children will look forward to feeding the colorful fish.
Dates and times: The complex is open from 10 AM to 5 PM, Tuesday through Sunday, except on major holidays.
Getting there: The address is 4000 Morikami Park Road in Delray Beach, 33446. GPS coordinates are N26° 25.6785', W080° 9.3061'.
Parking: Adequate, with overflow capability.
Fees and tickets: Prices at press time are $10 for adults, $9 for seniors, $6 for children six to seventeen years old, and free for museum members and children under the age of six.

Facilities
Restrooms: An ADA-accessible restroom is located within the gardens.
Other ADA compliance information: The gardens have a main path that is fully accessible throughout their length. Some narrower accessory paths have steps or obstacles. Little shade is available on the main path.
Places to eat or drink on-site: There is a well-regarded and reasonably priced Japanese restaurant within the Morikami Gardens complex. Sources of

cold water are plentiful throughout the gardens.

Picnic facilities: There is a pavilion as well as picnic tables and grills on the grounds close to the gardens.

Places to sit: Benches and flat-topped boulders provide places to sit and relax while appreciating the sights, sounds, and smells of the gardens. Be sure to apply mosquito repellant before coming. Mosquito wipes are sold at the museum store as well.

Places to stay on-site: None.

Educators

The Morikami has educational programs, and field trips can be arranged.

Contact Information

www.morikami.org

<hr>

Five Centuries in a Day

De Soto National Memorial, Bradenton, Manatee County

Historical Background

A timeline of Florida history since the landing of Hernando de Soto, as seen from the perspective of the Bradenton area.

What You'll Find

For covering five centuries, the day goes by pretty quickly. You'll experience:

- De Soto's Camp Uzita and his conquistadores roaming about the park on horseback
- A Seminole family that has made camp close to the sturdy walls of the visitor center in case of attack
- Florida Crackers watching from their base camp for any unclaimed cattle to round up
- Civil War–era soldiers enjoying some R & R under a brief truce
- Twentieth-century soldiers from World War I to Vietnam maintaining their equipment in camp, still prepared to serve if called

Planning Your Visit

Whom to bring: This is for the whole family. Dogs are permitted within the park only when on a leash no longer than six feet. Guide animals are welcome.

Dates and times: The event is held on the last weekend in March from 10 AM to 4 PM. See the park website for changes.

Getting there: GPS coordinates are N27° 28.4143', W082° 38.2171'. The address is 3000 75th Street NW in Bradenton, 34209. Boaters may access the park via the Manatee River, but the park has no boat ramp. Bicycles may be used on the road and in the parking lot, but not on the walking trails. Bike racks are provided at the picnic area.

Parking: Ample. ADA spaces are provided.

Fees and tickets: Free!

Facilities

Restrooms: ADA-compliant restrooms are across the parking lot at the visitors center. There are changing tables located in the women's restroom.

Other ADA compliance information: The hard-packed ground of the park is not as easy to negotiate in a wheelchair or a walker as is the concrete pavement approach, but it is nevertheless reasonably accessible. There is a special flat ADA-accessible surface for the parking of wheelchairs and scooters located adjacent to the bleachers. Shade is plentiful.

Places to eat: There are no concessions.

Picnic facilities: A ten-table picnic area is located adjacent to the parking lot and is available for visitors on a first-come basis. Grills and alcoholic beverages are not allowed within the park.

Places to sit: Bleachers are provided at Camp Uzita, and there are benches on the walkway to the visitors center.

Places to stay on-site: None. However, generations of soldiers have been pleased with Bradenton's many air-conditioned places of lodging after securing a weekend pass.

Reenactors
Needed are sixteenth-century Spanish military and civilians, Seminoles of the late eighteenth and nineteenth centuries, Civil War–era military and civilians, and twentieth-century U.S. military, all appropriately garbed. Amenities provided include food and drink. Call the park for more information.

Educators
There are no school days or field trips. Curriculum aids are at the National Park Service website for De Soto National Memorial.

Contact information
The De Soto National Memorial physical address is:
De Soto National Memorial
8300 De Soto Memorial Hwy.
Bradenton, FL 34209
941-792-0458

Appendices

Glossary

Adventuring - away from home, looking for excitement

Baccy - tobacco

Booshway - the leader of a party of mountain men, or of a rendezvous, whose authority is unquestioned

Ball - a bullet

Britches - trousers that end above the knee

Buffaloed - confused

Cackle fruit - hen's eggs

Careening camp - a temporary camp on the beach next to a ship situated in very shallow water for the purpose of cleaning the ship's hull of barnacles, seaweed, etc.

Conchs - Key West Crackers

Corn pone - a fried hoecake with milk in the batter instead of water

Cracker - "Florida Cracker" is a term of pride, meaning a member or descendent of a self-reliant pioneer family who settled and thrived in Florida in the years before air conditioning, bug spray, and other modern "necessities."

Cracklin' - fried hog fat, sometimes mixed into cornbread to make cracklin' cornbread

Dutch oven - a three-footed kettle with a dished lid, used for both baking and cooking

Farb - using inappropriate clothing or gear for the time period and not caring

First-person interpretation - a reenactor who does not drop character

Feelin' right pert - feeling pretty darn good

Fooferaw - fancy decorations for clothing, frequently given as gifts in colonial times

Fat pine - pine with a lot of pitch in it, useful for starting fires

Galena pill - lead balls or bullets

Galvanize - Used mainly of Civil War reenactors, this is the act of switching sides in order to make a better event such as a battle; many Civil War reenactors can present themselves as a Federal unit or a Confederate one, depending on the needs of the event they are participating in

Gone under - dead

Gewgaws - trinkets such as beads used for decoration

Gone - dead

Gone beaver - has been dead awhile

Grub - food

Hardtack - a hard biscuit made of flour and water that has been baked solid for long-term storage

Hawk - a Tomahawk

Hello the camp - traditional greeting given on approaching an unfamiliar camp, especially if one plans on walking back out rather than being carried out

Hoecake - a bread cake made of cornmeal, salt, and water that has been baked on a hoe over a fire

Jollification - a private celebration for reenactors held after a living history event. Surviving reenactors are responsible for cleaning up the following morning, excepting those whom the tides have already washed out to sea.

Jolly roger - the skull-and-crossbones flag of a pirate vessel

Lobo - a timber wolf

Military tattoo - a military drum performance, frequently accompanied by bagpipes and pageantry

Motel militia - reenactors who spend the night in a motel and not in the period camp

Naybobbin - foolish talk

No-see-um - stinging gnat

Palaver - to talk over

Pilgrim baiting - rude spectators trying to trick a first-person reenactor into dropping character

Possibles - miscellaneous items needed for survival such as flint and steel, cup, etc.

Prime beaver (also **real beaver**) - the best

Ramada rangers - see "Motel militia"

Rev War - American Revolutionary War

Ronnyvoo (Rondyvoo, Rondy) - rendezvous

Scurvy - sores on the lips and gums caused by vitamin C deficiency

Show his/her butt - defiant, misbehaving in a defiant manner

Shines - very high quality

Shinin' times - when things went very well; memorable times

Sutler - a merchant

Swamp cabbage - heart of Sabal palm, cooked like cabbage

Segundo - the second in command, especially of a rendezvous

Skookum - a borrowed Native American word meaning "good"

Square - a term of respect implying reliably good character

Square shooter - a person of consistently admirable character

Tattoo - see "Military tattoo"

Ten-foot rule - an authenticity test for reenactors: looking authentic at ten feet is good enough. Also used for females posing as males, such as Civil War soldiers

Togs - ordinary clothing

Truck garden - a garden large enough to have produce left over to take to market

White House - a white portable restroom; this is where reenactors are going when they say they are going to speak to the President.

Yellow jack - yellow fever

(Based on *A Glossary of American Mountain Men Terms, Words & Expressions* compiled by Walt Hayward and Brad McDade, and special thanks to Dana Ste. Claire for his help with many of the Florida Cracker terms)

Abusive but Handy Phrases for Spanish Settlers under Attack by the English

St. James and close Spain! (*¡Santiago y cierra España!*)

Blessed St. Augustine, save us! (*¡Bendito San Agustín, sálvanos!*)

Flee! (*¡Salgan!*) (Note: verb applies to more than one individual.)

English dogs! (*¡Perros ingleses!*)

Holy Mary, help me! (*¡Santa María, ayúdame!*)

Run for your lives! (*¡Apresúrense!*)

Heretical pirates! (*¡Piratas heréticos!*)

To the fort! To the fort! (*¡Al fuerte! ¡Al fuerte!*)

Where's my son/daughter?! (*¿En dónde está mi hijo(a)?*)

   (Note: *hijo* would be for "son" and *hija* for "daughter.")

They're going to kill everybody! (*¡Van a matar todos!*)

Where's Juan/Juana? (*¿En dónde está Juan/Juana?*)

It's a disaster! (*¡Es una desgraia!*)

We're doomed to hell! (*¡Somos fregados!*)

Gang of flea-bitten pirates. (*Banda de piratas pica-pulgas.*)

(Special thanks to Tim Burke of Calderone's Company.)

A Calendar of Living History Events

(for school days, see the event's chapter)

January

First weekend:

Living History Day at Fort Matanzas (1742–63, St. Augustine)
(Sat. only)   39

Union Garrison at Fort Clinch (1861–65, Amelia Island)   115

Candlelight Tour of Fort Clinch
(1861–65, Amelia Island) (Sat. only)   115

Cow Hunter Camp (1876, Lake Kissimmee State Park)   143

Dade Battlefield Reenactment (1835, Bushnell) (sometimes done the
last weekend of December instead)   53

Second weekend:

Fort Chokonikla's Living History Weekend
(1849, Bowling Green)   72

Birney's Raid (1861–65, Volusia County)   102

Turpentine Event at Topsail Hill
(1900, Walton County) (Sat. only)   170

Cow Hunter Camp (1876, Lake Kissimmee State Park)   143

Southwest Florida Heritage Festival (timeline, Sarasota County)   218

Liri Valley Campaign (1943–44, Ocala)   188

Third weekend:

Brooksville Raid (1861–65, Hernando County)   119

Alafia River Rendezvous opens for
reenactors only (pre-1830s, Polk County)   47

Cow Hunter Camp (1876, Lake Kissimmee
State Park, Polk County)   143

Fourth Friday:

Alafia River Rendezvous open to public (pre-1830s, Polk County)   47

Fourth weekend:

Alafia River Rendezvous open to public (pre-1830s, Polk County)   47

School of the Soldier and Point Washington Skirmish
(1861–65, Walton County)   97

Torchlight Tour of Fort Matanzas (1742–63, St. Augustine)   40

Koreshan Unity Ghost Walk (1900, Lee County)   172

Yesterdays Festival (timeline, Clay County) (Sat. only)   230

Cow Hunter Camp (1876, Lake Kissimmee State Park)   143

February

First Monday: A Day in Old Florida
(1500s-1600s, St. Johns County)   18

May

First weekend:

Change of Flags at St. Augustine (1763, St. Augustine)   41

Special Spring Union Encampment at Fort Clinch
(1861–65, Amelia Island)   115

Candlelight Tour of Fort Clinch
(1861–65, Amelia Island) (Sat. only)   115

Living History Day at Fort Matanzas (1742-63, St. Augustine)
(Sat. only)   39

Second weekend:

Military Muster at Mission San Luis (1656–1704, Tallahassee)   23

VE Day in Florida (1945, Lake County)   194

Third weekend:

A Firefight at Heritage Village (1861–65, Pinellas County)   122

Fort Foster Garrison (1836–38, Hillsborough County)   57

Fourth weekend:

World War II Event at Fort Clinch (1941–45, Amelia Island)   186

Memorial Day:

Morningside Farm closes for season (1870, Gainesville)   139

June

First weekend:

Drake's Raid (1586, St. Augustine) (Sat. only)   16

Living History Day at Fort Matanzas (1742–63, St. Augustine)
(Sat. only)   39

Union Garrison at Fort Clinch (1861–65, Amelia Island)   115

Candlelight Tour of Fort Clinch
(1861–65, Amelia Island) (Sat. only)   115

Third weekend:

Fort Foster Garrison (1836–38, Hillsborough County)   57

July

First weekend:

Living History Day at Fort Matanzas (1742–63, St. Augustine)
(Sat. only)   39

Union Garrison at Fort Clinch (1861–65, Amelia Island)   115

Candlelight Tour of Fort Clinch (1861–65,
Amelia Island) (Sat. only)   115

July 4:

Fourth of July at the Barnacle (1890s, Coconut Grove)   159

Third weekend:

Fort Foster Garrison (1836–38, Hillsborough County)   57

August

First weekend:
Dade Battlefield World War II Event (1939–45,
   Bushnell) (Sat. only)   181
A Day in the Life of Florida (timeline,
   Volusia County) (Sat. only)   232
Living History Day at Fort Matanzas (1742–63, St. Augustine)
   (Sat. only)   39
Union Garrison at Fort Clinch (1861–65, Amelia Island)   115
Candlelight Tour of Fort Clinch
   (1861–65, Amelia Island) (Sat. only)   115
Third weekend:
Fort Foster Garrison (1836–38, Hillsborough County)   57

September

Saturday of Labor Day Weekend:
Menendez Landing Event (1565, St. Augustine)   14
Sunday of Labor Day Weekend:
Dade City's Pioneer Days (1850–99, Pasco County)   99
Labor Day (First Monday):
Dade City's Pioneer Days (1850–99, Pasco County)   99
Morningside Farm opens for season (1870, Gainesville)   139
First weekend:
Living History Day at Fort Matanzas (1742–63, St. Augustine)
   (Sat. only)   39
Union Garrison at Fort Clinch (1861–65, Amelia Island)   115
Candlelight Tour of Fort Clinch (1861–65,
   Amelia Island) (Sat. only)   115
Third weekend:
Spanish-American War Event at
   Fort Clinch (1898, Amelia Island)   164
British Garrison at the Castillo (1763–84,
   St. Augustine) (Sat. only)   42
Fort Foster Garrison (1836–38, Hillsborough County)   57
Fourth weekend:
Olustee Civil War Expo
   (1861–65, Olustee Battlefield Historic State Park)   74
Fort King Festival (timeline, Ocala) (Sat. only)   234

October

First weekend:

Hillsborough River Raid (1863, Tampa) 84
Parrish Civil War Event (1861–65, Manatee County) 117
Dunedin's Dearly Departed (1899–1940s, Pinellas County) 175
Living History Day at Fort Matanzas (1742–63, St. Augustine)
(Sat. only) 39
Union Garrison at Fort Clinch (1861–65, Amelia Island) 115
Candlelight Tour of Fort Clinch (1861–65,
Amelia Island) (Sat. only) 115
Cow Hunter Camp (1876, Lake Kissimmee State Park) 143

Second weekend:

Confederate Garrison at Fort Clinch (1861–65, Amelia Island) 115
Torchlight Tour of Fort Clinch (Sat. only)
(1861–65, Amelia Island) 115
Munson Community Heritage Festival
(1851–1900, Santa Rosa County) 168
Cow Hunter Camp (1876, Lake Kissimmee State Park) 143

Third weekend:

Goat Day/Pioneer Day (1800s, Calhoun County) (Sat. only) 148
Fort Foster Garrison (1836–38, Hillsborough County) 57
Cow Hunter Camp (1876, Lake Kissimmee State Park) 143

Fourth Friday:

Heritage Day Festival (1863, Perry) 131
Siege of 1702 at St. Augustine
(1702, St. Augustine) (evening only) 32

Fourth weekend:

Siege of 1702 in St. Augustine (1702, St. Augustine) (Sat. only) 32
Paxton's Heritage Festival
(1861–1900, Walton County) (Sat. only) 128
Cow Hunter Camp (1876, Lake Kissimmee State Park) 143
Florida Forest Festival (late 1800s, Perry) (Sat. only) 131

November

First weekend:

Ocali Country Days (1851–1900, Silver Springs State Park) 153
Ocklawaha River Raid (1865, Ocala) 124
Rocky Bayou's Pioneer Day (late 1800s,
Okaloosa County) (Sat. only) 150
Baker's Heritage Day and Folk Festival (late 1800s, Okaloosa County)
(Sat. only) 155
Living History Day at Fort Matanzas (1742–63, St. Augustine)
(Sat. only) 39

Events for Reenactors Only

Reservation-Only Events

Year-Round Experiences

The following experiences are open year-round except for certain days (see individual listing for details):

Sample Questions for Children to Ask of Reenactors

Plopped into an alien situation and faced with oddly garbed, unfamiliar people, it is no wonder that many children will have no idea what to say or do. The longer they stay frozen and silent, obeying a lifetime of admonitions about talking with strangers or asking nosy questions, the more opportunity for education is lost.

Following are some starter questions for children until their natural inquisitiveness can take over and they begin exploring their new world on their own.

Where did you come from?

Why did you come here?

What is the hardest thing about what you do?

Are you glad you came? Why?

What are you doing?

When I have a birthday, we have cake, open presents, and sing "Happy
     Birthday." What do you do?

To soldiers:

     Why are you fighting?

     Do you get scared? When? What do you do when you're scared?

     What do you fight with? Show me.

     Have you ever been hurt? Where? What did it feel like?

     Where is your family? Do you miss them?

To pioneers:

     What do your kids do all day?

     What do you do for fun?

To pirates:

     Where do you keep your treasure?

     What is the name of your ship?

     How did you get to be a pirate?

     Are you always going to be a pirate?

Sunshine State Standards and Lesson Ideas

The purpose of this brief section is to emphasize the educational value of living history events by relating them to various benchmarks found in the Sunshine State Standards for education in Florida. These standards can be found and downloaded at www.floridastandards.org. The standards and their associated benchmarks were reviewed for grades K-12 in the disciplines of Social Studies, Science, Health, and Math.

The coded labels are listed for each benchmark that I thought would easily be addressed by attending almost any living history event in this book, whether as a participant or as a spectator. This applies to individuals, large classes on field trips, or homeschooling families. Suggestions are made as to how to address these benchmarks and standards through teaching activities.

Creative educators will do far more with this sample material than I can. It is my hope that this section will serve as an aid for planning, for justifying a class outing or opportunity for extra credit, or for completing a grant application to fund a field trip.

Social Studies Standards
Strands:
A= American History
G= Geography
E= Economics
C= Civics and Government
W= World History

Kindergarten:
SS.K.A.1.1-2; SS.K.A.2.1.4-5; SS.K.A.3.1-2
SS.K.G.3.3
SS.K.E.1.1, 3-4
SS.K.C.1.1-2; SS.K.C.2.1-3

First Grade:
SS.1.A.1.1; SS.1.A.2.2.1-2, 4; SS.1.A.3.1-2
SS.1.G.1.1.3; SS.1.G.3.1.6
SS.1.E.1.3-6
SS.1.C.1.1-3; SS.1.C.2.1-3; SS.1.C.3.1-2

Second Grade:
SS.2.A.2.1; SS.2.A.3.1
SS.2.E.1.1-3
SS.2.C.1.1-2; SS.2.C.2.2, 4-5; SS.2.C.3.2

Third Grade:
SS.3.A.1.1
SS.3.G.4.1
SS.3.E.1.1,3
SS.3.C.1.1-2; SS.3.C.2.1

Fourth Grade:
SS.4.A.1.1; SS.4.A.3.1-10; SS.4.A.4.1-2; SS.4.A.5.1.2; SS.4.A.6.2-3;
SS.4.A.7.3;
SS.4.A.8.3-4; SS.4.A.9.1
SS.4.G.1.3
SS.4.E.1.1

Fifth Grade:
SS.5.A.1.1; SS.5.A.1.2; SS.5.A.3.3; SS.5.A.4.4; SS.5.A.4.6; SS.5.A.6.6
SS.5.E.1.1; SS.5.E.2.1
SS.5.C.2.2, 4

Sixth Grade:
SS.6.W.1.1, 6; SS.6.W.2.1-2

Seventh Grade:
SS.7.C.2.14

Eighth Grade:
SS.8.A.1-7; SS.8.A.2.5, 7; SS.8.A.3.16; SS.8.A.4.3-5, 10, 17-18; SS.8.A.5.1-2,
4-8
SS.8.G.3.2; SS.8.G.5.1-2

Ninth–Twelfth Grades:
SS.912.A.1.3; SS.912.A.2.1-2, 7; SS.912.A.3.1, 4, 6, 13; SS.912.A.4.11;
SS.912.A.5.12;
SS.912.A.6.5, 12, 14
SS.912.W.1.6; SS.912.W.7.6; SS.912.W.7.11

Strategies for learning about Social Studies

Preparations for trip:

    Brief students for understanding regarding the destination's place
        on the timeline

    Go over the day's schedule on a timeline

    Give each student an assigned question or two to ask a reenactor

Have students observe:

    Correlation between actual destination and its map

    Different jobs or tasks being done

    Goods being produced and services provided

Have students ask about:

    Rules and laws of the times

    Basic economics, such as how people are paid for their
        goods or services

    Ways in which differing groups of people have learned to work together

    Causes of conflict between groups, especially regarding use of resources

    How resource availability and weather have influenced human settlement

    The significance in history of the day's destination

    Daily lives of Native Americans, soldiers, explorers, soldiers, or pioneers

    Effects of a Florida event or person upon areas outside Florida

Science Standards

Strands (Big Ideas):

N = Knowledge

E= Exploring

P= Properties

L=Life and its diversity

Kindergarten:

SC.K.N.1.1-5

SC.K.E.5.1-4

SC.K.P.8.1; SC.K.P.9.1

SC.K.L.12.1; SC.K.L.14.1

First Grade:

SC.1.N.1.2-3

SC.1.E.5.2, 4; SC.1.E.6.1-3

SC.1.P.8.1

Second Grade:
SC.2.N.1.1-3
SC.2.E.7.5
SC.2.P.13.3-4;
SC.2.L.17.1-2

Third Grade:
SC.3.E.5.4; SC.3.E.6.1
SC.3.P.8.3; SC.3.P.10.1-2; SC.3.P.11.1-2

Fourth Grade:
SC.4.E.6.3, 6
SC.4.P.9.1; SC.4.P.11.1-2
SC.4.L.17.2-4

Fifth Grade:
SC.5.E.7.7
SC.5.P.13.2-3
SC.5.L.15.1

Sixth Grade:
SC.6.E.7.7-8
SC.6.L.14.6

Seventh Grade:
SC.7.L.17.1, 3

Eighth Grade:
SC.8.N.4.1-2

Ninth-Twelfth Grades:
SC.912.E.7.8
SC.912.L.17.8, 12-14, 18, 20

Strategies for learning about Science
Preparations for trip:
    Divide students into groups with differing functions per member
        (e.g. recorder)
    Brief for understanding regarding the destination's place
        on the timeline
    Discuss awareness of and preparations for weather-related problems
    Give each group an assigned question and/or observation
    Note uses of the sun regarding the trip, e.g. counting days till leaving, light
of day for observations, warmth provided, and need for sunscreen

Have students observe:
    How different materials are used at the destination according
        to their properties
    Shelters against severe weather
    Which sense organs are used in making observations

Have students ask about:
    Useful properties of materials found in Florida by explorers,
        especially involving new solutions to old problems
    Relationship of available resources to human activity at the destination
    Whether the resources are renewable or reusable
    Effect of human use on the resources

Have students know how to report:
    Their observations and how they made them

Math Standards
Strands (Big Ideas)
A= arithmetic (numbers and operations)
G= geometry (shapes, including edges and vertices)

Kindergarten:
MA.K.A.1.1-3
MA.K.G.2.1-4; MA.K.G.3.1

First Grade:
MA.1.A.1.1-2
MA.1.G.3.1; MA.1.G.5.2

Strategies for learning about Math

Preparations for trip:

Distribute handouts and/or worksheets with labeled shapes

Brief for understanding regarding the destination's place
on the timeline

Have students observe:

Relate objects by attributes such as size, shape, length, weight,
height, or capacity

Find shapes at the destination, especially in 2-D or 3-D (a cannon
with a cannonball demonstrates a circle, cylinder, and a sphere.)

Count the number of sides or vertices in observed shapes

Do simple numerical operations involving objects observed at destination

Have students ask about:

How measurements are done during the destination's time period,
such as with balances

Health Standards

Strands (Big Ideas)

C= concepts

B= behavior

P= promotion

Kindergarten:
HE.K.C.1.1-4; HE.K.C.2.1-3
HE.K.B.2.1-4; HE.K.B.3.1-3
HE.K.P.1.1; HE.K.P.2.1

First Grade:
HE.1.C.2.2-3
HE.1.B.1.1; HE.1.B.2.2-4; HE.1.B.3.1-3
HE.1.P.1.1-2; HE.1.P.2.1

Second Grade: HE.1.C.1.1, 3-5
HE.2.C.1.3-4; HE.2.C.2.2-3
HE.2.B.2.1-4; HE.2.B.3.1-3
HE.2.P.1.1-2; HE.2.P.2.1

Third Grade:
HE.3.C.1.1,5; HE.3.C.2.1-2, 7
HE.3.B.2.1-2; HE.3.B.3.1
HE.3.P.1.1

Fourth Grade:
HE.4.C.1.1; HE.4.C.2.2-3
HE.4.B.2.1-4; HE.4.B.3.1,4
HE.4.P.1.1-2

Fifth Grade:
HE.5.C.1.1, 3-4; HE.5.C.2.2
HE.5.P.1.1-3

Sixth Grade:
HE.6.C.1.2
HE.6.B.1.3
HE.6.P.1.1-3

Seventh Grade:
HE.7.C.1.2; HE.7.C.2.2

Strategies for learning about Health
Preparations for trip:
> Distribute handouts and/or worksheets
> Address health concerns and prevention on the field trip
> Brief for understanding regarding the destination's
>> place on the timeline
> Discuss safety awareness and preparations
> Give each student an assigned question and/or
>> observation on group's behalf

Have students observe:
> Safety precautions, practices, and warnings
> Barriers against attack or environment, including shelters

Have students ask about:
> Health practices of reenactors and of the times
> Firearms safety, including artillery
> Fire safety, including campfires
> Dangers in environment (of the times), including endemic diseases
> Functions of clothing, armor, or shelter

Prevention measures
What to do in case of problems
Who are the medics?

Have students know how to report:
  When they need bathrooms, water, or shade
  When someone else appears to need help

At De Soto National Memorial, an unforgettable learning experience begins as a junior ranger encounters Hernando de Soto himself.

Scouting Awards

The educational value of living history events extends well beyond the classroom. The wide range of such events in Florida fulfill many requirements for an equally wide range of Scouting awards, including Boy Scout Merit Badges and Girl Scout Interest Project Awards. Those who are looking for opportunities to earn certain awards (especially those that are rarely given or that are required for higher rank) should obtain the requirements for those awards from their leaders and then see what is available at the living history venues in their area.

Boy Scout Merit Badges

Animal Science

Basketry

Camping

Indian Lore

Disabilities Awareness

Archaeology

American Cultures

American Heritage

Citizenship in the Nation

Girl Scout Brownie Try-Its

Our Own Council's Try-It

Building Art

Brownie Girl Scouts Through the Years

Listening to the Past

Girl Scout Junior Badges

Across Generations

Finding Your Way

Humans and Habitats

On My Way

Our Own Troop's Badge

Architecture

Folk Arts

My Heritage

Our Own Council's Badge

Yarn and Fabric Arts

Girl Scout Interest Projects Awards for Cadettes, Seniors, and Ambassadors

A World of Understanding

Folk Arts

Heritage Hunt

Performing Arts

Women Through Time

Camping

Generations Hand in Hand

Museum Discovery

Textile Arts

Acknowledgments

Some of life's most memorable journeys begin with a single misstep. This book started out as an idea and well-organized plan, but somehow got off track. Finally I decided maybe it wasn't such a good idea after all and discarded all my notes. I did not know that on my trek through Florida's timeline, I had acquired a couple of stowaways. Amanda Rigney and Brittany Glenn Abbott had been enthralled with the concept and had followed my every move. Upon hearing of the cancellation, they were aghast. For the next fourteen months I was relentlessly subjected to all the pleading, wheedling, cajoling, charm, conniving, and scheming that two determined thirteen-year-old girls can conjure up. I finally caved in. You're reading the result.

The chapters grew out of the briefings I gave the girls before each event they attended or participated in. The practical questions comprising each chapter were supplied by my neighbor Darise McLoughlin. John Powell (no relation, but I would be honored if there were) and Judge Nelson Bailey provided wise counsel and stories on the true history of Florida. Tyler Davis, Ed Dunham, and Harry Smid gave the girls and me the warmest possible welcome to the world of reenacting. Jim Busby and Elizabeth Eich showed me where to find many living history venues in Florida's Panhandle after a year of fruitless searching on my part.

Cindy Malin is a delightful person and an irreplaceable bridge to the Seminole Tribe of Florida. Long-suffering June Cussen of Pineapple Press performed the editorial alchemy of turning leaden scribbling into something better.

The task of writing was fueled by gallons of sweet tea from Sonny's BBQ and the occasional turbo boost came from unlimited quantities of strawberry lemonade from Ruby Tuesday's. Background vocals were performed by Bruce Springsteen and Bob Seger, with frequent instrumental interludes from Ray Lynch, George Winston, and Michael Jones.

Looking back at all the people to whom I owe so much, I have to wonder if I contributed anything at all. I, uh, let's see . . . I typed it. That's it! I typed it.

Further Reading

Readers should remember that reenactors research their areas of interest assiduously and that the websites listed under "Contacts" for many events are thus sources of reliable knowledge resulting from painstaking research. The following sources provide the interested reader with additional information well worth knowing:

A Voyage Long and Strange: Rediscovering the New World (Henry Holt and Co., 2008) and *Confederates in the Attic: Dispatches from the Unfinished Civil War* (Pantheon, 1998), both by Pulitzer Prize–winning author Tony Horwitz, are entertaining and instructive books. The first is about the history of North America 1492–1620. Both books include Mr. Horwitz's experiences with reenactors, some of them in Florida.

The Seminole Wars: America's Longest Indian Conflict by John and Mary Lou Missall (University Press of Florida, 2004) exemplifies what happens when solid scholarship encounters great material.

History of Florida in 40 Minutes by Michael Gannon (University Press of Florida, 2007) is a quick (really quick) winner. Included is the complete text of the book as a lecture by the author on a CD lasting (surprise!) 40 minutes.

Dream State by Diane Roberts (University Press of Florida, 2004) distills eight generations of family whispers, storytelling gifts, eccentricities, and wickedly funny revelations as to where all the bodies are buried as well as who buried them and why. It's Florida's history presented as irresistible gossip.

A History of Florida Forts by Alejandro M. de Quesada (History Press, Charleston, SC, 2006) will interest those who have wondered why almost every place in Florida started out as a fort.

Cracker: The Cracker Culture in Florida History by Dana Ste. Claire (University Press of Florida, 2006) gives the best answer to the question about what a Florida Cracker really is.

A Land Remembered by Patrick D. Smith (Pineapple Press, 1982) is an acknowledged fictional masterwork that follows three generations of a family of Florida pioneers.

St. Augustine and St. Johns County: A Historical Guide by William R. Adams (Pineapple Press, 2009) opens doorways into the past in America's ancient city.

www.seminoletribe.com is the online voice of the Seminole Tribe of Florida. Extremely well done, the site's history section is essential reading for persons wishing a more balanced view of the Sunshine State's past.

Old Florida Style: A Story of Cracker Cattle by Steve Kidd and Alex Menendez (Delve Productions, Inc., distributed by Pineapple Press, 2009). This DVD, filmed in crystal clear high-definition video, showcases Florida's Cracker heritage, particularly the Florida cow hunters and their culture. You'll see cracker cows being driven along the waterline of freshwater lakes and gator-infested swamps, hear first-hand accounts from a woman who lived the cow hunter's life, and meet a cowboy poet laureate and an African American cow man.

Florida's reenactors have three professional-quality **newsletters** to keep readers informed and up to date. The first one is from John Powell of the St. Augustine Garrison. His newsletter concentrates on events of the sixteenth through eighteenth centuries supported by the St. Augustine Garrison and/or Calderone's Company (of the Bradenton area). Send a request to powe7652@bellsouth.net to get onto the mailing list. Bob Niepert of Hardy's Brigade has two monthly newsletters on his website that deal mainly with events relating to the nineteenth century, especially the Civil War. The website is www.floridareenactorsonline.com.

Living History Events by Municipality

Living History Events by County

Photo Credits

Photos on pages 48, 49, 156, 233 courtesy of Glen McLean

Photos on pages 13, 239, 262 courtesy of De Soto National Memorial

Photo on page 8 courtesy of Collier County Museum,

Photos on pages 11, 26, 27 courtesy of Elizabeth Neily

Photos on pages 58, 60 courtesy of Fort Foster State Historic Site

Photos on pages 78, 80 courtesy of Jim Busby (Walton Guards)

Photos on pages 94, 95, 226 courtesy of James A. Callahan
    of Callahan Digital Art

Photos on pages 123, 124, 223 courtesy of Heritage Village

Photo on page 157 courtesy of Diane Burnett of 3-D Restorations, Inc.

Photo on page 116 courtesy of Amelia Island Chamber of Commerce

Photos on pages 207, 215 courtesy of Adventure Photos of Sea World

Photo on page 216 courtesy of Zero-Gravity Corporation

Photo on page 221 courtesy of Historic Pensacola Village

Photos on pages 211, 212 courtesy of Jules Undersea Lodge

Photos on pages 55, 56, 65, 66, 67, 70, 228 courtesy of
    The Seminole Tribe of Florida

Photos on pages 202, 203, 204, 205 courtesy of NASA

Photos on pages i, x, 4 courtesy of Kathy Heitman

All other photos taken by the author